Mastering Puppet 5

Optimize enterprise-grade environment performance with Puppet

Ryan Russell-Yates
Jason Southgate

BIRMINGHAM - MUMBAI

Mastering Puppet 5

Commissioning Editor: Vijin Boricha
Acquisition Editor: Meeta Rajani
Content Development Editor: Nithin George Varghese
Technical Editor: Komal Karne
Copy Editor: Safis Editing
Project Coordinator: Drashti Panchal
Proofreader: Safis Editing
Indexer: Tejal Daruwale Soni
Graphics: Tom Scaria
Production Coordinator: Shantanu Zagade

First published: September 2018

Production reference: 1280918

Published by Packt Publishing Ltd.
Livery Place
35 Livery Street
Birmingham
B3 2PB, UK.

ISBN 978-1-78883-186-4

www.packtpub.com

To those mentors who have helped me understand that the only important question in infrastructure is: "How can we do this better?"

`mapt.io`

Mapt is an online digital library that gives you full access to over 5,000 books and videos, as well as industry leading tools to help you plan your personal development and advance your career. For more information, please visit our website.

Why subscribe?

- Spend less time learning and more time coding with practical eBooks and Videos from over 4,000 industry professionals

- Improve your learning with Skill Plans built especially for you

- Get a free eBook or video every month

- Mapt is fully searchable

- Copy and paste, print, and bookmark content

packt.com

Did you know that Packt offers eBook versions of every book published, with PDF and ePub files available? You can upgrade to the eBook version at `www.packt.com` and as a print book customer, you are entitled to a discount on the eBook copy. Get in touch with us at `customercare@packtpub.com` for more details.

At `www.packt.com`, you can also read a collection of free technical articles, sign up for a range of free newsletters, and receive exclusive discounts and offers on Packt books and eBooks.

Contributors

About the authors

Ryan Russell-Yates is a technical consultant in the fields of automation, DevOps, and infrastructure architecture. He has helped numerous IT practitioners at companies of various shapes and sizes across a range of industries to implement automation best practices at scale. Ryan's true passion in the technology industry is teaching practitioners new tools, technologies, and strategies for dealing with today's complicated digital landscape.

Jason Southgate has been working in the IT industry for more than 15 years, has been using Puppet for more than 6 years, and has tackled some very large projects in Europe, most recently creating an IaaS/PaaS cloud for KPN, the Netherlands' premier telecommunications company, using Puppet Enterprise at a very large scale. Jason was certified in Puppet in 2014, and also has AWS and Azure certification.

About the reviewer

Deniz Parlak has worked with Linux/UNIX technologies for more than five years. He is a [Dev-Sys-Sec]Ops enthusiast. Deniz is currently working with [Dev-Sys-Sec]Ops applications, especially Docker, Ansible, Kubernetes, and cloud providers, and continues to share information about new technologies with people at many technical conferences and lectures. He has also published a book entitled *CentOS System and Server Management*, and is still writing Docker and Bash scripting books. His presentations on the Zeus tool and AWS hardening were selected for events such as Black Hat Asia 2018, DevOpsDays, and NuitDuHack.

Packt is searching for authors like you

If you're interested in becoming an author for Packt, please visit `authors.packtpub.com` and apply today. We have worked with thousands of developers and tech professionals, just like you, to help them share their insight with the global tech community. You can make a general application, apply for a specific hot topic that we are recruiting an author for, or submit your own idea.

Table of Contents

Preface

Puppet 5 remains the software configuration management software of choice, especially for larger-scale configurations.

Here are some examples of current real-world use cases of Puppet:

- Twitter uses Puppet for what is currently one of the larger social networking infrastructures (`https://blog.twitter.com/engineering/en_us/topics/infrastructure/2017/the-infrastructure-behind-twitter-scale.html`). Facebook uses Opscode Chef, the competitive product in the software configuration management category.
- Uber uses Puppet for its standard configuration management (`https://eng.uber.com/uchat/`).
- Walmart is also a very large Puppet user (`https://puppet.com/blog/how-walmart-scaled-puppet-55K-nodes-and-beyond`).

Although there are newer products, such as Ansible and Salt, Puppet remains – I believe – the premier tool, especially for such larger infrastructures (10,000+ servers). It is worth mentioning that Ansible has also become very popular, possibly due to its shallower learning curve and adoption by Red Hat.

Dealing with this level of scale and complexity is non-trivial. With this book, *Mastering Puppet 5*, we want to put the know-how at your disposal to tackle your own large-scale challenges, at mastery level.

Version 5 of Puppet, which is the version covered by this book, was announced with considerable fanfare at last year's PuppetConf (2017) by the new CEO, Sanjay Mirchandani, as *"Puppet's largest set of product innovations. Ever."* In this book, we've gone through these new technologies, including Puppet Discovery, Puppet Tasks, and Puppet Pipelines, to give you the know-how you need to use Puppet 5 in the real world with confidence.

Who this book is for

If you are a system administrator or developer who has already used Puppet and are looking for mastery-level skills and best practices with a view to using Puppet in an enterprise environment, at large scale, this book is for you. Some beginner-level knowledge of using Puppet would be necessary.

If you are looking for a gentle introduction to Puppet, before starting to use this book, please take a look at Puppet's own free self-paced training courses (`https://learn.puppet.com/category/self-paced-training`) or attend some instructor-led or private training (`https://puppet.com/support-services/training`).

What this book covers

Chapter 1, *Authoring Modules*, will really get you on the right path to higher quality Puppet modules and manifests, introducing 12 best practices for module writing.

Chapter 2, *Roles and Profiles*, introduces two additional layers of abstraction and improved interfaces for making your hierarchical business data easier to integrate, making system configurations easier to read, and making refactoring easier.

Chapter 3, *Extending Puppet*, covers three parts of the ecosystem that can still be accessed at the Ruby level for the purposes of extending Puppet to suit more advanced use cases; namely, custom facts, custom functions, and types and providers.

Chapter 4, *Hiera 5*, covers the latest incarnation of Hiera, which allows us to keep all site-specific and business-specific data out of our manifests, making our Puppet modules vastly more portable. We also take a quick look in this chapter at the three layers of configuration and data: global, environment, and module. We also cover how to set up an encrypted YAML backend. Lastly, we take a cursory look at using Jerakia to extend Heira.

Chapter 5, *Managing Code*, covers the use of r10k and Code Manager, allowing us to store all Puppet code in Git repositories and providing version control and rollback capabilities. We discuss directory environments, which give us multiple versions of code on a single master, and how they're supported by r10k and Code Manager. We build a Puppetfile and actively deploy our code to our Puppet Master.

Chapter 6, *Workflow*, covers a basic Puppet workflow. We'll be incorporating the PDK into our basic workflow more heavily, allowing us to write code more efficiently.

Chapter 7, *Continuous Integration*, covers tying Puppet into Jenkins as a **Continuous Integration (CI)** system. We'll discuss the components of a **CI/Continue Deployment (CI/CD)** pipeline, what it takes to achieve some of the milestones to get there, and actively improve our Puppet code in a CI system.

Chapter 8, *Extending Puppet with Tasks and Discovery*, covers Puppet Tasks and Puppet Discovery. Puppet Tasks allows us to run ad hoc commands and use them as building blocks for imperative scripts. We'll be building a task to inspect log files and planning to build an aggregated log file for our Puppet Master. Puppet Discovery allows us to inspect our existing infrastructure and determine ground truth on packages, services, users, and various other components of a virtual machine or container.

Chapter 9, *Exported Resources*, covers virtual and exported resources in Puppet. We'll explore exporting and collecting resources in our manifests, and the common use cases for exported and collected resources to include the following: a dynamic /etc/hosts file, load balancing, and automatic database connections. We'll also explore the file_line and concat resources to allow us to build dynamic configuration files based on these exported resources.

Chapter 10, *Application Orchestration*, covers the ordering of multiple node runs. We'll build application orchestration manifests, which allow us to tie nodes together and provide configuration values across multiple nodes, ensuring that our multi-node application runs in the order necessary, with the information it needs.

Chapter 11, *Scaling Puppet*, covers the horizontal and vertical scaling of Puppet. We'll explore some common settings for tuning, and inspect ways to horizontally scale Puppet services.

Chapter 12, *Troubleshooting and Profiling*, covers some common troubleshooting cases we see with Puppet. We'll focus on both Puppet service errors and catalog compilation errors, and inspect tuning and configuring our log files.

To get the most out of this book

Users with some prior Puppet experience will get the most out of this book, but every lesson is intended to be helpful to someone at any stage of learning about Puppet. To follow along in the book, users should install a trial version of Puppet Enterprise and attach some nodes to the Puppet Master. Each chapter will help set up the Puppet Master in a way to utilize the existing infrastructure.

Directions for installing Puppet Enterprise can be found at https://puppet.com/docs/pe/latest/installing_pe.html.

Download the example code files

You can download the example code files for this book from your account at
`www.packt.com`. If you purchased this book elsewhere, you can visit
`www.packt.com/support` and register to have the files emailed directly to you.

You can download the code files by following these steps:

1. Log in or register at `www.packt.com`.
2. Select the **SUPPORT** tab.
3. Click on **Code Downloads & Errata**.
4. Enter the name of the book in the **Search** box and follow the onscreen instructions.

Once the file is downloaded, please make sure that you unzip or extract the folder using the latest version of:

- WinRAR/7-Zip for Windows
- Zipeg/iZip/UnRarX for Mac
- 7-Zip/PeaZip for Linux

The code bundle for the book is also hosted on GitHub at `https://github.com/PacktPublishing/Mastering-Puppet-5`. In case there's an update to the code, it will be updated on the existing GitHub repository.

We also have other code bundles from our rich catalog of books and videos available at `https://github.com/PacktPublishing/`. Check them out!

Download the color images

We also provide a PDF file that has color images of the screenshots/diagrams used in this book. You can download it here: `https://www.packtpub.com/sites/default/files/downloads/9781788831864_ColorImages.pdf`.

Conventions used

There are a number of text conventions used throughout this book.

`CodeInText`: Indicates code words in text, database table names, folder names, filenames, file extensions, pathnames, dummy URLs, user input, and Twitter handles. Here is an example: "The earlier incarnations of Hiera (version 3 or earlier) used a single, entirely global `hiera.yaml`."

A block of code is set as follows:

```
lookup({
    'name'  => 'classification',
    'merge' => {
      'strategy'        => 'deep',
      'knockout_prefix' => '--',
    },
})
```

When we wish to draw your attention to a particular part of a code block, the relevant lines or items are set in bold:

```
lookup({
    'name'  => 'classification',
    'merge' => {
      'strategy' => 'deep',
      'knockout_prefix' => '--',
    },
})
```

Any command-line input or output is written as follows:

```
$ sudo /opt/puppetlabs/puppet/bin/gem install hiera-eyaml
```

Bold: Indicates a new term, an important word, or words that you see on screen. For example, words in menus or dialog boxes appear in the text like this. Here is an example: "We can reach the plugin page by clicking on **Manage Jenkins** on the left-hand side of the screen."

 Warnings or important notes appear like this.

Tips and tricks appear like this.

Get in touch

Feedback from our readers is always welcome.

General feedback: Email `customercare@packtpub.com` and mention the book title in the subject of your message. If you have questions about any aspect of this book, please email us at `customercare@packtpub.com`.

Errata: Although we have taken every care to ensure the accuracy of our content, mistakes do happen. If you have found a mistake in this book, we would be grateful if you would report this to us. Please visit `www.packt.com/submit-errata`, selecting your book, clicking on the Errata Submission Form link, and entering the details.

Piracy: If you come across any illegal copies of our works in any form on the internet, we would be grateful if you would provide us with the location address or website name. Please contact us at `copyright@packt.com` with a link to the material.

If you are interested in becoming an author: If there is a topic that you have expertise in and you are interested in either writing or contributing to a book, please visit `authors.packtpub.com`.

Reviews

Please leave a review. Once you have read and used this book, why not leave a review on the site that you purchased it from? Potential readers can then see and use your unbiased opinion to make purchase decisions, we at Packt can understand what you think about our products, and our authors can see your feedback on their book. Thank you!

For more information about Packt, please visit `packtpub.com`.

Authoring Modules

1

Authoring Puppet modules and manifests is the real heart of the work for your Puppet ecosystem.

So, you've perhaps already written at least a few modules for software components in your infrastructure, and there's already a great guide to getting started writing modules in the Puppet documentation at `https://puppet.com/docs/pe/2017.3/quick_start_guides/writing_modules_nix_getting_started_guide.html`, so I won't waste any time going over that material again. But I'm sure that, in pursuit of mastering Puppet v5, what you would really like to do is to write those modules correctly.

Let's take that step together toward better quality modules in this chapter. I've spent a lot of time in the trenches over the last few years, gathering together best practices from some of the best projects across Europe and applying practices and software principles I've learned from both my university education and 15+ years in the industry. I hope I can introduce you to some shortcuts and make your life easier!

The following are a set of recommendations that I feel will really get you on the right path to higher quality Puppet modules and manifests:

- Using a decent IDE and plugins
- Using a good module class structure:
    - Following the class-naming conventions
    - Having a single point of entry to the module
    - Using high cohesion and loose coupling principles
    - Using the encapsulation principle
    - Strongly typing your module variables

- Using the new Puppet Development Kit commands:
    - Creating the module framework and metadata
    - Creating the `init.pp`
    - Creating further classes
    - Validating your module
    - Unit testing your module
- Staying on the lookout for code smells
- Making sure you are not working with dead code
- Working with the community
- Using Puppet Forge
- Writing great documentation
- Adding module dependencies
- Adding compatibility data for your modules
    - Operating systems support
    - Puppet and PE version support
- Using the new Hiera 5 module level data
- Upgrading your templates from ERB to ERP syntax

Let's examine each of these best practices now in turn.

Using a decent IDE and plugins

Using a decent text editor with the plugins that equip you to write well for Puppet is a really good step toward better quality. There are quite a few options out there, and it's best to use whatever suits your own unique writing style. Personally, I have used Atom (`https://atom.io`) most successfully, and recently installed it locally on my workstation. I used Eclipse many years ago (this has also been known previously as Geppetto), which I in fact felt was unwieldy due to a large memory footprint. It's also nice to remain fairly handy with Vim, especially for working on the command line server-side, or if you use a Linux OS on your workstation. There's also TextMate, for an macOS X only editor that has all of Apple's look and feel.

Let's take a look at some of the various options for an **Integrated Development Machine (IDE)** available to us as Puppet developers.

Vim

Vim (http://www.vim.org) is, of course, still a mainstay for text file editing. It has a very long history in the Unix world, and it's a very lightweight command-line text editor. Vim is just about as raw a text editor as you can get. It can be used as a lightning fast and efficient IDE if you have the memory and patience to learn the myriad keyboard commands. My advice is to start out with a few basic commands, and make an effort to pick up a few more each time you use Vim.

You can pimp your Vim and make it better suited for editing Puppet manifests. Let's take a look at that, assuming you've just grabbed a fresh Vim installation, and you have Git installed.

Move to your home directory and clone the given repository with the following commands:

```
cd ~
git clone https://github.com/ricciocri/vimrc .vim
cd .vim
git pull && git submodule init && git submodule update && git submodule
status
cd ~
ln -s .vim/.vimrc
```

Cloning the repository into your home directory's `.vim` directory will configure your Vim settings for you. The repository contains several submodules containing the following:

- **Pathogen** (https://github.com/tpope/vim-pathogen) is Vim guru Tim Pope's general-purpose add-on that allows you to manage your Vim *runtimepath* with ease and install Vim plugins and runtime files each in their own private directories, rather than having file collisions.
- **Vim-puppet** (https://github.com/rodjek/vim-puppet) is the original Vim plugin written by Tim Sharpe, making Vim much more Puppet-friendly.
- **snipmate.vim** (https://github.com/msanders/snipmate.vim) is a Vim script that implements some of TextMate's snippet features for Vim.
- **Syntastic** (https://github.com/vim-syntastic/syntastic) is a syntax-checking plugin that runs files through external syntax checkers and displays any resulting errors. This can be done from the command line with the `pdk validate` command, or automatically as files are saved.
- **Tabular** (https://github.com/godlygeek/tabular) is used to line up your fat arrows (=>) according to the *Puppet Style Guide*, so that it will pass running the `pdk validate` command. (We will cover the `pdk validate` command in full later.)

- **vim-fugitive** (https://github.com/tpope/vim-fugitive) provides deep Git integration for Vim.

I can't promise this will be a perfect Vim setup for your own personal Vim style, but it will certainly get you on the right path, and you will have Pathogen installed, so you can further tweak your Vim settings until you have it just how you like it.

You might also want to fork this repository in GitHub, so you can keep all your settings and share them with your team.

TextMate

TextMate (http://macromates.com) is an macOS X only editor, and there's a TextMate bundle available (https://github.com/masterzen/puppet-textmate-bundle) for editing Puppet manifests. First, install TextMate and Git (available with the command-line developer tools), and follow these commands to set up the Puppet bundle:

```
$ mkdir ~/temp
$ cd ~/temp
$ git clone https://github.com/masterzen/puppet-textmate-bundle.git
Puppet.tmbundle
$ mv ~/temp/Puppet.tmbundle ~/Library/Application\
Support/TextMate/Bundles/
$ rm -fr ~/temp
```

Now select a manifest and open it with TextMate. In the **TextMate** dialog, select **Puppet** and **Install Bundle**, and you are all ready to rock.

Atom

Here's the IDE that I would recommend based on my own personal style, using my MacBook as the host OS. Atom (https://atom.io) is a fully featured IDE described as, *A hackable text editor for the 21st Century* and contains all the functionality you'd expect: cross-platform, package (that is, plugin) manager, auto-completion, file browser, multiple panes, find and replace, and so on.

GitHub has developed Atom, and they have built it with the goal of combining the convenience of a fully fledged IDE with the deep configurability of a classic but complex editor such as Vim.

There are literally thousands of open source packages that add new features and functionality to Atom, and here are the ones I recommend specifically for Puppet development:

- `language-puppet` (adds syntax highlighting and snippets to Puppet files)
- `linter-puppet-lint` (provides linter support to your Puppet manifests)
- `aligner-puppet` (aligns the fat arrows according to the Puppet Style Guide)
- `erb-snippets` (snippets and hotkeys for writing Puppet ERB templates)
- `linter-js-yaml` (parses your YAML files with JS-YAML)
- `tree-view-git-status` (displays the Git status of files in the tree view)

Visual Studio

If you're a developer in the Windows and .NET world, then look no further than the Puppet language support for Visual Studio Code extension (`https://marketplace.visualstudio.com/items?itemName=jpogran.puppet-vscode`).

It contains all the features you would expect for Puppet development in the Visual Studio IDE: syntax highlighting, code snippets, file validation, linting according to the Puppet Style Guide, IntelliSense for resources and parameters, importing from the `puppet resource` command, node graph previewing, and now, **Puppet Development Kit** (**PDK**) integration.

Using good module and class structure

This section contains a set of recommendations surrounding good module and class design. Bear in mind that Puppet development is, in principle, just like any other type of software development, and we've learned over many years in software development, and especially at O&O software, that certain modular and class design principles make our development better. I also feel that part of our journey toward *infrastructure as code* is making our Puppet code just as well-designed, structured, and tested as any other application code.

Following the class-naming conventions

There's a certain class-naming convention that has developed over time within the Puppet community, and it's really worth taking these into account when structuring your classes:

- `init.pp`: `init.pp` contains the class named the same as the module, and is the main entry point for the module.
- `params.pp`: The `params.pp` pattern (more on this later in the chapter) is an elegant little hack, taking advantage of Puppet's class inheritance behavior. Any of the other classes in the module inherit from the `params` class, so have their parameters set appropriately.
- `install.pp`: The resources related to installing the software should be placed in an `install` class. The install class must be named `<modulename>::install` and must be located in the `install.pp` file.
- `config.pp`: The resources related to configuring the installed software should be placed in a `config` class. The `config` class must be named `<modulename>::config` and must be located in the `config.pp` file.
- `service.pp`: The resources related to managing the service for the software should be placed in a `service` class. The service class must be named `<modulename>::service` and must be located in the `service.pp` file.

For software that is configured in a client/server style, see the following:

- `<modulename>::client::install` and `<modulename>::server::install` would be the class names for the `install.pp` file placed in the `client` and `server` directories accordingly
- `<modulename>::client::config` and `<modulename>::server::install` would be the class names for the `config.pp` file placed in the `client` and `server` directories accordingly
- `<modulename>::client::service` and `<modulename>::server::service` would be the class names for the `service.pp` files placed in the `client` and `server` directories accordingly

Having a single point of entry to the module

`init.pp` should be the single entry point for the module. In this way, someone reviewing the documentation in particular, as well as the code in `init.pp`, can have a complete overview of the module's behavior.

If you've used encapsulation effectively and used descriptive class names, you can get a very good sense just by looking at `init.pp` of how the module actually manages the software.

 Modules that have configurable parameters should be configurable in a single way and in this single place. The only exception to this would be, for example, a module such as the Apache module, where one or more virtual directories are also configurable.

Ideally, you can use your module with a simple include statement, as follows:

```
include mymodule
```

You can also use it with the use of a class declaration, as follows:

```
class {'mymodule':
  myparam => false,
}
```

The *Apache virtual directory* style of configuring a number of defined types would be the third way to use your new module:

```
mymodule::mydefine {'define1':
  myotherparam => false,
}
```

The anti-pattern to this recommendation would be to have a number of classes other than `init.pp` and your defined types with parameters expecting to be set.

Using high cohesion and loose coupling principles

As far as possible, Puppet modules should be made up of classes with a single responsibility. In software engineering, we call this high, functional cohesion. Cohesion in software engineering is the degree to which the elements of a certain module belong together. Try to make each class have a single responsibility, and don't arbitrarily mix together unrelated functionalities in your classes.

Using the encapsulation principle

As far as possible, these classes should use encapsulation to hide the implementation details from the user; for example, users of your module don't need to be aware of individual resource names. In software engineering, we call this encapsulation. For example, in a `config` class, we can use several resources, but the user doesn't need to know all about them. Rather, they just simply know that they should use the `config` class for the configuration of the software to work correctly.

Having classes contain other classes can be very useful, especially in larger modules where you want to improve code readability. You can move chunks of functionality into separate files, and then use the contain keyword to refer to these separated chunks of functionality.

 See `https://puppet.com/docs/puppet/5.3/lang_containment.html` website for a reminder about the contain keyword.

Providing sensible, well-thought-out parameter defaults

If the vast majority of the people using your module will use the module with a certain parameter set, then of course it makes sense to set that parameter with a default.

Carefully think through how your module is used, and put yourself in the position of a nonexpert user of your own module.

Present the available module parameters in a sensible order, with more often accessed settings before least accessed settings, as opposed to some arbitrary order, such as alphabetical order.

Strongly typing your module variables

In versions of Puppet proper to the new language features which came out in version 4, we would create `class` parameters with undefined data types, and then, if we were being very nice, we would use the `stdlib validate_<datatype>` functions to check appropriate values for those variables:

```
class vhost (
  $servername,
```

```
    $serveraliases,
    $port
)
{ ...
```

Puppet 4 and 5 have an in-built way of defining the data type that a parameterized class accepts. See the following example:

```
class vhost (
   String   $servername,
   Array    $serveraliases,
   Integer $port
)
{ ...
```

Using the new Puppet Development Kit commands

Some features to improve quality in your Puppet development, such as `puppet-lint`, `puppet-rspec`, and commands such as `puppet module create` have been around for some time, but previously, you had to discover these tools out there in the wild, install them, and figure out how to use them effectively yourself.

Puppet decided back in August 2017 to bring these things all together on the client side and make them a breeze to use with the new Puppet Development Kit version 1.0. I can certainly recall `puppet-rspec` always took some time to set up and get working correctly. Now it's all really easy.

Let's take a whistle-stop tour of the module development process using the new PDK 1.0.

- **Creating the module framework and metadata**: The `pdk new module` command runs in the same way as the old `puppet module create` command, as follows:

    ```
    $ pdk new module zope --skip-interview
    ```

- **Creating the** `init.pp`: There is now a set of creation commands for manifests inside modules, as follows:
    - `pdk new class` (https://puppet.com/docs/pdk/1.0/pdk_ reference.html#pdk-new-class-command)

- pdk new defined_type (https://puppet.com/docs/pdk/1.0/pdk_reference.html#pdk-new-definedtype-command)
- pdk new task (https://puppet.com/docs/pdk/1.0/pdk_reference.html#pdk-new-task-command)—see Chapter 6, *Workflow*, for more details on the new Puppet task functionality.

So, just use the name of the module to create init.pp:

```
$ pdk new class zope
```

These commands now negate any need for snippets in your text editor to create the comments, declarations, and other boilerplate code.

- **Creating further classes**: Create any further classes using the same command. See the following example:

```
$ pdk new class params
```

Validating your module

As you are working, you can use the new pdk validate command (https://puppet.com/docs/pdk/1.0/pdk_reference.html#pdk-validate-command) to assist with checking that the module compiles, conforms to the Puppet Style Guide, and has valid metadata:

```
$ pdk validate
```

Unit testing your module

The number one most important thing you can do to bring quality to your modules is to test them! Testing really is one of the most important aspects of software quality assurance in any field of software development. In the agile development community, we've been banging on the table about automated testing for more than 10 years!

Puppet RSpec (http://rspec-puppet.com/tutorial) has been allowing the Puppet community to unit test their modules for quite some time, but it's even easier now with the new PDK 1.0, as everything is set up ready, and you can just add your testing code and run the tests.

From a Puppet perspective, unit testing means *checking the output from the compiler*. Are the resources contained in the compiled relationship resource catalog, and is their order as expected, given the parameters passed and/or facts present?

When you begin to write tests in Puppet-RSpec, it seems at first like all you are doing is rewriting the Puppet manifests in another Ruby-like language. There is, however, really more to it than that. If there is some reasonable complexity to the module's functionality, for example, testing the dynamic content produced by Puppet templates, support for multiple operating systems, and different actions according to the passed parameters, then these tests actually form a safety net when editing or adding new functionality to your modules, protecting against regressions when refactoring, or upgrading to a new Puppet release.

Let's carry on from the previous two sections and use the development kit to unit test our module. Whenever you generate a class using the `pdk new class` command, PDK creates a corresponding unit test file. This file, located in your module's `/spec/classes` folder, already includes a template for writing your unit tests (see `http://rspec-puppet.com/tutorial`). You can then run the tests using the following command:

```
$ pdk test unit
```

Staying on the lookout for code smells

Be on the lookout for code smells, especially as your Puppet code base ages! The following link is a research project that describes a bunch of Puppet *code smells*, which is an XP (extreme programming) term meaning code issues—usually meaning either a poor design or implementation:

`http://www.tusharma.in/wp-content/uploads/2016/03/ConfigurationSmells_preprint.pdf`

Let's quickly run through using the `Puppeteer` Python-based tool used in the preceding research project:

1. Ensure you have the latest Java SDK installed.
2. Move to your `workspace` directory `~/workspace`, and clone the following Git repository:

```
$ git clone https://github.com/tushartushar/Puppeteer
$ cd Puppeteer
```

3. Download the PMD tool (`https://github.com/pmd/pmd`) and update the path in the shell script. PMD is an extensible static code analyzer with **copy-paste-detector (CPD)** built-in.

4. Update the folder path where all the Puppet repositories are placed.

5. Execute the `cpdRunner.sh` shell script to carry out clone detection using the PMD-CPD tool.

6. Update the `REPO_ROOT` constant in `SmellDetector/Constants.py`, which represents the folder path where all the Puppet repositories are placed.

7. Execute `Puppeteer.py`.

8. Analyze Puppet repository with `puppet-lint` (optional).

9. Execute `puppet-lintRunner.py` after setting the repository root.

10. Set the repository root in `Puppet-lint_aggregator/PLConstants.py`.

11. Execute `PuppetLintRules.py`, it will generate a consolidated summary of the analysis for all the analyzed projects.

Working with dead code

Another issue that can often hit you as your Puppet code base ages is unused code in your codebase. But, there's a tool out there in the wild we can use to keep on top of this issue.

`puppet-ghostbuster` essentially compares what is actually being used (stored in PuppetDB) to what you think you are using (in your code base directory). This give you the opportunity to slash and burn anything that's really unused. This is great from the point of view of software maintainability. A smaller code base is simply cheaper to maintain!

Let's quickly run through using this Ruby gem.

Make the following settings in your environment variables:

- `HIERA_YAML_PATH`: The location of the `hiera.yaml` file. It defaults to `/etc/puppetlabs/code/hiera.yaml`.
- `PUPPETDB_URL`: The URL or the PuppetDB. It defaults to `http://puppetdb:8080`.
- `PUPPETDB CACERT_FILE`: Your site's CA certificate.
- `PUPPETDB_CERT_FILE`: A SSL certificate signed by your site's Puppet CA.
- `PUPPETDB_KEY_FILE`: The private key for that certificate.

Run the command as follows:

```
$ find . -type f -exec puppet-lint --only-checks
ghostbuster_classes,ghostbuster_defines,ghostbuster_facts,ghostbuster_files
,ghostbuster_functions,ghostbuster_hiera_files,ghostbuster_templates,ghostb
uster_types {} \+
```

You can add to and remove from the comma-delimited items to check for unused classes, defined types, facts, files, functions, Hiera files, templates, and types.

Using Puppet Forge

It maybe goes without saying that there's no reason to reinvent the wheel when you are authoring your Puppet modules. A few minutes in Puppet Forge (`https://forge.puppet.com`) can really save you days and days of editing. There are, at the time of writing, more than 5,000 Forge modules, so it makes a great deal of sense to leverage all that hard work done by the Puppet community. Search the Forge first for that bit of software; it's more than likely that something already exists.

In my experience, I have found there is often something that *almost* does the job. Maybe there's a module (usually an unsupported and unapproved one) that maybe, for example, performs the management for the software you require, but it's only for Ubuntu, and you're using Red Hat. It's usually a better approach to fork that module, whatever shape it's in, and work on that, rather than start from scratch.

Working with the community

The best way for me to describe this best practice is to use an anti-pattern as an example.

I once came across a Puppet developer who would start a module completely from scratch, and then copy and paste lines of code from a Forge module into the new module. From then on, that module exists entirely outside the community! It's not a fork even, so to integrate changes that have been made over time from the community becomes a real pain. You would have to cherry-pick those changes to get the functionality into your own, and you will probably still be left with regression problems. Generally, a best practice is to always at the very least fork the Forge module! This means you get the Git history, which often contains the thoughts that have gone into producing that module.

You see, if you were ever a reader of the great book *The Cathedral & the Bazaar: Musings on Linux and Open Source by an Accidental Revolutionary* (`https://www.amazon.com/Cathedral-Bazaar-Musings-Accidental-Revolutionary/dp/0596001088`), then you will understand that the Linux-orientated philosophy of software development through a *bazaar*, collaborative working style trumps spinning off development into a cathedral, independent working style. Well, that's my take on this developer's working style. He was working cathedral-ly, as opposed to bazaar-ly. Effectively, you are making the decision to pit your cathedral team against the multitude of the bazaar, and to my mind, that's simply not wise project management when it comes to giving you a competitive advantage in the internet age.

Sometimes, modules on the Forge get a bit out of date. If the metadata for the module is out of date, you can always produce that again using the PDK `new module` command (`https://puppet.com/docs/pdk/1.0/pdk_generating_modules.html#create-a-module-with-pdk`) and commit the new metadata.

Of course, to be a great Puppet community member, it would be an even better practice to make pull requests for the changes you have made and contribute to the work of the community.

Writing great documentation

Another important recommendation is to simply write great documentation. There's nothing worse, I feel, as a developer, than to have to dig into the code to understand how a module works; it's like having to lift the hood of the car to understand how to drive a vehicle!

Get good at writing English to convey technical ideas! I really think it's a skill that every good developer really needs to master.

Grabbing yourself a Markdown editor

Puppet modules use markdown for their documentation formatting. So it makes sense to use either a standalone Markdown editor, or some plugins for your IDE, so that you can create your quality documentation appropriately. Following on from our selection of code IDEs that we considered earlier in the chapter, the corresponding markdown plugins follow.

Vim

You can use the vim-instant-markdown plugin (`https://github.com/suan/vim-instant-markdown`) if you're a vim fan.

TextMate

You can use the TextMate markdown bundle (`https://github.com/textmate/markdown.tmbundle`) if you enjoy the Apple look and feel of TextMate.

Atom

If, like me, you enjoy using Atom, you can use the Markdown Preview Plus package (`https://atom.io/packages/markdown-preview-plus`).

Visual Studio

If you're a developer in the Windows and .NET world, then look no further than the Markdown editor extension (`https://marketplace.visualstudio.com/items?itemName=MadsKristensen.MarkdownEditor`).

Standalone Markdown editors

If you would rather use a standalone Markdown editor, I can recommend personally MacDown for macOS X. My (very) short list of standalone Markdown editors for various operating systems follows.

Remarkable

If you're using Linux, then Remarkable is probably the best standalone editor. It also works on Windows. Some of its features include live preview, exporting to PDF and HTML, GitHub markdown, custom CSS, syntax highlighting, and keyboard shortcuts.

MacDown

If you would rather use a standalone Markdown editor, I can recommend MacDown for macOS X, which is free (open source). It's heavily inspired by Mou, and is designed with web developers in mind. It has configurable syntax highlighting, live preview, and auto-completion. If you're looking for a lean, fast, configurable standalone Markdown editor, this might be the one for you.

Adding module dependencies

Edit the module's `metadata.json` file to add module dependencies. See the following example:

```
"dependencies": [
    { "name":" stankevich/python",
      "version_requirement":">= 1.18.x"
    }
]
```

The `name` key is the name of the requirement, namely, `"pe"` or `"puppet"`. The `version_requirement` key is a semver (`http://semver.org`) value or range. See the following examples:

- `1.18.0`
- `1.18.x`
- `>= 1.18.x`
- `>=1.18.x <2.x.x`

These would all be valid values for `version_requirement`.

Check the `metadata.json` file for validity afterwards using the new PDK command, as follows:

```
$ pdk validate metadata
```

The great thing about adding module dependencies is the fact that, when you run the `puppet module download` command, Puppet will download all the module dependencies accordingly.

Adding compatibility data for your modules

This section introduces you to adding compatibility data for the module designed for your version of Puppet or Puppet Enterprise and the operating system you want to work with. To begin with, Edit the module's `metadata.json` file to add compatibility data.

Operating systems support

Express the operating systems your module supports in the module's `metadata.json`, as shown in the following example:

```
"operatingsystem_support": [
        { "operatingsystem": "RedHat", },
        { "operatingsystem": "Ubuntu", },
]
```

The Facter facts `operatingsystem` and `operatingsystemrelease` are expected. Here's a more complete example:

```
"operatingsystem_support": [
        {
            "operatingsystem":"RedHat",
            "operatingsystemrelease":[ "5.0", "6.0" ]
        },
        {
            "operatingsystem": "Ubuntu",
            "operatingsystemrelease": [
                "12.04",
                "10.04"
            ]
        }
    ]
```

Check the `metadata.json` file for validity afterwards using the new `pdk` command:

```
$ pdk validate metadata
```

Puppet and PE version support

The `requirements` key in the `metadata.json` file is a list of external requirements for the module in the following format:

```
"requirements": [ {"name": "pe", "version_requirement": "5.x"}]
```

name is the name of the requirement, for example "pe" or "puppet".
version_requirement can be a semver (http://semver.org) version range, similar to
dependencies.

Again, you can check the metadata.json file for validity afterwards using the new PDK
command, as follows:

```
$ pdk validate metadata
```

Using the new Hiera 5 module level data

For quite some time when module writing, we've been using the params.pp pattern. One
class in the module, by convention called <MODULENAME>::params, sets the variables for
any of the other classes:

```
class zope::params {
  $autoupdate = false,
  $default_service_name = 'ntpd',


  case $facts['os']['family'] {
    'AIX': {
      $service_name = 'xntpd'
    }
    'Debian': {
      $service_name = 'ntp'
    }
    'RedHat': {
      $service_name = $default_service_name
    }
  }
}
```

So, you can see here that we are using some conditional logic depending on the
os::family fact, so that the service_name variable can be set appropriately. We are also
exposing the autoupdate variable, and giving it a default value.

This params.pp pattern is an elegant little hack, which takes advantage of Puppet's
idiosyncratic class inheritance behavior (using inheritance is generally not recommended in
Puppet). Then, any of the other classes in the module inherit from the params class, to have
their parameters set appropriately, as shown in the following example:

```
class zope (
  $autoupdate   = $zope::params::autoupdate,
```

```
    $service_name = $zope::params::service_name,
) inherits zope::params {
  ...
}
```

Since the release of Hiera 5, we are able to simplify our module complexity considerably. By using Hiera-based defaults, we can simplify our module's main classes, and they no longer need to inherit from `params.pp`. Additionally, you no longer need to explicitly set a default value with the = operator in the parameter declaration.

Let's look at the equivalent configuration to the `params.pp` pattern using Hiera 5.

First of all, in order to use this new functionality, the `data_provider` key needs to be set to the `heira` value in the module's `metadata.json` file:

```
...
"data_provider": "hiera",
...
```

Next, we need to add a `hiera.yaml` file to the root directory of the module:

```
---
version: 5
defaults:
  datadir: data
  data_hash: yaml_data
hierarchy:
  - name: "OS family"
    path: "os/%{facts.os.family}.yaml"


  - name: "common"
    path: "common.yaml"
```

We can then add three files to the `/data` directory (note that the `datadir` setting in the `hiera.yaml` file). The first file of these three is used to set the AIX `service_name` variable:

```
# zope/data/os/AIX.yaml
---
zope::service_name: xntpd
```

The second file is used to set the Debian `service_name` variable:

```
# zope/data/os/Debian.yaml
zope::service_name: ntp
```

And finally, there is the common file, and Hiera will fall through to this file to find its values if it doesn't find a corresponding operating system file when looking for the `service_name` setting, or a value for `autoupdate` when searching the previous two files:

```
# ntp/data/common.yaml
---
ntp::autoupdate: false
ntp::service_name: ntpd
```

We will look at Hiera 5 in much more detail in Chapter 4, *Hiera 5*.

Summary

In this chapter, we have covered a lot of ground, and I've introduced a bunch of best practices you can use to produce better quality component modules.

In the next chapter, we'll still be covering development in Puppet DSL, and turn our attention to two special modules: role and profile, which can help us to build reusable, configurable, and refactorable site-wide configuration code.

2
Roles and Profiles

The *roles and profiles pattern* became common knowledge in the Puppet community following Craig Dunn's seminal blog post (https://www.craigdunn.org/2012/05/239/), and has been rapidly taken up by the rest of the community. It's now a widely adopted pattern or best practice. It's a reliable way to build reusable, configurable, and refactorable site-wide configuration code, and it's an approach to dealing with the interfaces of your infrastructure—using the software development paradigms of *encapsulation* and *abstraction*.

Before the pattern developed, the Puppet language itself provided just two levels of abstraction, as follows:

- The component module (https://puppet.com/docs/puppet/5.3/modules_fundamentals.html)
- The node definition (https://puppet.com/docs/puppet/5.3/lang_node_definitions.html)

But it soon became clear that further intermediate abstraction was needed to break up, restructure, and clarify these two.

Let's consider the overarching task: we want to assign classes (and their corresponding business data) to nodes, and we want to do this in a way that encapsulates and hides complexity away at each stage of this abstraction process: moving from looking at the node in its context within the whole infrastructure, as a software stack, and drilling down into the technology components and their configuration, which comprise elements of that software stack.

I've seen nodes being defined in the very long-hand way, using only these two levels of abstraction. I've also seen other approaches, such as using a Hiera-based micro **external node classifier** (**ENC**). I've helped to transition companies to using the roles and profiles pattern, and I've used both the Puppet Enterprise console and Foreman as ENC. I've defined nodes in Puppet code, using Hiera in many ways to assist node classification, and I've even used the PE console API for node classification, so I hope I've picked up a few best practices along the way that I can now pass along to you.

In this chapter, let's look together at the roles and profiles pattern, and how this can help you to manage your infrastructure professionally and achieve our next milestone in *Mastering Puppet 5*.

Summary of the pattern

The roles and profiles pattern adds two additional layers of abstraction between your *node classification* at the highest level and *component modules* at the lowest, thus providing three levels of abstraction in your Puppet modules. The following descriptions go from the most complex to the least:

- **Component modules**: These are modules for the management of software for your business. There will no doubt be a bunch of these that you've downloaded from the Forge (for example, puppetlabs/apache, puppetlabs/mysql, hunner/wordpress, and so on), and no doubt also some that you have developed for your own business-specific purposes.

We've discussed these already at length in `Chapter 1`, *Authoring Modules*, so here's the rub:

- **Profiles**: A set of encapsulated *technology-specific* classes that use one or more component modules and corresponding business data to configure part of a solution stack
- **Roles**: A set of encapsulated *business-specific* classes that comprise profiles to build a complete system configuration

These two additional layers of abstraction and improved interfaces make hierarchical business data easier to integrate, system configurations easier to read for both business people and technologists, and they make refactoring easier.

The following UML diagram shows the relationship between the elements in the pattern more clearly:

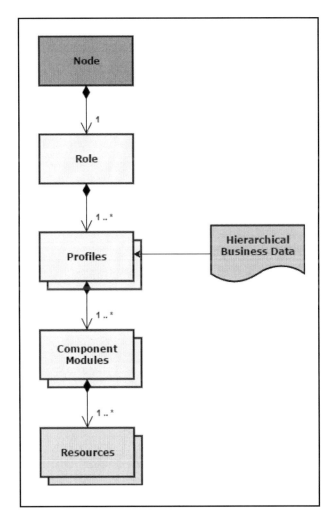

From the preceding diagram, we can see the following:

- A **Node** has *exactly* one **Role**
- A **Role** comprises *one or more* **Profiles**
- **Profile** comprise *one or more* **Component Modules** and corresponding **Hierarchical Business Data**
- **Component Modules** comprise *many* **Resources**

Puppet resources should already be very familiar to you, and we've already covered component modules in `Chapter 1`, *Authoring Modules*, so in the following two sections, let's take a deep dive into the *profile* and *role* part of the pattern.

Profiles

First, let's take a step back and consider what we want to achieve with profiles.

The overarching exercise is to produce usable chunks of technology that can be fitted together, in a building-brick fashion, to compose what we call in the industry these days *technology stacks* or *solution stacks*. The most well-known example of a stack would be the LAMP stack (Linux, Apache, MySQL, PHP), and more recently, Ruby or Python have sometimes superseded PHP as the primary scripting language. Node.js is being rapidly adopted across the industry, too.

Considering the LAMP stack, what we want to do is create chunks of technology for the Apache, MySQL, and PHP components. Profiles are, therefore, these smaller chunks of technology that will eventually comprise these full solution stacks. Profiles are the three *building bricks* that we piece together, as follows:

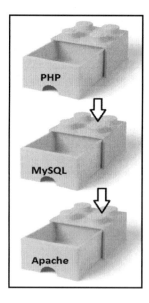

Let's look at this LAMP stack with some fully functional Puppet **domain specific language (DSL)** code:

```
# LAMP stack profiles


# apache profile
class profile::web::apache (
  String $directory = '/var/www',
  String $vhost,
) {
  include apache
  apache::vhost { $vhost:
    port    => '80',
    docroot => "/var/www/${vhost}",
  }
}


# mysql profile
class profile::db::mysql (
  String $username = '/var/www',
  String $password,
) {


  include mysql::server
  mysql::db{ 'mysqldb':
    user     => $username,
    password => $password,
    grant    => 'ALL',
  }
}


# php profile
class profile::programming::php
{
  class { '::php':
    ensure       => latest,
    manage_repos => true,
    fpm          => true,
    dev          => true,
    composer     => true,
    pear         => true,
    phpunit      => false,
    settings    => {
      'PHP/max_execution_time'  => '90',
```

```
        'PHP/max_input_time'       => '300',
        'PHP/memory_limit'         => '64M',
        'PHP/post_max_size'        => '32M',
        'PHP/upload_max_filesize'  => '32M',
        'Date/date.timezone'       => 'Europe/Berlin',
      },
   }
 }
```

As you can see, in these classes, we are producing an *abstraction* for the remaining, AMP section of the LAMP stack and *encapsulating* the functionality of the underlying component modules. Linux is already installed, of course!

Profiles best practices summary

Here are the best practices you should note in the development of your own profiles, referring to the preceding LAMP stack as an example:

- Design for use of the `include` keyword
- Use subdirectories for sensible, readable profile class groups
- Hide complexity with parameters, defaults, and abstraction
- Decide how to set the parameters for component classes
- Decide to use either automatic class parameter lookup or the `lookup` function

Let's examine each of these best practices now in turn.

Designing for use of the include keyword

The single interface of your profiles should be their adoption in the corresponding roles part of the pattern using the Puppet `include` keyword. Bear this in mind when writing your profiles. We would simply write the following in any role that requires PHP to be installed on that node:

```
  ...
  include profile::programming::php
  ...
```

With regard to the Puppet `include` keyword:

- Multiple declarations are OK
- It relies on external data for parameters

Syntax: Accepts a single class name (for example, `include apache`), or class reference (for example, `include Class['apache']`)

Using subdirectories for sensible, readable profile class groups

We are using the component modules puppetlabs/apache, puppetlabs/mysql, and mayflower/php, and encapsulating these into the profile `classes web::apache database::mysql` and `programming::php`, respectively. You can see that I have used some sensible subdirectories and class names to reflect their contribution to the stack, namely `web`, `db`, and `programming` subdirectory locations for the Apache, MySQL, and programming profiles, respectively.

Hiding complexity with parameters, defaults, and abstraction

You can see that, in the Apache profile, we have hidden the complexity of the vhost-defined type quite considerably, so that you just need to provide the name of the vhost as a string. Additionally, you can overwrite the value of the root `internet` directory. I believe it's the same location on all Linux operating systems. This reduction in the size of the interface really reduces complexity, and provides a simple, neat abstraction, which is fine if you don't need multiple Apache vhosts.

Deciding how to set the parameters for component classes

As the Puppet documentation on roles and profiles states (`https://puppet.com/docs/pe/2017.3/managing_nodes/roles_and_profiles_example.html#the-rules-for-profile-classes`), there is a trade-off regarding how to set the parameters provided to component modules, and we should base our decision on *how readable the code is* versus *how flexible the business data needs to be*.

That is, if we always use the same value for a certain parameter, we can *hardcode it* (highly readable), we can compute the value for a parameter based on, for example, facts (quite readable and somewhat flexible), or we can look up the value of a parameter in our business data hierarchy (highly flexible).

Deciding to use either automatic class parameter lookup or the lookup function

For the third consideration in the previous best practice, there's another decision to make around how data arrives into the profile class from your business data hierarchy:

- In these profiles, we have used the automatic class parameter lookup (`https://puppet.com/docs/puppet/5.3/hiera_automatic.html`) to request data from our business data hierarchy. Using the interface of the profile's parameters is a reliable and well-known way to look for the profile's configuration settings, and allows better integration with external tools, such as Puppet Strings (`https://github.com/puppetlabs/puppet-strings`), the YARD-based (`https://yardoc.org`) documentation extraction and presentation tool.
- When we wrote the code for the `profile` class, we also could have omitted all the parameters and instead used the `lookup` function:

```
$jenkins_port = lookup('profile::jenkins::jenkins_port',
{value_type => String, default_value => '9091'})
$java_dist    = lookup('profile::jenkins::java_dist',
{value_type => String, default_value => 'jdk'})
$java_version = lookup('profile::jenkins::java_version',
{value_type => String, default_value => 'latest'})
# ...
```

This approach is an alternative if you aren't comfortable with the automagic nature of an automatic class parameter lookup. I have certainly found it more comfortable to make an explicit data lookup, and then deal with the returned value there and then in the more robust Puppet DSL. I found earlier versions of Hiera notoriously cryptic when trying to track down bugs (`https://puppet.com/blog/debugging-hiera`), and this approach really helps. You can check data types and make further validations directly. By having the full lookup key written out in the profile, we can globally `grep` for it across our entire Puppet DSL codebase, and thus make a definitive link between Puppet manifests and the business data servicing them:

```
grep -nr 'profile::web::apache::vhost*' .
```

You can then use the new `Puppet lookup` (https://puppet.com/docs/puppet/5.3/man/lookup.html) command (previously, the `hiera` command line invocation). Since it's the CLI equivalent of the `lookup` function, you can be sure during debugging that you are getting *exactly* the business data value you require:

```
Puppet lookup ' profile::web::apache::vhost *' .
```

Actually, I also have certain issues with YAML as a language itself (see, for example, https://arp242.net/weblog/yaml_probably_not_so_great_after_all.html), and being able to rely on the robustness of the more explicit Puppet DSL compensates for what I feel are YAML's native weaknesses during debugging.

Take a close look at this blog post: https://puppet.com/blog/debugging-hiera-redux, which is an update to debugging Hiera with the latest commands, and of course ensure you are at the very least using a YAML parser.

Also, bear in mind that Hiera really does have its limitations, especially for larger and more diverse infrastructures (https://www.craigdunn.org/2015/09/solving-real-world-problems-with-jerakia).

So, moving on, let's now look at the higher level of abstraction in the pattern: *roles*.

Roles

Let's take another step back and consider what we want to achieve with the roles part of the pattern. The overarching task is to piece together these *building-brick-like* profile classes into full tech stacks, which we call *roles*, and are now the second part of our full pattern:

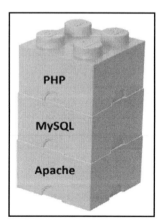

Here you can see that we have taken the composite profiles from our previous example, and stacked them one on top of the other, to produce a full tech stack. We are also utilizing two additional shared profiles:

- `profile::base` is included in all machines, including workstations. It manages security baselines and so on, using conditional logic for OS-specific profiles; for example, `profile:: base::ubuntu`, `profile::base::redhat`, and so on, as needed.
- `profile::server` is included in all machines that provide a service over the network, and configures services such as NTP, firewalls, monitoring, logging, and so on.

Let's look again at the fully functional LAMP stack as an example in Puppet DSL:

```
# LAMP stack


class role::lamp {
  include profile::web::apache
  include profile::db::mysql
  include profile::programming::php
  include profile::server
  include profile::base
}
```

Roles best practices summary

Here are the best practices you should note in the development of your own roles, referring to the preceding LAMP stack as an example:

- Construct roles only with the `include` keyword
- Name roles in your business's conversational name
- Decide on the granularity of roles for your nodes

Let's examine each of these best practices now in turn.

Constructing roles only with the include keyword

As the Puppet documentation states regarding roles, in rules (`https://puppet.com/docs/pe/2017.2/r_n_p_full_example.html#the-rules-for-role-classes`), the only thing roles should do is declare profile classes with the puppet `include` keyword. That is, they don't themselves have any class parameters. Roles also shouldn't declare any component classes or resources—that's the purpose of profiles.

Naming roles in your business's conversational name

The name of a role should be based on your business's conversational name for the type of node it manages. So, if you generally call the machine a *web server*, you should prefer a name such as `role::web`, as opposed to naming it according to any underlying profile technology such as `web::apache` or `web::nginx`. This adds a layer of abstraction and hides the complexity of the profile code, again utilizing good programming practices.

Another advantage to this best practice is the benefit of communication within your organization: testers, project managers, and even business people can understand the simple language of roles, yet Puppet developers communicate more readily at the deeper *profile* level of abstraction.

Profiles expose an appropriate interface to roles. Roles, correspondingly, also expose a neat interface to your ENC, and this allows even fewer technical company personnel to be responsible for node classification.

Deciding on the granularity of roles for your nodes

You should start with roles that are entirely fine-grained, with every role being just a simple list of the profiles it contains.

If you have a lot of only slightly different nodes, you could begin to introduce more complex roles that just contain one profile per line, for example, conditional logic or even nested roles.

Summary

In this chapter, we have broadened our skills in writing Puppet modules to encompass the roles and profiles pattern, with reference to two special cases which provide a reliable way to build reusable, configurable, and refactorable site-wide configuration code.

Next, we stay in the development frame of mind, but look at how we can cover some of those possible edge cases where we may need to extend Puppet beyond its regular usage scenarios.

3
Extending Puppet

The Puppet ecosystem, which is over 10 years old now, was originally written in Ruby.

There has been a lot of progress made toward moving the main code base to the Clojure language (especially the main Puppet Server and PuppetDB components); however, there are still several parts of the ecosystem that can still be accessed at the Ruby level for the purposes of extending Puppet to suit more advanced use cases, namely the following:

- Custom facts
- Custom functions
- Types and providers

Let's consider each of these in turn, and see how we can extend Puppet on both the client and server side using firstly some rudimentary and then later some more advanced understanding of Ruby code.

Custom facts

Custom facts are a client-side technology for extracting arbitrary information from the node during the execution of the agent run, and they may be utilized in Puppet manifests or templates, along with any other distributed facts. Facts are executed on the Puppet agent.

The best way to create and distribute a new custom fact is to place it in a module, in the `facter` subdirectory of the `lib` directory, and it will then be distributed to the agent machine via `pluginsync`.

 This documentation page at `https://puppet.com/docs/puppet/5.3/plugins_in_modules.html#adding-plug-ins-to-a-module` shows you exactly where in a module to place your code, and the section at `https://puppet.com/docs/puppet/5.3/plugins_in_modules.html#installing-plug-ins`, in the same documentation, shows the technical details for `pluginsync`.

The following diagram illustrates the `pluginsync` process that precedes a normal catalog request. Usually, a GET method is called on the Puppet server using the FQDN, which then initiates the `pluginsync` process, and the appropriate facts, types, and providers are distributed back to the agent:

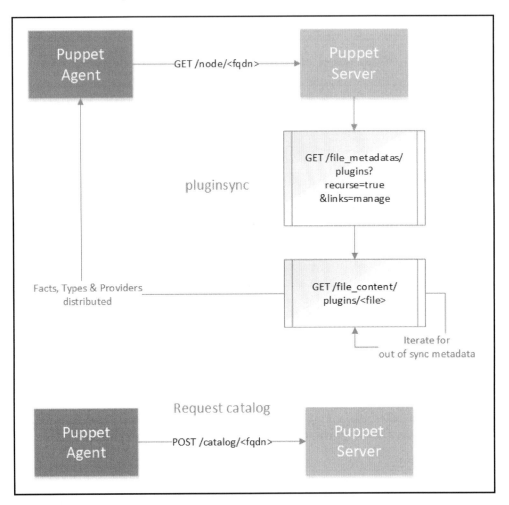

You can review the exact details for all the HTTPS communication between the Puppet agent and Puppet Server at `https://puppet.com/docs/puppet/5.3/subsystem_agent_master_comm.html`.

Most of the time, I have found that a fact is generally just an execution of an arbitrary command-line expression, and that is a good way to think generally about facts: they effectively consist of a Ruby wrapper, usually around a command-line expression that makes itself available to the Puppet ecosystem via Facter.

The following code would be a good snippet to use as a template for further development:

```
# <modulepath>/lib/facter/mycustomfact.rb
Facter.add(:mycustomfact) do
    confine :kernel => "Linux"
    ...
    myvar = Facter::Core::Execution.exec("foo")
  ...
  end
```

Do make sure that you `confine` your fact appropriately. There's nothing worse than when you introduce a new operating system to your infrastructure only to find that you are now executing failing facts because they don't use a certain command syntax. Or, what if we suddenly introduce a handful of Windows nodes, only to find that Windows doesn't, of course, understand most Linux commands?

Bear this in mind during your authoring of custom facts.

Debugging facts

You can debug Facter by using a `facter.debug` statement anywhere in your custom fact's Ruby code, as shown in the following:

```
Facter::Type.newtype(:mycustomfact) do
    ...
    Facter.debug "foo is the value: #{foo}"
    ...
  end
```

During debugging, running Facter by itself won't pick up your new custom fact since it would usually require the `pluginsync` process to distribute it. You must set the `FACTERLIB` environment variable to shortcut this process when you are developing and debugging the new code on your development node. Let's say you have the `some_facts` and `some_other_facts` subdirectories in your personal working directory, where you are editing the Ruby code for a new fact you are developing. You would set the code up as follows:

```
$ ls ~/some_facts
mycustomfact.rb
```

```
$ ls ~/some_other_facts
 myothercustomfact.rb
$ export FACTERLIB="~/some_facts: ~/some_other_facts"
$ facter mycustomfact myothercustomfact —debug
```

Custom functions

This is where custom facts allow us to run arbitrary code on the client side. Custom functions are a *server-side* technology that assist you in the compilation of a catalog. Functions are executed on the Puppet server. Puppet already includes several functions that are built-in, and additional ones are contained in Puppet Forge modules, particularly the `stdlib` module (see `https://forge.puppet.com/puppetlabs/stdlib`).

There are, in fact, three possible ways to create custom functions, although you are unlikely to use the first two, so I will just leave you with some links to the Puppet documentation for those options:

- You could write the function in Puppet DSL (see `https://puppet.com/docs/puppet/5.3/lang_write_functions_in_puppet.html`), although you'll be unable to take advantage of the more powerful Ruby API.
- You could write the function in the legacy Ruby functions API (see `https://puppet.com/docs/puppet/5.3/functions_legacy.html`), although this is to be avoided unless you must specifically support Puppet 3.
- You could write the function in the modern Ruby function API. This is what we'll concentrate on for the remainder of this section.

The best way to create and distribute a new custom function is to place it in a module, in the `puppet/functions/<modulename>` subdirectory of the `lib` directory, and it will then be distributed via `pluginsync`, as shown in the following code:

```
#<modulepath>/lib/puppet/functions/mymodule/myfunction.rb
Puppet::Functions.create_function(:'mymodule::myfunction') do
  dispatch :up do
    param 'String', :a_string
  end
  def up(a_string)
    a_string.upcase
  end
end
```

Types and providers

Puppet already has a very rich lexicon of built-in resource types (see `https://puppet.com/docs/puppet/5.3/type.html`), and these have also been extended with additional modules. Windows-specific resource types would be a very good example of where Puppet has had its resource types successfully extended (see `https://puppet.com/docs/puppet/5.3/resources_windows_optional.html`).

The following are some indications that you may want to consider writing a type and provider as an alternative to regular modules and manifests in Puppet DSL:

- You have several `exec` statements in your Puppet DSL with convoluted `onlyif` and `unless` conditional properties
- Puppet doesn't handle situation very well where:
  - Your Puppet DSL is not a powerful-enough API, and you need access to pure Ruby to manipulate data
  - Your Puppet DSL code has significant and quite convoluted conditional logic

Types

Go through the following steps to create your type:

1. Create and distribute the type
2. Add the `namevar` special attribute
3. Add additional type properties
4. Add the optional `ensure` property
5. Add type parameters
6. Set the property and parameter defaults
7. Check the input value with a validate block
8. Check the input value against a `newvalues` array
9. Check datatype compatibility with `munge`
10. Use `AutoRequire` for implicit relationships
11. Use `Arrays` to list the values of an attribute
12. Use the `desc` method to add inline documentation

Check out the official documentation page on Puppet types at `https://puppet.com/docs/puppet/5.3/custom_types.html`. Gary Larizza's blog also offers an alternative set of useful examples of types at `http://garylarizza.com/blog/2013/11/25/fun-with-providers/`.

Let's now go through each of these steps to create your new type in more detail in the following sections.

Creating and distributing the type

The best way to create and distribute a new custom type is to place it into a module, in the `puppet/type` subdirectory of the `lib` directory, and it will then be distributed to the agent machine via `pluginsync`, as we already saw with custom facts in the previous section.

The filename should match the name of the type under development, as shown in the following code:

```
<modulepath>/lib/puppet/type/mynewtype.rb

Puppet::Type.newtype(:mynewtype) do
...
end
```

Adding the namevar special attribute

After we make use of the special attribute of the type, that is its `namevar`, we can then actually use a declaration of our resource using the Puppet DSL. The `namevar` should identify the resource uniquely within the underlying operating system, and must be something that can be prespecified, as shown in the following code:

```
Puppet::Type.newtype(:mynewtype) do

  mynewparam(:name, :namevar => true) do
  end

end
```

Now, we can declare our resource in the Puppet DSL. In this case, the `namevar` defaults to the resource title, as shown in the following code:

```
mynewtype { 'foo': }
```

The resource title is used to make a reference to the resource uniquely inside the Puppet catalog. Hence, the `namevar` indicates the underlying system's name for that resource, as shown in the following code:

```
mynewtype { 'foo':
    name => 'bar',
  }
```

Then, run the following command:

```
$ puppet apply -e "mynewtype { 'foo': }"
notice: Finished catalog run in 0.09 seconds
```

Adding additional type properties

Type properties are attributes that reflect the current state of that resource on the underlying operating system.

During the Puppet run, these values are actively enforced, so they should be both *discoverable* and *updatable*. If the attribute can't be updated, it could be implemented as a read-only property. In the following code, we are extending our example type's interface to define a version property:

```
Puppet::Type.newtype(:mynewtype) do
   ...
   mynewproperty(:version) do
   end
   ...
  end
```

Now we start to use that property in the Puppet DSL, as shown in the following code:

```
mynewtype{ 'foo':
    version => '2.2',
  }
```

But it won't allow the catalog to compile yet, since there's no implementation for that property in any corresponding provider, as shown in the following command:

```
$ puppet apply -e "mynewtype { 'foo': version => '2.2' }"
err: /Stage[main]// Mynewtype[foo]: Could not evaluate: undefined method
'version' for nil:NilClass
notice: Finished catalog run in 0.04 seconds
```

Adding the optional ensure property

Although optional, most native Puppet resource types do have an ensure property, although there are exceptions—for example, . exec and notify. You simply give the resource type the ensure property by immediately calling ensurable:

```
Puppet::Type.newtype(:mynewtype) do
  ensurable
  ...
end
```

The corresponding providers for this type would then implement the ensure property through the use of create, exists?, and destroy methods.

In Puppet DSL, the ensure property should be the first attribute in the resource (according to the Puppet style guidelines), and it supports the present and absent keywords (present being the default, so it may be omitted for the sake of brevity), as shown in the following code:

```
mynewtype { 'foo':
  ensure => absent,
}
```

Adding type parameters

Type parameters differ from properties in that they don't directly relate to actual discoverable and updatable resources on the underlying system. Rather, they do one of the two following things:

- Allow you to specify additional informational context for interacting with properties and resources on the underlying system
- Provide a layer of abstraction allowing you to override the expected behavior on the underlying system

Let's add a source parameter to our new type using the newparam method:

```
Puppet::Type.newtype(:mynewtype) do
  ...
  newparam(:source) do
  end
  ...
end
```

Setting property and parameter defaults

Let's say we wanted to add an additional `override` parameter, which we wanted to configure with a default value of `false`. Here's the Ruby code to express that:

```
Puppet::Type.newtype(:mynewtype) do
  ...
  newparam(:override) do
    defaultto :false
  end
  ...
end
```

Checking the input value with a validate block

We can validate the provided value of a new property called `version` with a `validate` block and, for example, a `regex` expression, as shown in the following code:

```
Puppet::Type.newtype(:mynewtype) do
  ...
  newproperty(:version) do
    validate do |value|
      fail("Invalid version specified") unless value =~
        /^(\d+\.)?(\d+\.)?(\*|\d+)$/
    end
  end
  ...
end
```

Checking the input value against a newvalues array

We can also validate the provided value of the property with an array of values using the `newvalues` method, as shown in the following code:

```
Puppet::Type.newtype(:mynewtype) do
  ...
  newparam(:override) do
    defaultto :true
    newvalues(:true, :false)
  end
  ...
end
```

Checking datatype compatibility with munge

To decide whether an underlying provider property should be updated, a simple equality comparison is made between the provided value and the value retrieved using the provider.

The `munge` method can ensure that the data supplied by the user has a consistent datatype with that expected to be returned from the provider. For example, we could call the `munge` method to make sure that the user-supplied datatype of `integer` or `numeric string` is compatible with the `integer` required by the provider, as shown in the following code:

```
Puppet::Type.newtype(:mynewtype) do
  ...
  newparam(:identifier) do
    munge do |value|
      Integer(value)
    end
  end
  ...
end
```

Using autorequire for implicit relationships

To make it easier for users of your type, you can use `autorequire` to avoid tediously specifying a lot of explicit relationships in longhand between resources. The `autorequire` method establishes implicit ordering between resources in the catalog. A typical example of this would be filing resources depending on their parent directories.

For example, in our type, if the `source` parameter is a file path, then we should ensure the corresponding `file` resource is managed first, as shown in the following code:

```
Puppet::Type.newtype(:mynewtype) do
  ...
  autorequire(:file) do
    self[:source]
  end
  ...
end
```

Manually specified dependencies in the Puppet DSL have a higher precedence for the compiler than the implicit dependencies that are put in place by virtue of the `autorequire` method.

Using arrays to assign a list of values to an attribute

When the expected value of an attribute is an array, the `array_matching` option should be included in the call to `newproperty` with a value of `all`. All values of the array are then used for that attribute, as shown in the following code:

```
Puppet::Type.newtype(:mynewtype) do
  ...
  newproperty(:myarray, :array_matching => :all) do
  end
  ...
end
```

Using the desc method to add inline documentation

Users of your new type can use the `puppet describe` and `puppet doc` commands to fetch the inline documentation you've configured. For a full description of all the types currently configured in your environment, including custom resources, run the following command:

```
$ puppet describe -list
```

Let's finish our type example now by adding some inline documentation using the `desc` method:

```
Puppet::Type.newtype(:mynewtype) do

  ensurable

  newparam(:override) do
    desc 'whether or not to override'
    defaultto :true
    newvalues(:true, :false)
  end

  newproperty(:version) do
    desc 'the version to use for mynewtype'
    validate do |value|
      fail("Invalid version") unless value =~
        /^(\d+\.)?(\d+\.)?(\*|\d+)$/
    end
  end

  newparam(:identifier) do
    desc 'the identifier for mynewtype'
    munge do |value|          '
```

```
        Integer(value)
      end
   end

end
```

Providers

Providers are the implementation of the resources on a system. Types express the interface used in describing the resources, whereas providers provide the implementation about how the resources interact with the underlying system.

The separation between the interface and its implementation allows multiple providers to be developed for a type.

The `package` type provided as part of a Puppet installation, for example, has many separate providers that interact with systems, including `rpm`, `apt`, `yum`, `zipper`, `chocolatey`, and so on. All that's needed for a new provider to be developed is for it to adhere to the interface defined in its type.

 You can check out the official documentation pages on Puppet providers at `https://puppet.com/docs/puppet/5.3/custom_types.html#providers` and `https://puppet.com/docs/puppet/5.3/provider_development.html`. Gary Larizza's blog also offers an alternative set of useful examples on providers at `http://garylarizza.com/blog/2013/11/26/fun-with-providers-part-2/`.

Go through the following steps to create a new provider for your type:

1. Create and distribute your provider
2. Indicate the suitability of the provider to the type in the following ways:
    - Using the `confine` method
    - Using the `defaultfor` method
    - Using the `commands` method
3. Implement the `ensure` property
    - Using the `exists?` method
    - Using the `create` and `destroy` methods
4. Use the GET and SET methods to manage type properties
5. Implement the `self.instances` method

Let's now go into more detail for each of these steps for creating your new provider in the following sections.

Creating and distributing the provider

The best way to create and distribute a new provider for your type is to place it into the same module, in the `puppet/provider/<typename>` subdirectory of the `lib` directory, and it will then be distributed to the agent machine via `pluginsync`. Note that the filename should match the name of the provider, as shown in the following code:

```
# <modulepath>/lib/puppet/provider/mynewtype/myprovider.rb

Puppet::Type.type(:mynewtype).provide(:myprovider) do
  ...
end
```

Indicating the suitability of the provider to the type

The `confine` and `commands` methods are used to ascertain which providers are valid for the type, and the `defaultfor` method is used to indicate the default provider where there are multiple providers. Let's take a look at each of these methods.

Using the confine method

The `confine` method can be used with a fact, as shown in the following code:

```
Puppet::Type.type(:mynewtype).provide(:myprovider) do
  ...
  confine :osfamily => :redhat
  ...
end
```

The `confine` method could also use `exisits` to base its conditions on whether a certain file is present on the system under management. The following example demonstrates how the provider is restricted to only those systems where Puppet's `.config` file exists:

```
Puppet::Type.type(:mynewtype).provide(:myprovider) do
  ...
  confine :exisits => Puppet[:config]
  ...
end
```

Another possibility is to base the conditions of the `confine` method on certain Puppet features (they are all listed in the source code directory at `https://github.com/puppetlabs/puppet/tree/master/lib/puppet/feature`), as shown in the following code:

```
Puppet::Type.type(:mynewtype).provide(:myprovider) do
  ...
  confine :feature => :selinux
  ...
end
```

Finally, `confine` can accept a Boolean expression to restrict your provider, as shown in the following code:

```
Puppet::Type.type(:mynewtype).provide(:myprovider) do
  ...
  confine :exisits =>  Puppet[:config]
  ...
  confine :true => begin
    if File.exists?(Puppet[:config])
      File.readlines(Puppet[:config]).find {|line| line =~ /^\s*\[agent\]/
}
    end
  end
  ...
end
```

Using the defaultfor method

The `confine` method is fine, but its usage may still result in multiple valid providers for a particular resource type. In this circumstance, the type should specify its preferred provider using the `defaultfor` method.

The `defaultfor` method uses a fact name and value as its arguments, which are then used to determine the default provider for certain types of underlying system.

For example, on Red Hat systems, both `yum` and `rpm` would be valid as providers to the package resource type, but the `defaultfor` method would be used to indicate that for Red Hat systems, `yum` is in fact the default provider, as shown in the following code:

```
Puppet::Type.type(:mynewtype).provide(:yum) do
  ...
  confine :osfamily =>  :redhat
  defaultfor: osfamily => :redhat
  ...
end
```

Using the commands method

Confining providers may also be based on the availability of certain commands from the system path using the `commands` method.

More importantly, by using the special methods generated by `commands`, we can also inform Puppet of the correct commands for interacting with the underlying system. This is preferable over Ruby's own methods for command execution, such as `%x{cmd}` or `cmd` for the following reasons:

- Puppet displays commands invoked this way when the `--debug` flag is set
- They are documented as a requirement for the provider
- Exceptions are handled consistently by raising a `Puppet::ExecutionFalure`

This is shown in the following code:

```
Puppet::Type.type(:mynewtype).provide(:yum) do
...
  commands :yum => 'yum', :rpm => 'rpm'
...
 end
```

Implementing the ensure property

In order to implement the `ensure` property, the providers need to be able to ascertain whether the resource exists, create the resource where it doesn't exist, and destroy resources that exist. This is implemented by virtue of the `exists?`, `create`, and `destroy` methods, which we will look at in the following sections.

Using the exists? method

The `exists?` method retrieves the `ensure` state of the resource. A Boolean is returned, as shown in the following code:

```
Puppet::Type.type(:mynewtype).provide(:yum) do
  ...
  confine :osfamily =>   :redhat
  defaultfor: osfamily => :redhat
  ...
  def exists?
    begin
      rpm('-q', resource[:name])
    rescue Puppet::ExecutionFailure => e
```

```
          false
        end
      end
      ...
    end
```

Using the create and destroy methods

The existence state of a resource is modified with reference to the declaration of the resource with the ensure property by the user in the Puppet DSL by using the create and destroy methods.

The create method is called when both of the following criteria have been met:

- The ensure property has been set to present in the resource declaration
- The false value is returned by the exists? method (to indicate that the resource doesn't already exist)

The destroy method is called when both of the following criteria have been met:

- The ensure property has been set as absent in the resource declaration
- The true value is returned by the exists? method (to indicate that the resource already exists)

The following code shows how you can use these methods:

```
Puppet::Type.type(:mynewtype).provide(:yum) do
  ...
  def create
    package=resource[:version] ?
      "#{resource[:name]}-#{resource[:version]}]" : resource[:name]
    yum('install', '-y, package')
  end
  ...
  def destroy
    yum('erase', '-y', resource[:name])
  end
  ...
end
```

Using the GET and SET methods to manage type properties

Each property defined in the type should implement a GET and SET method in the provider.

Puppet will then invoke these methods during a Puppet run to manage the property as follows:

1. The GET method is called initially to retrieve the current value
2. This is subsequently compared against the value declared by the user in the Puppet DSL
3. If the values are different, then the SET method is invoked to update that value if necessary.

This is shown in the following code:

```
Puppet::Type.type(:mynewtype).provide(:yum) do
  ...
  def version
    version = rpm('-q', resource[:name])
    if version =~ /^#{Regexp.escape(resource[:name])}-(.*)/
      $1
    end
  end

  def version=(value)
    yum('install', "#{resource[:name]}-#{resource[:version]}")
  end
  ...
end
```

Implementing the self.instances method

Puppet provides an additional mode of operation, that being the discovery of resources using the puppet resource command. The self.instances method should implement the return of any instances of a particular resource type that the provider is able to find on the underlying system.

The following example illustrates the use of the `rpm -qa` command to query for all packages installed on the underlying Red Hat system:

```
Puppet::Type.type(:mynewtype).provide(:yum) do
  ...
  def self.instances
    pkgs = rpm('-qa','--qf','%{NAME} %{VERSION}-%{RELEASE}\n')
    pkgs.split("\n").collect do |entry|
      name, version = entry.split(' ', 2)
      new( :name => name,
        :ensure => :present,
        :version => version
      )
    end
  end
  ...
end
```

Each resource returned by `self.instances` stores the attributes in the `@property_hash` instance variable. All the other methods in the provider have access to the property hash, so we could implement the `exists?` and `version` methods in our provider in a much simpler way, as shown in the following code:

```
Puppet::Type.type(:mynewtype).provide(:yum) do
  ...
  def exists?
    @property_hash[:ensure] == :present
  end

  def version
    @property_hash[:version]
  end
  ...
end
```

Summary

In this chapter, we looked at extending Puppet with client-side facts, server-side custom functions, and custom types and providers. You can see that with some Ruby know-how, you can easily extend the Puppet ecosystem to cover some of your own unique requirements.

In the next chapter, we'll be taking a look at Hiera 5, which we'll use to create a separation between code and business data.

4
Hiera 5

Hiera 5 is now a fully fledged member of the Puppet ecosystem. We've all been using Hiera for several years already, to provide a so-called *separation of concerns* between Puppet code and configuration data. Essentially, Hiera lets us separate the *how* (Puppet modules and manifests) from the *what* (configuration data). This allows us to keep all site-specific and business-specific data out of our manifests, making our Puppet modules vastly more portable. I can recall some time ago in the Puppet community, when Kelsey Hightower first gave us a presentation about separating manifests from data. Well, Hiera 5 finally comes of age in this version, and now allows us complete mastery over this aspect of our infrastructure design.

Hiera provides a key/value lookup facility for configuration data, allowing external lookups of values, and then exposing that data to Puppet DSL and hence, the Puppet compiler. Hiera data is kept in a pluggable database comprised of usually nothing more than simple text-based files. What we should aim to achieve is the design of a data hierarchy that essentially cascades through our server categories. Hiera then searches through all the tiers in this hierarchy, merging all the results into either a single value, array, or hash.

Although Hiera typically has a pluggable design, the sources for Hiera data are written in easy-to-read YAML. This means that it's often not necessary for Puppet developers to always be involved with site configuration, so some server configuration can now be done by other, less technical professionals in your organization.

Separation of concerns between code and data

Hiera separates Puppet DSL from business data, allowing us to use some of the same generic Puppet DSL repeatedly. In fact, as much as 80% of the Puppet DSL most organizations use is entirely generic; only the business data varies. Hiera allows us to make this full separation of concerns between functionality and business data, instead handily passing in the business data to our modules as parameters.

Hiera works by first setting business values at the widest catchment (that is, site-wide, or *common* in Puppet parlance), and then moving up the hierarchy, overriding this global value at the appropriate level.

Data specific to infrastructure lends itself incredibly well to a hierarchical model. Infrastructure always tends to consist of sets of configurable attributes: IP addresses, ports, hostnames, and API endpoints. There is a ton of settings that we configure within our infrastructures, and most of them are best represented hierarchically.

A lot of infrastructure data starts out with a default, let's say, the DNS resolver your data center uses. You first set this as a key-value pair in the `common.yaml` data file. After Puppet is first installed, the hierarchy hash inside `hiera.conf` provides initially just this common (default) level:

```
---
version: 5
hierarchy:
  - name: Common
    path: common.yaml
defaults:
  data_hash: yaml_data
  datadir: data
```

Introducing a frame for the environment

Here's a typical scenario for Hiera: you find yourself having to override the DNS setting for your development environment because that environment can't connect to the production resolver on your network. You then deploy your production in a second data center, and you need that location to be different. Hiera allows us to model settings such as *the production DNS resolver is* `10.20.1.3`, *and the development DNS server is* `10.199.30.2`.

To accommodate this type of scenario, we can introduce what's best described as an environment *frame* within the Hiera hierarchy, as follows:

```
---
version: 5
 hierarchy:
    - name: "Per-node data"
      path: "nodes/%{trusted.certname}.yaml"

    - name: "Per-environment data"
      path: "%{server_facts.environment}.yaml"

  - name: Common
      path: common.yaml
```

The percent-braces `%{variable}` syntax denotes a Hiera interpolation token. Wherever you use these interpolation tokens, Hiera will evaluate the variable's value and inserts it appropriately into the hierarchy.

 See the Puppet documentation for specifics on the Hiera 5 configuration syntax: `https://puppet.com/docs/puppet/5.3/hiera_config_yaml_5.html#config-file-syntax-hierayaml-v5`.

If we are using the data `datadir` and using the YAML backend by default, we can completely omit the defaults hash, as these are the default settings.

A more complete hierarchy

We are just handling simple hierarchies, so instead of programming a complex conditional statement in Puppet DSL to determine how a DNS resolver gets resolved, we can build a hierarchy that best represents our infrastructure, such as the following:

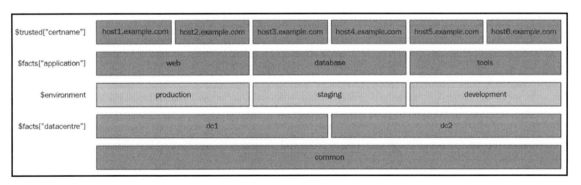

This example hierarchy would be represented with the following `hiera.yaml`:

```
---
version: 5
  hierarchy:
    - name: "Per-node data"
      path: "nodes/%{trusted.certname}.yaml"

    - name: "Per application data"
      path: "%{facts.application}.yaml"

    - name: "Per environment data"
      path: "%{server_facts.environment}.yaml"

    - name: "Per datacenter data"
      path: "%{facts.datacenter}.yaml"

    - name: "Common data"
      path: common.yaml
```

The `facts`, `trusted`, and `server_facts` hashes are the most useful hashes to interpolate in `hiera.yaml`.

Note, if you need to reference the node's `fqdn`, use `trusted.certname`. In order to reference the environment of a node, the `server_facts.environment` fact is available.

 See the Puppet documentation for more specifics on interpolation in Hiera: `https://puppet.com/docs/puppet/5.3/hiera_merging.html#interpolation`.

Hiera 5 summary

Let's step through some of the key differences between Hiera 3 and Hiera 5 now, as follows:

- Global, environment, and module layers
- Encrypted YAML backend
- Lookup function
- Debugging Hiera

Global, environment, and module layers

The earlier incarnations of Hiera (version 3 or earlier) used a single, entirely global `hiera.yaml`. Since its hierarchy is entirely global, it's not actually possible to change it without changing all environments simultaneously. Environments are usually used to control code changes, so this really makes a single `hiera.yaml` file quite inappropriate. Hiera 5 uses three layers of configuration and data:

- Global layer:
    - In Hiera 3, this was the only layer
    - Useful for very temporary overrides, for example, when your operations team must bypass regular change processes
    - The legacy Hiera 3 backends are still supported—so it can be used while migrating to Hiera 5
    - This layer should generally now be avoided. All regular data should now be specified in the environment layer

- Environment layer:
    - The environment layer is now where most of the Hiera data definition happens
    - Available across all modules in the environment
    - Overrides the module layer

- Module layer:
    - As we discussed in `Chapter 1`, *Authoring Modules*, the module layer can now configure default values and merge behavior for a module's class parameters. It is a handy alternative to using the `params.pp` pattern.
    - To get the identical behavior, as we are used to with the `params.pp` pattern, the `default_hierarchy` setting is advisable, as those bindings aren't in merges.
    - Data set in the environment layer overrides the default data configured by the author of the module.

Encrypted YAML backend

In Puppet 4.9.3, a `hiera-eyaml` backend was added to the Hiera functionality, allowing you to store encrypted data values. So, you can now hide away all your secret values, such as passwords, certificates, and so on, rather than using plain text in your Hiera data files. Let's go through the steps you can take to get this facility up and running.

Installing hiera-eyaml

To set up `eyaml` with Puppet Server, install the `hiera-eyaml` gem with the following command:

```
$ sudo /opt/puppetlabs/bin/puppetserver gem install hiera-eyaml
```

You'll also need to install the Ruby gem a second time with the following command:

```
$ sudo /opt/puppetlabs/puppet/bin/gem install hiera-eyaml
```

Creating the encryption keys

Use the `eyaml createkeys` command to create the public and private encryption keys, as follows:

```
$ eyaml createkeys
```

This command will create the public and private keys with their default names in the default `./keys` directory.

Securely storing away the encryption keys

Let's now copy the two keys into the `/etc/puppetlabs/puppet/eyaml` directory and set up the appropriate permissions, giving the Puppet user ownership, and excluding all other users from being able to access the two keys:

```
$ mv -t /etc/puppetlabs/puppet/eyaml ./keys/*.pem
$ chown -R puppet:puppet /etc/puppetlabs/puppet/eyaml
$ chmod -R 0500 /etc/puppetlabs/puppet/eyaml
$ chmod 0400 /etc/puppetlabs/puppet/eyaml/*.pem
$ ls -lha /etc/puppetlabs/puppet/eyaml
-r-------- 1 puppet puppet 1.7K Apr 25 08:08 private_key.pkcs7.pem
-r-------- 1 puppet puppet 1.1K Apr 25 08:08 public_key.pkcs7.pem
```

Changing hiera.yaml

Make the following settings in `hiera.yaml` to enable the `hiera-eyaml` backend, and provide access to the keys and data files:

- Set the `lookup_key` property to the value `eyaml_lookup_key` in order to use the new `eyaml` backend
- Add the locations of the encryption keys to the `options` hash
- Change all the file paths to `eyaml` rather than YAML file extensions:

```
---
version: 5
hierarchy:
  - name: "Encrypted and regular data"
    lookup_key: eyaml_lookup_key      paths:
      - "nodes/%{trusted.certname}.eyaml"
      - "%{facts.application}.eyaml"
      - "%{server_facts.environment}.eyaml"
      - "%{facts.datacenter}.eyaml"
      - "common.eyaml"
    options:
      pkcs7_private_key:
/etc/puppetlabs/puppet/eyaml/private_key.pkcs7.pem
      pkcs7_public_key:   /etc/puppetlabs/puppet/eyaml/public_key.pkcs7.pem
  defaults:
    datadir: data
```

With this configuration, you can store both encrypted and plaintext keys and values into your `eyaml` data files.

Lookup function

It's worth mentioning the fact that we should now be using the new `lookup()` function in our Puppet DSL to retrieve Hiera values. The `lookup()` function replaces the now deprecated set of Hiera functions:

- `hiera( )`
- `hiera_hash( )`
- `hiera_array( )`
- `hiera_include( )`

These each have an equivalent way of achieving the same result, so some fairly simple find-and-replace work on your Puppet DSL code base will soon have you moving away from the deprecated roadmap.

The lookup function syntax

The `lookup` function syntax has three specific styles of usage, as follows:

- With mandatory <name> and set of three optional arguments: <value type>, <merge behavior> and <default value> in that given order and separated by commas. For example, lookup(<name>, [<value type>], [<merge behavior>], [<default value>]).
- With optional <name>, and mandatory <options hash> arguments. For example, lookup([<name>], <options hash>).
- With mandatory <name> and <lambda expression> arguments. For example, lookup(<name>, <lambda expression>).

Lookup function arguments

Arguments to the `lookup` function shown in [ ] are not mandatory which is covered in the preceding section.

- <name>:
    - Must be of the data type string or array.
    - The key name in the Hiera hierarchy to retrieve.
    - An array of keys may also be provided. If the resulting Hiera lookup doesn't provide a result for the first key, it will iteratively try retrievals for the subsequently given keys, finally resorting to the default if none of the array keys succeed in returning a value.
- <value type>:
    - Must be a valid data type
    - The Hiera lookup (and hence the compilation of the catalog) will fail if the datatype of the returned value does not match the data type given here
    - Defaults to Data (that is, any normal value will not fail the Hiera lookup)

- `<merge behavior>`:
    - Must be either a `string` or a `hash` (please see the following *Deep merge lookup settings explained* section).
    - Explains whether and how to merge multiple values encountered at different hierarchy levels. This overrides the merge behavior that's been specified in the Hiera data sources.
    - Defaults to no value, meaning that, if present, Hiera will first use the merge behavior defined in the data sources; otherwise it will simply use the first lookup strategy (please see the following *Lookup strategies* section).

- `<default value>`:
    - If provided, the Hiera lookup will return the value provided here when it cannot find a value in the Hiera hierarchy
    - The values found by the Hiera lookup are never merged with the given default(s)
    - The `default type` and `value type` must match
    - `no value` is the default; meaning that whenever the Hiera lookup cannot retrieve a normal value, the Hiera lookup (and hence the compilation) will fail

As explained in the *The lookup function syntax* section, there's also an alternative way of providing the lookup function arguments, using an `<options hash>`:

- `<options hash>`:
    - Must be of type `hash`
    - If using this alternative `<options hash>` style of syntax, you can't combine it with any of the preceding regular arguments except `<name>`
    - Permissible keys for the options hash are as follows:
        - `name`: Identical to the first `<name>` argument described previously. You can pass this either as an argument or in the options `hash`, but not both.
        - `value_type`: Identical to the second `<value type>` argument described previously.
        - `merge`: This is the same as the third `<merge behavior>` argument described previously.
        - `default_value`: This is the same as the fourth `<default_value>` argument described previously.

- `default_values_hash`: This is a hash of lookup keys and their respective default values. If a normal value cannot be retrieved from a Hiera lookup, this hash will be checked for the key before Hiera gives up. This can be combined with either `default_value` or a lambda expression, which will be substituted if the value is unable to be retrieved from the Hiera hierarchy. An empty hash is the default.

- `override`: This value is a hash of Hiera lookup keys and their respective override settings. Hiera checks in the overrides hash for the key; if it is found, it returns that value finally, ignoring any merge behavior. An empty hash is the default.

Additionally, as explained in the *Lookup function syntax* section, there is a third alternative to providing the arguments to the `lookup()` function using a single lambda expression. If the Hiera lookup is unable to retrieve a value, the requested key is passed into the lambda expression, the result of which becomes the `default_value`:

```
lookup('my::key') |$my_key| {"Hiera couldn't find '${my_key}'. Did you forget
to add this key-value pair to your hierarchy?"}
```

Here, `<lambda_expression>` is returning a custom string to provide feedback to the user and to handle Hiera being unable to retrieve the required key gracefully , which in previous versions of Hiera would fail silently, causing all sorts of mischief.

We could also add our fact values and so on to help the user find the right place to insert their key-value pair (please refer to the *A more complete hierarchy* section at the beginning of this chapter):

```
lookup('my::key') |$my_key| {"Hiera couldn't find '${my_key}' using certname
'${trusted.certname}', application '${facts.application}', environment
${server_facts.environment}, and datacenter ${facts.datacenter}. Did you
forget to add this key-value pair to your hierarchy?"}
```

Lookup function examples

Let's just quickly run through the main use cases for the `lookup( )` function, also showing the equivalent usages of the old `hiera( )` function:

- The following usage is a completely regular lookup:

```
lookup('ntp::user')
  # equivalent to hiera('ntp::user')
```

- The following usage is a regular lookup, while providing a default:

```
lookup('ntp::user','root')
  # equivalent to hiera('ntp::user','root')
```

- The following usage is an array lookup:

```
lookup('my_ntp_servers', Array, 'unique')
  # equivalent to hiera_array('ntp_servers')
```

- The following is a deep-merge lookup:

```
lookup('users', Hash, 'deep')
  # equivalent to hiera_hash('users') with deep
```

- The following is a classification lookup:

```
lookup('classes', Array[String], 'unique').include
  # equivalent to hiera_include('classes')
```

Lookup strategies

The merge strategy is no longer set globally as it was in previous versions of Hiera, and this is a big improvement. The valid merge strategies are as follows:

- `first`: A retrieval of the first match is made; this is equivalent to the traditional `hiera()` default behavior
- `unique`: This is an array merge, equivalent to the old `hiera_array()` function
- `hash`: This is equivalent to the old `hiera_hash()` function without deep merging enabled

- deep: This is equivalent to the old `hiera_hash()` function with `deeper` merging enabled (`deep` is no longer supported)

 Check the official Hiera 3.3 documentation to understand the concept of deep and deeper merges fully: `https://puppet.com/docs/hiera/3.3/lookup_types.html#example`. Note, `deeper` merges in Hiera 3 are equivalent to a `deep` merge in Hiera 4+.
`deep` merges are no longer supported.

Deep merge lookup settings explained

Let's now look together at these commonly misunderstood merge settings, to make sure we have our Hiera know-how at the mastery level.

knockout_prefix setting

Here is an example of a deep merge, using the `knockout_prefix` setting to specify a prefix to indicate a value should be removed from the result:

```
# common.yaml
---
classification:
  classes:
     - paessler
     - other
# mynode.myorg.net.yaml
classification:
  classes:
     - -- paessler
     - nagios
     - webserver
```

Here, we are indicating that `mynode.myorg.net.yaml` is not using Paessler for monitoring, but rather Nagios. The use of this lookup returns the correct value, as follows:

```
lookup({
 'name' => 'classification',
 'merge' => {
 'strategy' => 'deep',
 'knockout_prefix' => '--',
 },
 })
```

sort_merge_arrays setting

We could also sort the merged arrays with the `sort_merge_arrays` setting, and remove the data that matches `knockout_prefix`. An array member or entire keys can be removed from the resulting hash:

```
lookup({
  'name'  => 'classification',
  'merge' => {
    'strategy'          => 'deep',
    'knockout_prefix'   => '--',
    'sort_merge_arrays' => true,
  },
})
```

merge_hash_arrays setting

If a certain array member contains a hash and you desire these to be merged together, this is possible by using the `merge_hash_arrays` setting.

unpack_arrays setting

Finally, there's the `unpack_arrays` setting. Let us change the data for our node again to look as follows, while leaving the common data the same:

```
# mynode.myorg.net.yaml
 classification:
   classes:
     - --paessler,nagios
     - webserver
```

The `unpack_arrays` setting takes each string, splits it according to the `,` delimiter, creating an array of, in our example, ["--paessler", "nagios"], and then merging it; in our example knocking out the `paessler` value, since it was indicated with the `knockout_prefix` as follows:

```
lookup({
   'name'  => 'classification',
   'merge' => {
     'strategy'          => 'deep',
     'knockout_prefix' => '--',
     unpack_arrays      =>',',
   },
})
```

Debugging Hiera

Hiera's data lookups are all done with reference to the details of the node being configured, and it's that node's scope which informs Hiera the datasets it should select, how to order the data, and how to interpolate certain values.

 See the Hiera documentation for more specifics on debugging and the lookup function: `https://puppet.com/docs/puppet/5.3/hiera_quick.html#testing-hiera-data-on-the-command-line` and `https://puppet.com/docs/puppet/5.3/man/lookup.html`.

Old debugging techniques

Previously, we have run `hiera` from the command line with the `-debug` argument, and provided the setting, for example, `mysetting`, we would like to look up, as follows:

```
$ hiera -c /etc/puppetlabs/puppet/hiera.yaml --debug mysetting
```

The preceding command runs `hiera` in the debug verbosity necessary, but we also need to collect the node's facts and other relevant information (particularly the environment and `fqdn`):

```
$ hiera -c /etc/puppetlabs/puppet/hiera.yaml --debug --json facts.json
mysetting environment=production fqdn=mynode.example.local
```

Another earlier debugging method was to use the `hiera` lookup function inside `puppet apply` using the `-e` (execute) argument:

```
$ puppet apply --debug -e '$foo = hiera(mysetting) notify { $foo: }'
```

Equivalent debugging technique

The `hiera` command has now been completely replaced with the `puppet lookup` command, so we can run the following and use the `--node` argument to provide the node to which the lookup pertains:

```
$ puppet lookup --node mynode.example.local --debug mysetting
```

The key difference here is that the `puppet lookup` function will now query `puppetdb` to gather all the appropriate facts for the given `node` argument.

We can also now use the `--explain` argument to give a complete description of how Hiera fetches the data in its hierarchy.

Beyond Hiera using Jerakia

If you would like to transcend single-customer and small-scale hierarchical data classifications and open up the possibilities of modeling larger, more complex and diverse environments, you should consider the use of Jerakia (`http://jerakia.io`), using Jerakia as a Hiera backend, or configuring Puppet to accept Jerakia as a data-binding terminus.

Jerakia advanced use cases

Here are some questions around advanced use cases for Jerakia:

- How can I use a different Hiera backend for just one module?
- How can I allow a team the use of a separate hierarchy, exclusively for their own application?
- How can I allow access to a smaller subset of data to a certain user or team?
- How can I use `eyaml` encryption without being forced to use YAML?
- How can I implement a dynamic hierarchy rather than hard coding it?
- How can I group together application-specific data into separate YAML files?

Jerakia allows us to implement some of these corner cases.

Installing Jerakia

Jerakia is installed from a RubyGem. Simply run the following command:

```
$ gem install jerakia
```

Configuring Jerakia

Set up the `jerakia.yaml` configuration file as follows:

```
$ mkdir /etc/jerakia
$ vim /etc/jerakia/jerakia.yaml
```

This is the simplest configuration:

```
---
policydir: /etc/jerakia/policy.d
logfile: /var/log/jerakia.log
loglevel: info
eyaml:
 private_key: /etc/puppetlabs/puppet/eyaml/private_key.pkcs7.pem
 public_key: /etc/puppetlabs/puppet/eyaml/public_key.pkcs7.pem
```

If you intend to use encryption, you should also provide the keys in the `private_key` and `public_key` settings as indicated.

Creating your default Jerakia policy

All requests for data from Jerakia are processed according to the so-called **policy**. The filenames for policies should be the same as the actual name of the policy, and are loaded from the directory indicated by the `policydir` setting in your `jerakia.yaml` configuration file. If a certain policy name is not indicated by the lookup request, then the name `default` is used. Let's create the default policy, as follows:

```
$ mkdir /etc/jerakia/policy.d
$ vim /etc/jerakia/policy.d/default.rb
```

A Jerakia `policy` is a container of the so-called `lookup`, which is performed in the indicated order. A lookup consists of a `datasource` that should be used for the data lookup, along with any plugin functions.

There follows a simple example, using the `file` data source to provide data from simple YAML files:

```
policy :default do

  lookup :default do
    datasource :file, {
      :format    => :yaml,
      :docroot   => "/var/lib/jerakia",
      :searchpath => [
```

```
          "hostname/#{scope[:fqdn]}",
          "environment/#{scope[:environment]}",
          "common",
        ],
      }
    end

  end
```

Let's change the default policy to accommodate settings for another configuration team, based in, let's say, denmark:

```
policy :default do

  lookup :denmark do
    datasource :file, {
      :format    => :yaml,
      :docroot   => "/var/external/data/ie",
      :searchpath => [
        "project/#{scope[:project]}",
        "common",
      ]
    }

    confine scope[:location], "dk"

    confine request.namespace[0], [
      "apache",
      "php",
    ]
    stop

  end

  lookup :default do
    datasource :file, {
      :format    => :yaml,
      :docroot   => "/var/lib/jerakia",
      :searchpath => [
        "hostname/#{scope[:fqdn]}",
        "environment/#{scope[:environment]}",
        "common",
      ],
    }
  end

  end
```

Using Vault as an encryption backend

The version 2 release of Jerakia now supports integration with Vault via the transit secret backend.

Vault is an open source platform for encrypting, securing, storing, and tightly controlling access to passwords, tokens, certificates, and other secret settings for your infrastructure. Vault also handles those tricky aspects of secret management, such as leasing, rolling, revocation, and auditing.

So, Vault provides something like an *encryption as a service* backend for Jerakia.

Installing and configuring Vault

See the Vault documentation to install and configure Vault: https://www.vaultproject.io/docs/install/index.html

Unsealing Vault

Follow the procedures in the Vault documentation to unseal Vault: https://www.vaultproject.io/docs/concepts/seal.html

Enabling the transit backend

Enable the transit backend by mounting it as follows:

```
$ ./vault mount transit
```

Creating an encryption key

Let's create a key Jerakia will use for encrypting and decrypting. By default, the key is simply called `jerakia`:

```
$ ./vault write -f transit/keys/jerakia
```

Creating a policy for encrypting and decrypting

Now we need to create a policy which restricts Jerakia to using only the encryption and decryption endpoints.

In order to create this policy, we'll create a new file, `jerakia_policy.hcl`, and then import it into Vault using the `policy-write` Vault command:

```
# jerakia_policy.hcl
path "transit/decrypt/jerakia" {
   policy = "write"
 }
 path "transit/encrypt/jerakia" {
   policy = "write"
 }
$ ./vault policy-write jerakia jerakia_policy.hcl
```

Checking the encryption is working correctly

We can now try to encrypt a value on the command line using the Jerakia transit key and the policy that we've just created:

```
$ echo -n "Lorem ipsum dolor sit amet" | base64 | ./vault write
transit/encrypt/jerakia plaintext=- -policy=jerakia
vault:v1:Xv3R5CugxnCLhL/T2eJ+rN+UilHzo78evxd0tf5efx0M2U2qIgaI
```

> See the Vault documentation for more specifics on the `read` and `write` commands: `https://www.vaultproject.io/docs/commands/read-write.html`.

Allowing Jerakia to authenticate with our Vault

AppRole authentication is the recommended method of authenticating with Vault.

When using this authentication method, Jerakia is configured with a role ID (`role_id`) and a secret ID (`secret_id`), and Jerakia uses these values to acquire a limited-lifetime token from Vault to interact with the API of the transit backend.

Upon token expiry, Jerakia will request a new token using `role_id` and `secret_id` again.

First, we'll create an AppRole for Jerakia, giving it a TTL of 15 minutes. This has to be associated with the access policy we created earlier using the policies argument:

```
$ ./vault write auth/approle/role/jerakia token_ttl=15m policies=jerakia
```

Now, we can check the Jerakia AppRole and ascertain the `role_id`:

```
$ ./vault read auth/approle/role/jerakia/role-id
Key      Value
---      -----
 role_id bfce3860-0805-43dc-ab6d-fe789559fe32
```

We also need to create a `secret_id`:

```
$ ./vault write -f auth/approle/role/jerakia/secret-id
Key                   Value
---                   -----
 secret_id            94f23dba-7355-426c-ae1e-5768dbb70280
 secret_id_accessor   f7b0f10a-99f4-4c7e-b69d-7bbd27a3c016
```

Now that we have `role_id` and `secret_id`, we can proceed to integrate Jerakia with Vault.

Configuring Jerakia for encryption

In the `jerakia.yaml` configuration file, we configure the encryption option with a provider of Vault and the specific configuration that our provider requires:

```
encryption:
   provider: vault
   vault_addr: http://127.0.0.1:8200
   vault_use_ssl: false
   vault_role_id: bfce3860-0805-43dc-ab6d-fe789559fe32
   vault_secret_id: 8a2fa99c-7811-5e65-a74a-8ab2ba9b6389
   vault_keyname: jerakia
```

We should now be able to `encrypt` and `decrypt` using Jerakia:

```
$ jerakia secret encrypt mySecret
 vault:v1: d3HftM8HAJDwWeSfLkBcdpAdTFy8fBu3mj4Kf3mHADSLuevwCbjZ
$ jerakia secret decrypt
vault:v1:d3HftM8HAJDwWeSfLkBcdpAdTFy8fBu3mj4Kf3mHADSLuevwCbjZ
 mySecret
```

Encryption-enabling our Jerakia lookups

We enable encryption by using the `output_filter` method to our lookup in our policy:

```
policy :default do

  lookup :default do
    datasource :file, {
      :format    => :yaml,
      :docroot   => "/var/lib/jerakia",
      :searchpath => [
        "hostname/#{scope[:fqdn]}",
        "environment/#{scope[:environment]}",
        "common",
        ],
      }
    output_filter :encryption
  end

end
```

This instructs Jerakia to pass everything to the encryption filter and to match all the retrieved values against the signature of the encryption provider. If a match is made, the encryption provider will be used to decrypt the value before it is returned.

Summary

In this chapter, we have taken a close look at the main differences between Hiera 5 and its earlier incarnations. We have also described how you can now quickly set up the encrypted YAML backend, so you no longer have to save your secret Hiera values in plain text.

We've also looked at Jerakia, which you can use to cover more advanced use cases, such as providing different hierarchies to different teams, and integrating Vault to provide something like an *encryption as a service* backend for Jerakia.

In the next chapter, let's continue our master class by examining the management of Puppet code.

5
Managing Code

Code management has gone a lot of changes over the lifetime of Puppet. In earlier versions of Puppet, code management was largely left to individual users. Most users started by simply editing code directly on the Puppet Master. One organization that I worked for created Yum RPMs for every module, allowing us to roll back and forth between individual modules on multiple Puppet Masters, prior to the introduction of Puppet environments. Many users stored their Puppet code in Git or subversion and checked the code out to directories in the Puppet Master.

Each of these models comes with significant overhead management, and two solutions have risen to the top of the Puppet community during the transition from Puppet 2 to Puppet 3: Puppet Librarian and r10k. Puppet Librarian manages code like a Ruby bundle file, bringing in all the listed modules and dependencies with a single command. Automatic dependency management from the Forge has some issues, as well. Some modules include dependency lists for all operating systems, including ones that are not in your infrastructure. Some modules do not receive updates for a period of time, linking to old versions of a dependency while your organization is using a newer version. Finally, dependencies in Puppet modules are often listed as a range of versions rather than a single version, and if these modules are used across multiple manifests, it can be difficult to resolve conflicts.

Some users of Puppet Librarian use `puppet-librarian-simple`, which does not manage dependencies. Although `puppet-librarian-simple` is easier to install than r10k, it does not maintain feature parity with r10k; r10k has become the most commonly used code management solution, for both enterprise and open source users. r10k allows users to point to a remote repository that contains a set of instructions to build a Puppet environment. Puppet Enterprise comes with an expansion to r10k, known as Puppet Code Manager.

This chapter will cover the following topics:

- Efficiently managing code
- Code Manager
- Git

- r10k
- Control repository
- Installing and using r10k
- Multitenant control repository

Efficiently managing code

Although writing code directly to the disk on a Puppet Master is the easiest way to get started with Puppet, it is the least efficient model for managing infrastructure changes with Puppet. Manual changes leave the users to manage the following issues individually:

- Backup and recovery
- Change management
- Replication of Puppet Masters
- Replication of Puppet environments

Without code management, backups are often performed via disk snapshots, or by simply bundling code and moving it to a separate location in case of emergencies. Manual code placement leaves the organization responsible for maintaining a cadence and process for backing up and restoring, and for change management. Without any code management, replication of code to Puppet Masters and Puppet environments is a fully manual process, which leaves all Puppet code testing and implementation to dangerous manual processes, instead of processes within a controlled environment.

Although placing code in RPMs can solve the backup and recovery issue, change management, and the replication of Puppet Masters, it struggles with Puppet environments. An RPM has to be created for each Puppet environment, and this creates a confusing set of build files that consistently place code in multiple environments. Also, RPMs do not lend themselves to short-lived environments that are used to test individual code features.

Using Code Manager or r10k to manage code drastically simplifies these problems. Code is never written directly to the disk; instead, a list of requirements is pulled from one remote repository, and all relevant code is placed on the Puppet Master. One of the primary benefits of this model is that every change in code can be versioned in Git, and each change can be explicitly referenced (by tag, branch, or commit hash) and placed on the master. All of the code is always stored remotely, and is not reliant on the Puppet Master itself for backup and recovery. Rollbacks are now as easy as changing a single file in a remote repository. Code management also allows for the scaling of multiple Puppet Masters, with both long-lived and short-lived Puppet environments.

Code Manager

Code Manager provides Enterprise RBAC and additional code distribution features to r10k. Code Manager will automatically set r10k up for you, but using it requires that you understand how r10k calls code, and how to store your code in a Git repository.

Git

This book is not intended to be a complete resource on Git, but to use Code Manager effectively, you should know some basics about Git.

Git is a modern code repository that allows for asynchronous work on the same code set by multiple users. It accomplishes this by distinguishing every code commit as the difference between the previous code commit. Every commit is the unique delta in code between the last commit and the current changes. The first commit might add hundreds of lines of code to a code base, but the following commit might be as simple as removing one line and replacing it with another. When this code is cloned (or copied) by another user, it brings down the latest code and allows the user to roll back to previous commits.

As an introduction to Git, let's walk through a scenario. Suppose that you are using Git to redecorate your living room. The current commit is how your living room looks right now. If you liked how it looked last summer, before you replaced your couch, you could roll back to the previous commit and set your living room back to a previously accepted state. Commits should be seen as accepted states of code, or, in this case, accepted states of your living room.

First and foremost, we don't want to break our living room while building a new one, so we'll clone it with `git clone`. This makes a copy of the current living room, and its entire change history is bundled in. To keep things simple, we'll use the most recent version of our living room. If we wanted to make a change to the living room, we could purchase a new couch, a new TV, and two new lamps. Let's suppose that we love the lamps, but we're not sure about the couch and the TV. If we use `git add` on the lamps, it will add those lamps to the staging directory. Git will report the following:

```
$ git status
On branch master
Changes to be committed:
  (use "git reset HEAD <file>..." to unstage)

new object: Lamps

Changes not staged for commit:
```

```
(use "git add <file>..." to update what will be committed)
(use "git checkout -- <file>..." to discard changes in working directory)

modified: Couch
modified: Television
```

We've asked Git to track the changes on the new lamps that we love. When we type `git commit`, we're asked to write what the change is, and then, Git will commit the new living room to memory:

```
$ git commit -m 'Beautiful New Lamps'

[master 0b1ae47] Beautiful New Lamps
 1 object changed, 0 insertions(+), 0 deletions(-)
 create mode 100644 Lamps
```

Notice that the couch and TV are not included in this manifest of changes. In our working directory, or our current living room, the couch and TV are still present, but they're not permanent changes until we also add and commit them. Optionally, we could send our new commit (the lamps) back to our remote repository for safekeeping, and to let any other decorator use our most current living room composition with `git push`.

In short, we clone (copy) a living room format. We make changes to that format at will. The changes that we're sure we like, we add and commit. The changes that we're unsure about remain present, but only in our current working directory (or the current state of our living room). We could either add and commit our couch and television, or simply `git stash` and return our living room to the last known good state, which is now our previous living room, plus the new lamps. This pattern gives us the option to try drastic changes, and only commit the ones that we're sure about as a checkpoint in time. Once we have a commit (checkpoint) that we're willing to stand behind, we can then push that back to the version of the living room that everyone can see.

Let's go over using Git against code, instead of in the living room. The first step is to clone, or copy, a repository. The command `git clone` copies an entire repository and its history, and brings it to the local workstation. This copy of code is entirely separate from where it was cloned (its origin). `git clone` creates an entirely standalone copy of the original repository.

When a user first enters a code repository, all of the code is in the working directory. A user can make changes to the code at will here, and Git will track the delta between the last commit and what is currently in the repository. Git has a command called `git status` that allows a user to inspect what files are different from the last commit. In the following example, a module has been cloned, values have been changed in `init.pp`, and the user has run the `git status` from inside the directory of the module:

```
Changes not staged for commit:
  (use "git add <file>..." to update what will be committed)
  (use "git checkout -- <file>..." to discard changes in working directory)

  modified: init.pp
```

You may have noticed `Changes not staged for commit`. Git recognizes the working directory, changes staged for a commit, and every commit in the repository history. The standard workflow is to clone a repository, make changes, stage them for a commit, and make a new atomic commit, before pushing it back to a central repository.

Although we generally don't make changes to a module procured from the Puppet Forge (the primary external repository for Puppet Code), let's go over what it's like to clone, change, commit, and (optionally) push our code back to the original repository, which Git automatically tags as `origin`.

First, we'll clone and make a local copy of `puppetlabs/ntp`:

```
$ git clone git@github.com:puppetlabs/puppetlabs-ntp.git
Cloning into 'puppetlabs-ntp'...
remote: Counting objects: 7522, done.
remote: Compressing objects: 100% (13/13), done.
remote: Total 7522 (delta 5), reused 18 (delta 5), pack-reused 7504
Receiving objects: 100% (7522/7522), 1.64 MiB | 0 bytes/s, done.
Resolving deltas: 100% (4429/4429), done.
```

Notice that it cloned the repository and applied 4,429 deltas. We now have a local copy of the entire repository contained on GitHub. It will create a directory called `puppetlabs-ntp`, which we must enter by using a change directory to continue in the local repository.

Next, we'll edit the files that we intend to edit. In this case, I added a single comment to manifests/init.pp in the repository. I can check how Git views the repository with the command git status:

```
$ git status
On branch master
Your branch is up-to-date with 'origin/master'.
Changes not staged for commit:
  (use "git add <file>..." to update what will be committed)
  (use "git checkout -- <file>..." to discard changes in working directory)

  modified: init.pp

  no changes added to commit (use "git add" and/or "git commit -a")
```

Git now sees the change to the local repository. I want to ensure that this change is committed to the repository, so next, I'll add it to the staging directory, highlighting it for a commit with git add manifests/init.pp. If we run another simple git status, we will notice that our code is no longer not staged for commit, but is now under Changes to be committed:

```
$ git status
On branch master
Your branch is up-to-date with 'origin/master'.
Changes to be committed:
  (use "git reset HEAD <file>..." to unstage)

  modified: manifests/init.pp
```

With init.pp in the staging directory, I can commit this code to a new version. Running the command git commit will open your default editor, allowing you to comment and name your commit. I will run the command with an -m flag, which allows me to pass the message on the command line, rather than by opening up my default editor:

```
$ git commit -m 'Simple Clarification Comment added to init.pp feature'
[master 4538890] Simple Clarification Comment added to init.pp feature
 1 file changed, 1 insertion(+)
```

Now, my local repository has the new commit locally. I can view this commit with the command git log:

```
commit 45388902ef5cf125ea2109197e115f050d603406 (HEAD -> master)
Author: Ryan Russell-Yates <rary@packt.com>
Date: Sun Apr 8 16:28:26 2018 -0700

    Simple Clarification Comment added to init.pp feature
```

Most notably, this change is only on the local repository on my laptop. To share this code, I want to push my commit back to where I retrieved the original code from. When you run `git clone` locally, it also records where the code came from, and, by default, names the remote repository `origin`. If I run the command `git remote -v`, I can actually see the URL that the repository came from:

```
$ git remote -v
origin git@github.com:puppetlabs/puppetlabs-ntp.git (fetch)
origin git@github.com:puppetlabs/puppetlabs-ntp.git (push)
```

If I had permission to push directly to this repository, I could send my new commit to the source with the simple command, `git push origin master`. Master is the name of the branch, or the specific code set inside of a repository I'm working on.

Branches are a concept in Git that allow us to create a copy of code and work on it in what is similar to a separate directory. By default, Git creates a master branch, which is the intended location of the most up-to-date functional code. We can create a new branch in Git and change code without impacting the original branch that it came from. The most efficient use of Git is for trunk-based development, where we start on the master branch, create a new branch that contains new features, test those features, and eventually, merge our branch back into the master branch. This model allows us to work on, share, test, and even implement code, without impacting the original code set.

When we type `git checkout -b new_branch`, we create a new branch, based on the original branch that we were on. We can then work here, add additional commits, and even push it back to the source, without impacting the original code. Only when the code is merged back into the original branch does it have an impact on that branch. Think of it as the Git equivalent of copying a set of code to a new directory, working on it, testing it, and then copying it back to the original source when finished.

r10k

r10k is the primary driver behind Puppet Enterprise Code Manager. It is centered around a single repository, called the **control repository**. The control repository contains files that describe an entire Puppet environment. This collection of files holistically makes up a version of Puppet code intended to be pushed to a particular set of nodes. Every time r10k is run, it redeploys everything contained in the control repository.

Control repository

The control repository is the heart of code management for r10k and Code Manager. It is a single point of entry, represented as a Git repository, that describes one or more environments of one or more Puppet Masters.

r10k is designed to provide the following to a Puppet environment, from a control repository:

- Each Puppet module required to make a code set via the `Puppetfile`
- A Hiera hierarchy
- Hiera data
- An environment-specific configuration
- Any additional code (such as `site.pp`, roles, or profiles)

Multiple states on a single Puppet Master can be achieved by using a concept that was launched in Puppet 3: Puppet environments. In Puppet 3, we gained the ability to use multiple directories to store code, and to select which code directory each agent uses individually. Code Manager and r10k expand on this concept by treating every branch of the control repository as a completely separate environment.

If a control repository contains multiple branches, r10k can deploy each branch individually, as a separate environment. This does make our control repository branches a little different from a standard Git repository. Traditionally, the best model is trunk-based development, which gives us one master branch that is intended to receive all of the finished code changes. A Puppet control repository usually contains multiple long-lived and short-lived branches, with varying levels of intention to merge code between the branches. In the best scenario, we merge our code with the different levels of environments, until we reach production. Our `Puppetfile`, covered later in this chapter, is often the file that differs the most between the environments.

In a situation where an organization has formal production, preproduction, and development environments, and users actively working on Puppet code, we may see the following branches:

- `Production`
- `Preproduction`
- `Development`
- `Feature1`
- `Feature2`

`Feature1` and `Feature2` would be considered short-lived branches, with changes intended for merging into the development environment. Puppet environments are not required to be one for one with what an organization would consider their own environments, and often should not be. Do not feel restricted to making your Puppet environments exactly conform to the organizational boundaries of servers.

One of the easiest ways to view these environments is to categorize your `control-repo` branches internally as `production-like` and `non-production-like`.

production-like environments

`production-like` environments are formal lanes of code that an organization can expect to retrieve and get a stable code set for individual Puppet agents. When I work with organizations setting these up for the first time, I often describe them as, *any environment you may be called in to work on if it goes down on nights or weekends*. An organization may have a `dev` environment, but if it requires support from an infrastructure team to maintain, that environment should be treated like a production environment. Any environment meant to be used daily by another group in an organization should be controlled more tightly than `non-production-like` environments.

A few key points on managing `production-like` branches are as follows:

- If you're strong in CI/CD and deploying code to production often, deploy your modules by branch
- If you're deploying updates in regular cycles (such as quarterly), deploy your modules by tag, as a version number
- Make these branches protected branches in your Git repository
- Decide on an organizational RBAC and governance policy

More information on deploying modules via tags and branches will be covered in the *Puppetfile* section of this chapter.

If you're using a hosted Git solution, such as Bitbucket, GitLab, or GitHub, enable protected branches on `production-like` branches in the control repository. Protected branches ensure that only elevated administrator accounts can push directly to the branch or approve merge requests generated from other branches. This ensures that code is peer reviewed before being accepted into these controlled environments.

An organization should decide on an RBAC and governance policy surrounding these protected branches, and should select technical people to review code and formally accept code into these `production-like` environments. Like an open source project, this allows any member of an organization to recommend a change to a controlled environment via Git, but requires a trusted individual to accept this code into the controlled code base.

`non-production-like` environments, on the other hand, require significantly less management, and can be used to test new features before merging code into environments that support direct business needs.

non-production-like environments

We manage `non-production-like` environments differently from `production-like` environments. Where `production-like` environments need management to ensure that only trusted code is deployed, our `non-production-like` branches are hampered by these same protections.

The primary goal of these `non-production-like` branches is to facilitate rapid code deployment and testing cycles. Patterns like protected branches and governance policies intentionally slow development to add stability, and should not be used on these Wild-West Style development branches.

The two most common examples of `non-production-like` environments are Puppet staging environments and feature-branches. Puppet staging environments are built to allow all Puppet users to integrate and test changes in a single environment, prior to shipping code to a `production-like` environment.

If your organization needs a staging environment, you should only use a single staging environment, as merging between multiple staging environments can be difficult. Feature-branches are built exclusively to build and test new code in isolation, before sending it to staging, or directly to a `production-like` branch in absence of a staging environment, for organizations with robust CI/CD practices. We want to minimize overhead on these branches, to facilitate asynchronous code commits and testing without needing a trusted agent to approve every change.

A common workflow to develop Puppet code in environments at larger organizations is as follows:

- Clone the control repository
- Check out a new branch, based on the branch that you intend to make changes to (usually staging)

- Add one or more nodes to this environment via the PE console, or set the environment in the agents `puppet.conf`
- Iterate over code: write code and test it
- Merge your code with the staging environment and delete the short-lived branch
- Promote the staging environment through the multiple levels of production-like branches

With these concepts in mind, let's inspect what's contained inside of a Puppet control repository.

Puppetfile

The heart of the control repository is the `Puppetfile`. The `Puppetfile` acts as a list of Puppet modules to be imported on each run of r10k and deployed into a Puppet environment matching the branch name of the control repository. It allows us to bring in modules from two places: the Puppet Forge and remote Git repositories.

Pulling modules from the Puppet Forge can be written in shorthand, and at the very top of the file you can select a location to search for Forge modules. By default, the control repository will direct us to `https://forge.puppet.com`, which allows us to write the module we want to bring in in shorthand. Entering `mod "puppetlabs/ntp"` in the `Puppetfile` will pull in the latest version. By simply adding a version, such as `mod "puppetlabs/ntp", "7.1.1"`, r10k will ensure that only a specific version from the Forge is deployed to an environment. It is generally considered a best practice to always include a version with Forge modules, so as to not deploy a new major version into an environment unexpectedly.

Additionally, we can point directly to Git repositories. The most common use of this is for Puppet modules developed internally by a user or an organization. Like the Forge, we can specifically target a version of a Git repository and deploy it into an environment. The following is an example of this:

```
mod 'ourapp',
  :git => 'git@git.ourcompany.com:ourapp.git',
  :ref => '1.2.2',
```

Each line of this entry into the `Puppetfile` actually signifies something to r10k. The first line, `mod 'ourapp'`, tells r10k to deploy this repository under the name `'ourapp'`, and will deploy the module as that name. This name must match the namespace of the module, and, in this case, `config.pp` would need to contain `class ourapp::config`.

The :git reference tells r10k where to go to retrieve the code. r10k must have SSH keys available to reach this repository, unless the repository allows for anonymous cloning. The ref tag will actually search for commits, git tags, and branches, until it finds one that matches the reference. If this repository contained a git tag named 1.2.2, r10k would use that particular version of code. Note that this method of calling the repository can be troublesome if there is a branch named 1.2.2 and a tag named 1.2.2. ref is a shorthand that allows you to call a tag, branch, or commit, but they can also be directly called by the :tag, :branch, or :commit lines, respectively.

The following code is an example of a Puppetfile that provides the following:

- Sets the Forge to the HTTPS version of forge.puppet.com
- Includes the latest puppetlabs/ntp
- Includes puppetlabs/stdlib version 4.25.1
- Includes puppetlabs/nginx version 0.11.0
- Includes three internal applications, called by branch, tag, or commit

```
forge "https://forge.puppet.com"

# Forge Modules
# Always take latest version of NTP, notice no version listed
mod "puppetlabs/ntp"

# Specific versions of stdlib and nginx.
mod "puppetlabs/stdlib", "4.25.1"
mod "puppetlabs/nginx", "0.11.0"

# Modules from Git

# Pointing to Master Branch
mod 'ourapp',
    :git     => 'git@git.ourcompany.com:ourapp.git',
    :branch => 'master',

# Pointing to the 1.2.2 tag
mod 'ourapp2',
    :git => 'git@git.ourcompany.com:ourapp2.git',
    :tag => '1.2.2',

# pointing to an explicit git commit
mod 'ourapp3',
    :git     => 'git@git.ourcompany.com:ourapp3.git',
    :commit => '0b1ae47d7ff83489299bb7c9da3ab7f4ce7e49a4',
```

hiera.yaml

One of the best features of Hiera in Puppet 5 is that it is included by default, and does not require an additional installation. As noted in the previous chapter, Puppet 5 gives us three levels of Hiera: global, environment, and data, in modules. The environment level of Hiera is contained in the control repository, giving us separate data in each environment and allowing us to store all of our Hiera data in a single repository.

This model allows us to version control all of our data layer in Puppet 5 easily, and even merge our data across branches, if we want to iterate development of our Hiera data in the same way that we iterate over the development of Puppet code. We can use the same Hiera v5 configuration from the Chapter 4, *Hiera 5*, shown as follows, to set up our data in environments:

```
---
version: 5
 hierarchy:
 - name: "Per-node data"
 path: "nodes/%{trusted.certname}.yaml"
 - name: "Per-environment data"
 path: " %{server_facts.environment}.yaml"
 - name: Common
 path: common.yaml
```

This will use the default datadir in the control-repo, data, to store our Hiera data. If we were to use this hierarchy, our control repository might contain the following:

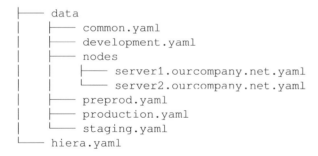

```
├── data
│   ├── common.yaml
│   ├── development.yaml
│   ├── nodes
│   │   ├── server1.ourcompany.net.yaml
│   │   └── server2.ourcompany.net.yaml
│   ├── preprod.yaml
│   ├── production.yaml
│   └── staging.yaml
└── hiera.yaml
```

site.pp

The site.pp is one of the oldest files found on a modern Puppet Master. The original intention of site.pp was to classify nodes, assigning classes and resources to a node to create a catalog. It accepts both regex and string match names, and, if used to place code and resources directly on a system, it would contain code such as the following:

```
node 'application.company.com' { include role::application }
```

Today, most users no longer store classifications in site.pp. Classification is handled by an **external node classifier** (**ENC**), such as the Puppet Enterprise Console. Hiera has also become a common method of classification, in lieu of an ENC. Any code that is not contained to a node in site.pp is applied to all nodes in the Puppet environment. The following code, placed outside of a node specification, searches all levels of a node's Hiera hierarchy for unique classes in an array named classes, removes anything contained in arrays named class_exclusions, and then applies them to each node. This allows Hiera to act as the classifier for Puppet nodes.

The following code enables Hiera as a classification strategy, when placed in site.pp:

```
#This section ensures that anything listed in Hiera under classes can be
used as classification

$classes = lookup('classes', Array[String], 'unique')
$exclusions = lookup('class_exclusions', Array[String], 'unique')
$classification = $classes - $exclusions

$classification.include
```

If we had a server named snowflake.ourcompany.com, and the following was contained in our Hiera hierarchy, we would include role::ourapp and profile::partners::baseline, but exclude profile::baseline, even though it was listed as a class in common.yaml. This ensures that profile::baseline is applied everywhere in the infrastructure, except for where it is explicitly excluded:

```
# common.yaml
---
classes:
  - profile::baseline
```

We can also use our above class exclusions to remove baseline from a particular node:

```
# nodes/snowflake.ourcompany.com.yaml
---
classes:
  - profile::partners::baseline
  - role::ourapp
class_exclusions:
  - profile::baseline
```

`site.pp` also allows us to set some sane defaults to our Puppet code, across our entire environment. In the following example, any Windows machine will use the package provider `Chocolatey`, by default. `Chocolatey` is a free and open source solution to a Yum-like package manager on Windows. If you haven't tried it yet in your Windows environment, it is a significant improvement on installing directly from `.msi` or `.exe`:

```
# Set Default Package Provider to Chocolatey on Windows

if $::kernel = 'windows' {
  Package {
    provider => 'chocolatey'
  }
}
```

environment.conf

The `environment.conf` file is an optional file in a control repository that allows you to override some settings in your Puppet environment. As of version 5.5, five settings are available for `environment.conf`, as follows:

- `modulepath`: Where to search for Puppet modules.
- `manifest`: Where to search for `site.pp`, or a directory of node manifest files, parsed alphabetically.
- `config_version`: A user-defined script to generate the version produced by running the Puppet agent.
- `environment_timeout`: How long the Puppet environment caches data about an environment.
- `static_catalogs`: An advanced configuration that internally versions files served from the Puppet Master. It is on, by default.

Additionally, `environment.conf` is able to use variables produced from Puppet configurations. In the following example, we set two of the most common settings found in an `environment.conf` file:

```
# Extend Modulepath
# Using $basemodulepath to ensure all default modulepaths are still
preserved
# This will now search for modules at $codedir/site, allowing us to place
modules
# directly into the control repo. Often used for Roles and Profiles
modulepath = site:$basemodulepath
# Set version that appears during a Puppet run with a custom script
# Contained in base on control repo config_version = 'scripts/version.sh'
```

Roles and profiles

In a previous chapter, we discussed roles and profiles. It is a common practice for many small organizations to place their roles and profiles in the control repository, as a simple place to get started writing puppet code for your organization. Using the previous `environment.conf`, our roles and profiles would be found at `/etc/puppetlabs/code/environments/<environment>/site`, as a roles directory and a profiles directory. These would be contained in the Git repository, in a `site` folder at the base of the repository.

For many larger organizations, accepting commits to a standalone role and standalone profile module can be easier to maintain than bundling them into the control repository. This provides each environment with the ability to call tagged versions of the role and profile modules specifically. Both methodologies are valid, and produce the same results on the agents utilizing the code.

At the end of this chapter, you will find a guide on a multitenancy control repository, which is easier to manage if the role and profile modules are separate from the control repository.

Control repository example

If we use everything in the control repository as designed in the previous examples, a single branch of our control repository will look as follows:

```
$ tree control-repo
control-repo
├── data
│   ├── common.yaml
│   ├── development.yaml
│   ├── nodes
│   │   ├── server1.ourcompany.net.yaml
│   │   └── server2.ourcompany.net.yaml
│   ├── preprod.yaml
│   ├── production.yaml
│   └── staging.yaml
├── environment.conf
├── hiera.yaml
├── manifests
│   └── site.pp
└── site
    ├── profile
    │   └── manifests
    │       └── application.pp
    └── role
```

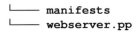

```
└──── manifests
└──── webserver.pp
```

Installing and using r10k

Generally, if you have Puppet Enterprise, you should use Code Manager instead of r10k. If you are a Puppet open source user, or if your environment is a mix of both open source and Enterprise nodes, consider a direct installation of r10k. There is a Puppet module available on the Forge that installs r10k on an existing Puppet Master by Vox Pupuli. It can be found at `https://forge.puppet.com/puppet/r10k`.

Once r10k is installed, an environment can be deployed by running `r10k deploy environment <branch> -p` on each master as the root user, or as a user with `sudo` access. Often, when r10k is used in place of Code Manager, a CI/CD system is used to automate the deployment over r10k.

Code Manager

Now that r10k has been detailed, let's explore the Puppet Enterprise version of it: Code Manager. Code Manager adds four main features to r10k, as follows:

- File Sync and Rsync across masters from **Master of Masters (MoM)**
- RBAC and pe-client-tools provides RBAC access
- Automatic environment isolation
- Easy installation

The primary reason to use Code Manager over r10k in Puppet Enterprise is the robust RBAC model provided by Puppet Enterprise. Without Git, r10k hooks require that you log in to the Puppet Master over SSH or the console and run a command to deploy one or more environments. The PE client tools provided by Puppet allow a user to generate a short-lived RBAC access token, which is checked against RBAC in the Puppet Enterprise Console remotely. This remote RBAC model allows you not only to give individuals different levels of access to environment deployment, but it also does not require a user to log in to the Puppet Master at all. The PE client tools are run from a local workstation and deploy the environment through the Puppet Enterprise web API.

The second major feature is file syncing. r10k deploys code directly into the code directory on a single Puppet Master. If an organization has multiple Puppet Masters controlled by a Master of Masters, a single command can deploy the code base to a code-staging directory on the MoM, which will then be deployed synchronously to all Puppet Masters in the environment. Instead of logging in to multiple Puppet Masters, you can run the command once, remotely, and allow the MoM to distribute code across all of your masters.

Code Manager also ensures that all environment isolation commands are run across your system, ensuring that type resources don't accidentally spill over into other environments. The open source equivalent to this command is `puppet generate types -- environment <environment>`.

The final major feature of Code Manager is an easy install. Everything needed to enable Code Manager is self-contained in Puppet Enterprise.

Enabling Code Manager

Enabling Code Manager across your architecture is easy in Puppet Enterprise, because it's prebundled in the system. The only artifact that must be generated on each master is the SSH key used to access the control repository and any other Git repositories in the `Puppetfile`. These SSH keys should be created with no password, and should be protected on the Puppet Master. Additionally, if you are using a Git service that supports it, enter this key as a deploy key, rather than a user key. Deploy keys only have the ability to check out code, and cannot submit code back to the Git server. For a single master, the following commands can be run as the root user or with `sudo`, to generate an SSH key:

```
# Create SSH Directory
$ sudo mkdir -p /etc/puppetlabs/puppetserver/ssh

# Generate SSH Key - With No Password
$ sudo ssh-keygen

Generating public/private rsa key pair.
Enter file in which to save the key (/var/root/.ssh/id_rsa):
/etc/puppetlabs/puppetserver/ssh/id-control_repo.rsa
Enter passphrase (empty for no passphrase):
Enter same passphrase again:
Your identification has been saved in /etc/puppetlabs/puppetserver/ssh/id-control_repo.rsa.
Your public key has been saved in /etc/puppetlabs/puppetserver/ssh/id-control_repo.rsa.pub.
The key fingerprint is:
SHA256:Random key root@server
The key's randomart image is:
```

```
+---[RSA 2048]----+
Random Art
+----[SHA256]-----+

# Ensure pe-puppet owns the directory and the keys
$sudo chown -R pe-puppet:pe-puppet /etc/puppetlabs/puppetserver/ssh
```

The simplest way to enable Code Manager after the generation of a key is to enter the classification of a PE Master, underneath the PE Infrastructure in the Puppet Enterprise console. Add the following parameters under the `puppet_enterprise::profile::master` class:

- `r10k_private_key`: Location of the private key generated and made available on the Puppet Master.
- `r10k_remote`: Location of the control repository—should be a Git URL.
- `code_manager_auto_configure`: Set to true. This lets Puppet set it up automatically.
- `r10k_proxy` (Optional): Set the URL of a proxy to reach the Forge, if your master can only reach the internet via a proxy.

An example of this classification without a proxy is as follows:

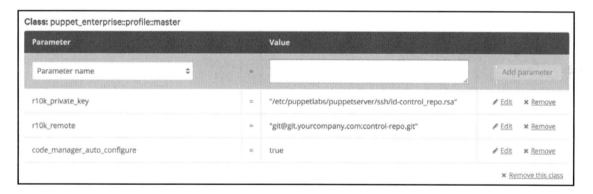

Some organizations would prefer to store their changes to Puppet in code, rather than in the PE console. The following code is also representative of the preceding changes, but the Puppet Master will fail to compile catalogs until `puppet_enterprise::profile::master` is removed from the PE console. To enable Code Manager with a profile instead of through the console, apply the following to the master, after removing the same class from the console:

```
class profile::pe_master {

  sshkey {'codemanager':
    ensure => present,
    key    => 'Long String of Private Key',
    target => '/etc/puppetlabs/puppetserver/ssh/id-control_repo.rsa',
    type   => 'ssh-rsa',
  }

  class puppet_enterprise::profile::master {
    code_manager_auto_configure => true,
    r10k_remote                 => 'git@git.ourcompany.com:control-
repo.git',
    r10k_private_key            => '/etc/puppetlabs/puppetserver/ssh/id-
control_repo.rsa',
  }

}
```

Each of these methods enables Code Manager on the master, enabling remote PE client tools to deploy environments from a separate workstation.

Code Manager RBAC

The simplest way to get started with Code Manager and RBAC is to add users to the existing user role, Code Deployers. Code Deployers have the ability to deploy any environment using the PE client tools. While this may seem too loose of a restriction at first, remember that Code Manager is only deploying an existing branch of the control repository. It is highly recommended not to prestage your code in Git, hoping that users do not run a code deployment and deploy the latest version of code. Code deployments should also be considered idempotent, and a user should be free to deploy environments at will, usually not overwriting any code at all if it is done by mistake.

In the following example, I have added myself as a user, added the user to the **Code Deployer** role, and maintained the ability to deploy any environment:

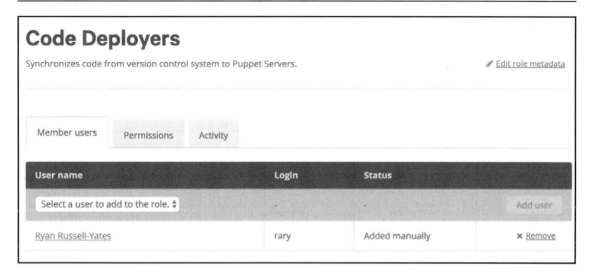

You can see the permission details in the following screenshot:

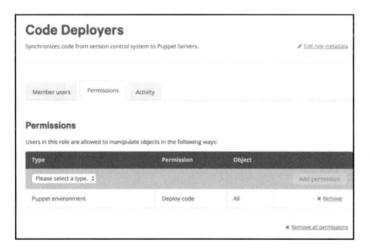

PE client tools

Code Manager is utilized through the PE client tools. These tools are installed by default on the Puppet Master, but for security reasons, we'd rather install them on user workstations, to allow for the remote deployment of code and to keep users off the Puppet Master. The PE client tools provide us with two new commands: `puppet-access login` and `puppet-code deploy <environment>`.

`puppet-access login` provides us with an RBAC token with a default lifetime of 5 minutes. Users can override this lifetime by adding the `--lifetime=<time>` flag to `puppet-access`. Time can be represented in minutes, hours, days, or years, with a number followed by `m`, `h`, `d`, or `y`, respectively. To give a half-day login, for example, a user should run `puppet-access login --lifetime=4h`. The maximum and default lifetime of these tokens is determined by the `puppet_enterprise::profile::console` class. The `rbac_token_auth_lifetime` parameter sets the default token that users will receive. `rbac_token_maximum_lifetime` sets the maximum lifetime of a token a user can request with the `--lifetime` flag. An organization should consider its standard login security practices before setting this value.

`puppet-code deploy <environment>` deploys a particular environment from the control repository, and can only be performed with a valid token from `puppet-access`. Once the token expires, the user will need to request access through `puppet-access` again. Adding the `-w` flag to `puppet-code deploy` will cause the deployment to wait and return a message about the status of the deployment. It is recommended that users run the `-w` flag when deploying manually, and omit it when a system runs a deploy automatically, such as a CI/CD system or a Git hook.

The first step is to download the PE client tools from the **Downloads** page of Puppet. It is provided for multiple operating systems, including Linux, macOS X, and Windows.

There are both a system-level configuration file and a user-level configuration file that can be set for the PE client tools. User configurations will override system configurations. There are two files that we must manage for PE client tools: `puppet-access.conf` and `puppet-code.conf`.

System-level configurations are contained at `C:/ProgramData/PuppetLabs/client-tools/` on Windows and `/etc/puppetlabs/client-tools` on all other operating systems. User configurations are contained at `~/.puppetlabs/client-tools` on all operating systems, which will override the system-level configurations.

Both `puppet-access` and `puppet-login` require a valid CA for the web API. By default, this can be found at `/etc/puppetlabs/puppet/ssl/certs/ca.pem` on any agent connected to the appropriate Puppet Master. You should copy this file locally, if performing development on a machine not managed by Puppet.

`puppet-access.conf` is used to provide configuration for the command `puppet-access login`, which connects to the Puppet Enterprise RBAC API, and grants a temporary login token to be used to deploy code. A `puppet-access.conf` usually contains at least the two following attributes:

- `service-url`: The RBAC API URL for the Puppet Enterprise installation
- `certificate-file`: A valid SSL certificate provided by the master

```
#puppet-access.conf
{
  "service-url": "https://pemaster.ourcompany.com:4433/rbac-api",
  "certificate-file": "/etc/puppetlabs/puppet/ssl/certs/ca.pem"
}
```

`puppet-code.conf` is similar to `puppet-access.conf` in that it requires a certificate and a `service-url` to call. Two things should be noted about `puppet-code.conf` in comparison to `puppet-access.conf`. The first thing is that the service URL will be different. `puppet-access` calls the RBAC API, while `puppet-code` calls the code-manager API. Additionally, although both use the exact same certificate from the Puppet Master, you'll notice that `puppet-code.conf` calls it `cacert` instead of `certificate-file`:

```
#puppet-code.conf
{
  "service-url": "https://pemaster.ourcompany.com:8170/code-manager",
  "cacert": "/etc/puppetlabs/puppet/ssl/certs/ca.pem"
}
```

Once setup is complete, a user can use the Code Manager workflow to perform the following:

- Check out code
- Make changes
- Push it back to the origin
- Run `puppet-access login` to receive a token
- Run `puppet-code deploy` to deploy the environment
- Check results
- Repeat, if necessary

Multitenant control repository

Larger organizations may need a multitenant setup of Puppet Enterprise Code Manager. While fundamentally, the workflow is the same, the way that we structure the control repository is slightly different.

We attempt to minimize the impact of the control repository, turning it into a call to libraries of sorts. We want to position our control repository to store references to code, rather than code itself. Moving role and profile manifests to external repositories allows us to manage them as a versioned artifacts, and declare which version is available to each and every enviroinment directly. Our control repository only contains the `Puppetfile`, things applied globally with `site.pp`, and values that we'd like to make available to the whole organization, to use in Hiera.

We make a few minor changes to the workflow to facilitate larger groups, as follows:

- Roles and profiles are exported to standalone modules, tagged with versions, and imported by the `Puppetfile`.
- Only values that serve for use across multiple modules, such as LDAP settings, are maintained in the environment-level Hiera. All direct calls to a class, such as `profile::ntp::servers`, are stored in data, in modules in the appropriate repo (in this case, the profile repository).

Roles and profiles are migrated to be standalone modules, and each team receives their own module, as well. These modules then incorporate their own robust Hiera layer in the module, and can be used to provide roles and profiles to each team. If we had a team developing an application called `myapp`, they would create a module called `myapp` and include a `role` and `profile` folder. Our namespacing changes a little bit, but allows us to look at modules as a collection of roles and profiles per team. The original `role` and `profile` repositories become a house for code commonly used by the whole organization, such as security baselines or web server defaults.

The following code can then be produced by the `myapp` team, which provides the strengths of Hiera, roles, and profiles to each of these repositories:

```
class myapp::role::app_server {
  # Global Baseline used by entire organization
  include profile::baseline
  # Profile generated specifically by myapp team
  include myapp::profile::application
}
```

```
class myapp::profile::application {
  # Profile has some custom code from the Myapp Team
  include myapp::application
  # Profile also uses the standard Webserver profile of the organization
  include profile::webserver
}
```

This methodology, combined with other practices in this chapter, such as protected branches, allows teams to work at different paces on different projects, while not holding other teams in the organization back. It limits the control repository to describing an environment, and opens up roles and profiles to receive code contributions from anywhere in the organization, with RBAC and governance in place to ensure that proper code reviews are performed before accepting code for the entire organization.

Our significantly smaller control repository now looks as follows:

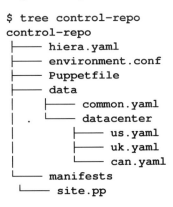

```
$ tree control-repo
control-repo
├── hiera.yaml
├── environment.conf
├── Puppetfile
├── data
│   ├── common.yaml
│   .└── datacenter
│       ├── us.yaml
│       ├── uk.yaml
│       └── can.yaml
└── manifests
    └── site.pp
```

And our team module acts like a small control repo for us, with a hiera hierarchy, roles and profiles:

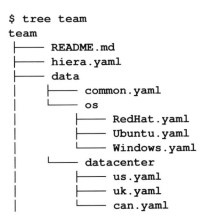

```
$ tree team
team
├── README.md
├── hiera.yaml
├── data
│   ├── common.yaml
│   └── os
│   │   ├── RedHat.yaml
│   │   ├── Ubuntu.yaml
│   │   └── Windows.yaml
│   └── datacenter
│       ├── us.yaml
│       ├── uk.yaml
│       └── can.yaml
```

```
├──── files
├──── manifests
│     ├──── profile
│     │     └──── myapp.pp #team::profile::myapp
│     └──── role
│           └──── myapp.pp #team::role::myapp which includes team::profile::myapp
├──── metadata.json
└──── templates
```

Summary

In this chapter, we discussed Git, r10k, and Code Manager. We highlighted the logical separation of production-like and non-production-like environments. The contents of a control repository were laid out: Puppetfile, hiera.yaml, environment.conf, site.pp, and various types of code, such as roles and profiles. We covered enabling Code Manager and using the PE client tools to interact with Puppet Code Manager. Finally, we discussed a multitenant, Enterprise-focused control repository format that exports roles and profiles to standalone modules and uses data in modules to provide a Hiera hierarchy to each team in an organization.

In the next chapter, we'll focus on integrating a workflow to our code development. We'll expand our work into the PDK and inspect good development practice.

6
Workflow

In this chapter, we'll discuss the workflow in Puppet. We'll cover what makes a good technical workflow, how to apply that to Puppet, and how to use the **Puppet Development Kit (PDK)** to improve our workflow. We'll investigate the following qualities of a good workflow: ease of use, rapid feedback, ease of onboarding, and quality control. We'll use Puppet Git repositories to provide a basic Puppet workflow that can be tuned to any system of management. We'll also explore the new PDK released by Puppet, which can improve our workflow.

The following topics will be covered in this chapter:

- Puppet workflow
- Designing a Puppet workflow
- Using the PDK

Puppet workflow

A workflow is a series of processes that work flows through, from initiation to completion. As the Puppet environments become more complex in an organization, a trusted and shared workflow will make sharing work easier. A Puppet workflow should allow us to access code, edit code, test our code, and, eventually, deploy our code back to the Puppet Master. Although it is not required, it is highly recommended that an organization or group of workers adopt a shared workflow. A shared workflow possesses a few main benefits, as follows:

- A measurable ease of use
- Rapid feedback
- Ease of onboarding
- Quality control

Ease of use

The primary reason to design and begin a workflow is to provide for ease of use. A team should design a workflow around their code base, allowing them to understand how to retrieve specific code, how to edit that code, and the impacts of the new edits. A workflow also provides a standardized way of packaging the code, to be delivered and used by the existing code base. Each step in the workflow should be clear, concise, communicated, and repeatable. It is important that everyone on the team understands not only how the workflow works, but why each step of the workflow exists, so that they can troubleshoot and contribute to the workflow, should something change in the organization.

One of the primary benefits of a shared workflow, as opposed to individualized workflows, is the ability to measure the impact of the workflow on the organization. To measure our workflow, we first separate standard and nonstandard units of work. The edits that we make to our code often vary in size and complexity, and are not easy to measure in standard units. On the other hand, code is generally checked out, tested, and deployed in the same way every time, leaving us with a good estimate of how long it will take to go through our workflow, minus the code edits.

If our workflow takes about 30 seconds to clone the code repository, an unknown amount of time to edit code, 5 minutes to run a test, and another 30 seconds to deploy the code in our environment, our workflow, with a single test, will take about 6 minutes. If we have eight members of our team, who each run through this workflow 10 times a day on average, our workflow actually constitutes about 8 hours a week of our combined work (*8 x 10 x 6 = 480* minutes, or 8 hours). Cutting this testing time in half reduces our total time as a team spent on the workflow by about 3 1/3 hours per week. Because of this measurable amount of time that can be saved in a workflow, a team should consider optimizing their workflow whenever possible.

Generally, you won't need more than a rough estimate of the time it takes to perform the standard functions of the workflow, but you will need to know which pieces might be performed more than once. With Puppet, a user will likely write, push, and test code more than they will pull it down. You can inspect each piece of the workflow separately and seek to improve a part of the process, but you should consider the ramifications of a change to the rest of the workflow.

Rapid feedback

A good workflow should provide constant feedback to its users. Each step should be clearly defined, with strict pass or fail criteria. For example, Git will warn a user whenever it detects a problem, such as being unable to pull code or push code back to the origin repository. We can extend this with Git commit hooks, both server-side and client-side, which perform checks to ensure that the code is in a proper state before being accepted into an organizational Git server from the local repository. Running Puppet itself within our test criteria, we expect clean and idempotent runs. The Puppet catalog should not produce failing resources, nor should it manage the same resource with every Puppet run.

The time it takes to solve problems with Puppet shrinks as more feedback is provided by a workflow to the engineer. If you work in a workflow that requires pushing code to an environment on the Puppet Master, and you are testing on a true agent, a simple run of `puppet parser validate` can save a lot of time. The parser validation will quickly tell you if Puppet code can be compiled, rather than what it will do. This simple command can reduce the number of times that we `git commit` on the code, push it to the Git repository, deploy it to an environment, log in to the test machine, and wait for the Puppet agent to trigger a catalog error. We can even ensure that this command is run before every commit with a precommit Git hook. Automated testing tools, such as RSpec and Beaker, can extend this methodology, and, combined with a CI/CD pipeline (discussed in the next chapter), can provide even more rapid feedback to code developers.

Ease of onboarding

A well-built workflow naturally facilitates the ease of adding new members to a project, whether open source or a part of an organization. A simple tool suite and guide can be invaluable to those new members, and can help them to get over the hurdle of the first commit. Even a simple getting started `README` can go a long way, if properly maintained. Onboarding new members to a project is costly, and quality workflow can minimize the time spent by the new member. Bringing on new project members also requires some information and time from existing project members. If your project is an ongoing development effort, it's highly likely that you'll have some turnover, and saving time for existing members while shortening the time for new members to reach effectiveness should be a priority in your workflow.

Quality control

A good workflow should always seek to reduce mistakes and increase code quality. Every built-in safety mechanism in a workflow allows a team to iterate over more complex features more quickly. Simple things, such as preventing pushes directly to production branches and basing production environments on semantically versioned code, allow for rapid development, without any worries about toppling critical infrastructure.

The following lists a few examples of workflow improvements designed around security and stability:

- Preventing direct code pushes to production on the control repository
- Preventing direct code pushes to masters on individual modules
- Running Puppet parser validation on all manifests prior to a push back to the repository of origin
- Running code reviews prior to merging into a master or `production-like` branches of the control repository
- Automated testing

Designing a Puppet workflow

Puppet has undergone a lot of changes in code management since its beginnings. Even the general workflow has changed drastically. This section will help you to understand some of the history of code management in Puppet, some of the challenges, and, most importantly, some of the solutions for designing and working with a strong Puppet workflow.

Originally, we wrote Puppet manifests directly to the disk. We logged on to the Puppet Master via SSH and edited our manifests directly, treating most of our code like configuration files for remote machines. This model required custom backups and recovery for code applied to agents, and did not provide easy rollbacks. If something went wrong in a deployment, you were forced to take snippets of code from a backup manually and deploy it to a system. Some members of the community took to storing their Puppet code in Git. As the number of individual repositories grew in organizations, manually bringing in Git repositories individually became more troublesome, and some community open source projects formed that were focused on staging Git code.

Components of the Puppet workflow

Although r10k is not the only Puppet Code Manager, it has become the standard Code Manager deployed to enterprise organizations. We'll break the work down into tasks and repositories, as follows:

- Repositories:
    - Control repository
    - Module repositories
- Tasks:
    - Clone
    - Create new branch
    - Edit relevant code
    - Add and commit
    - Push
    - Puppet login and deploy
    - Classify
    - Test (automatic or manual)

Repositories

Code management requires that all code be stored in Git. Splitting your code up into multiple repositories and placing the code on the master allows for references to different versions of code. Each of your modules should reside in a separate repository, allowing for versioning and governance on a per-module basis. The `Puppetfile` will call these repositories by using the Puppet Forge, or pointers at your own local Git instance.

Control repository

Our control repository, as described in the previous chapter, is nothing more than a Git code repository. The only unique quality that you need to keep in mind when working with it, is that branch names correspond to Puppet environments. If you create a Git branch named `feature` and deploy the code, the Puppet Master will deploy that code to `/etc/puppetlabs/code/environments/feature`. Generally, the Master branch is replaced with another protected branch named `production` in the control repository, so that agents can check in to a production branch by default.

Module repository

Module repositories are standard Git repositories. Generally, we want to protect the master branch and keep it from receiving direct commits. Contributors to component modules should instead submit pull requests to the repository and allow for a code review before accepting the code into the master branch. The master branch should be a functional version of the module at all times, although it need not be a version ready to be deployed into production. Treating the master as stable code allows non-production environments to point reliably at the master branch of all repositories, to get the latest accepted code during development. When it comes to deploying to production, we'll actually use a Git tag to create a version, such as 1.2.0. We can then deploy our latest code into non-production and formally accept code into production.

Tasks

The primary driver of the workflow in a Code Manager or r10k-based system is a Git workflow. There are multiple models of Git workflows, such as GitHub flow and Git flow, but the primary focus of this book isn't on Git, so we'll start with a minimal set of commands and procedures. The most effective way to get started is to work on the temporary environments provided by our control repository. In this workflow, we assume that a Git solution is already implemented on-site, or is provided by a managed service provider, and the Puppet Master is using Code Manager to deploy environments.

The first step of the workflow is to identify the components that need to change. In this workflow example, we'll assume that we're performing a change on a component module and a profile embedded in the control repository. We'll include remediation steps during the manual test phase, to include new code deployments and new pushes to the Git repository.

Clone and edit the component repositories

First, we'll clone the component module, change to a new feature branch, and perform edits on the files in the repository. We'll ensure that we use a Git branch during development, so that we can send our code to the upstream Git repository without impacting the original code. We'll end this step with a new snapshot of code on a separate branch of an existing module, so that we can test this code in isolation. This set of steps is the general workflow for the following:

1. Making a copy of the upstream repository for an individual module (`git clone/pull`)
2. Creating a branch of the module, separate from the Master (`git checkout`)

3. Making any and all edits to the code (IDE of choice)
4. Creating a snapshot of the current state of the code (`git add` and `commit`)
5. Sending the snapshot back to the upstream repository (`git push`)

In action, the code is as follows:

```
# Clone the remote git repository for the module. You can skip this step if
the
# repository is already present on your local system
git clone git@gitserver.com:puppet/module.git

# If the repository is already local on the system, we'll just want to
update our
# local master branch
git pull origin master

# Check out a new environment based on the existing master branch, which is
the
# default branch of a git repository, and the branch we should start on on
a clone.
git checkout -b new_feature

# We'll edit some files to add new features

# Adding new paramters to init
vim manifests/init.pp - Adding new parameters to init
# Adding a new feature to config
vim manifests/config.pp
# Ensuring the new feature is represented in the deployed template
vim templates/file.epp

# Add all edited files to git staging, assuming you're at the base of the
repository
git add .

# Add an atomic commit, not only describing what the commit is, but why it
was done
git commit -m 'Added new code to support feature requested by client'

# Push this code back to the origin repository as the new branch
git push origin new_feature
```

Our edits are now in the upstream repository, in a `new_feature` branch. The master branch will continue to serve as a reference point for further development for others, and for testing in a staging environment. So that we can begin to test this code, we'll create a new Puppet environment, designed specifically for testing and iteration over this code set.

Cloning the control repository

The first step starts like the last one: cloning the Git repository. One thing to remember about Puppet environments is that a branch of this repository corresponds to a Puppet environment. Most users of Puppet don't have a master environment, but rather, the production environment that Puppet places nodes into by default. If your organization has any environments prior to production, as many do, you'll want to make sure that you begin on the existing branch before creating a new branch. The `git checkout -b` command creates a new branch, starting from the branch that you are currently on. The following are the steps for creating a new environment, modeled after an existing environment:

1. Make a copy of the control repository from the upstream repository (`git clone`).
2. Check out the environment that you want to write new code against (`git checkout`).
3. Check out a new branch, based on the current branch (`git checkout -b`):

```
# This step is not needed if the repository is already on the local
file system
git clone git@gitserver.com:puppet/control-repo.git

# We'll assume integration is the pre-production branch used by the
organization
# to stage changes before moving into production-like branches
# Remember, there usually is no master branch in a control
repository, so we want
# to target a specific branch to work against.
git checkout integration

# If this repo has been freshly cloned, git pull shouldn't provide
any new updates,
# but it's safe to run either way. If the repository has already
been cloned in the
# past, you definitely want to run this command to pull the latest
commits from
# upstream.
git pull origin integration

# We'll perform a second checkout, with the -b flag to indicate a
new branch based on the existing branch
git checkout -b new_feature
```

Like the steps we took for our component module repository, this set of commands ensures that we have a local copy of the repository with the latest commits to the integration branch, and that we started a new branch based on the existing code. We're in a state to edit files found directly in our control repository, such as the Puppetfile, hieradata, and embedded roles and profiles (if you keep them in the control repository, rather than as separate, individual repositories). Once we have the code, we will want to edit the relevant files, create a new commit, push the code back to the origin repository, and deploy the environment.

Editing the control repository

Once we're inside of the local copy of the intended environment, it will be the right time to make changes to the code. We generally spawn these additional short-lived environments so that simple commands can be used to deploy new code. We have a few files to target, because we think of the control repository as a configuration file for the rest of the environment. The Puppetfile is used to manage dependencies, including any component modules (from the Forge or your own environment). roles and profiles are often kept in the control repository, as well, and code can be edited directly in these environments. The workflow for making changes in the control repository is as follows:

1. Edit the files (in the IDE of your choice).
2. Make a snapshot of the current state of the code (git add and commit).
3. Send the environment back to the remote repository (git push):

```
# Edit our files

# Change the branch of the component module to new_feature
vim Puppetfile

mod 'module',
  git => git@gitserver.com:puppet/module.git,
  branch => 'new_feature'

# Make a change in the profile that utilizes the component modules
vim site/profiles/manifests/baseline.pp

# Add our new changes, to be staged for a commit
git add .

# Commit our changes
git commit -m 'Supporting new Feature to support <effort>'
```

```
# Push our code back to the control repository as a new branch
intended to be
# realized as a new environment on the Puppet Master
git push origin new_feature
```

At this point, we've edited a module and files in the control repository and pushed them back to the origin. We'll now deploy the branch we made in the preceding code, and we will tweak our profile to use the module changes. Unless you have set up Git hooks or a CI/CD solution, you'll also have to trigger an environment deployment on the Puppet Master.

Deploying the new environment on the Puppet Master

Puppet provides the PE Client Tools, as described in Chapter 5, *Managing Code*, specifically for deploying code. If these tools are not available on your workstation, you can also log in to the Puppet Master, where they are already available for use. Assuming that you are using Code Manager, the following steps remain the same whether you are on a local workstation or a remote server:

1. Retrieve the login token from Puppet Enterprise (puppet-access login).

2. Deploy an environment from the upstream repository branch (puppet-code deploy):

```
# If PE Client Tools are not installed locally, the Puppet Master
comes with them
# installed by default. We'll assume that the PE client tools are
not already
# installed and log in to the Puppet Master
ssh user@puppet.org.net

# Generate an authorization token to allow your PE Console user to
deploy code
puppet-access login

# Use our access token to deploy our new environment. Notice the -w
flag, which
# triggers the client tools to wait and give you a pass or fail
message on the
# status of the deployment.
puppet-code deploy new_feature -w
```

Now our code has been deployed as a fresh environment on the Puppet Master. We're still missing a step to classify our test system and ensure that it is placed in the proper environment. For a Puppet Enterprise user, you can both classify and declare an environment by using a node classifier group in the PE console. To create a new node group, select an environment, check the environment group box, name it, and click **Create**. Enter your new environment group, pin your test node to the group, and add any relevant classes to the classification page.

You can also classify via `manifests/site.pp` in the control repository, as follows:

```
node 'test.node' {
  include relevant_role_or_profile
  include new_feature
}
```

The code for classification via Hiera is as follows:

```
# data/host/test.node.yaml
---
classification:
  - relevant_role_or_profile
  - new_feature

# manifests/site.pp

# Notice the lack of a node group around the include statement
include $::classification
```

There are multiple ways to classify that are commonly used by Puppet users, but without automated testing, we'll have to do some classification and run the agent to check the results of our tests.

Testing the changes

After your test node is properly attached to the environment group, you can log in to the node and trigger an agent run with puppet `agent -t`. Alternatively, you can run the Puppet agent through the PE console and read the log there. If you don't see any changes, there are a few possible reasons, as follows:

- The agent has already run, between when you classified the node in the console and ran the Puppet agent.
- A step was missed and the code was not properly deployed.
- Your code does not trigger any new changes on the system, and you should modify the system to see if Puppet corrects the change.

Ensure that you check the resources targeted by your change to see whether the agent has already deployed the new changes. You might also want to verify that the code deployment was done properly, and that you pushed your code back to the Git repository. If your code does not trigger any changes on the system, or if it triggers undesired changes, you can perform the following shorter workflow until the code is resolved properly:

1. Edit the code in the target repository: the control repository or the module repository (with the IDE of choice)
2. Make a snapshot of the code (`git add` and `commit`)
3. Push the code back to the remote repository (`git push`)
4. Redeploy the environment (`puppet-access login` and `puppet-code deploy`)
5. Trigger an agent run on the test machine (`puppet agent` or PE console)
6. Check for changes on the target system
7. Repeat until the desired state is achieved:

```
# Start in the repository with the change. This could be a
component module
# or the control repository. We're assuming each repository is
still on the
# branch from the last step, and no pulls or branch changes are
necessary.

# Edit the file with the targeted changes
vim manifests/manifest.pp

# Add the file to the git staging area
git add manifests/manifest.pp

# Commit the file to the repository
git commit -m 'Fixing specific bug'

# Push the repository back to upstream origin
git push origin new_feature

# From the Puppet Master, or a workstation with PE Client Tools

# Log in with RBAC
puppet-access login

# Deploy the environment
puppet-code deploy new_feature -w

# On the test node
```

```
# Run the agent, observe the results
puppet agent -t

# Repeat as necessary until issues are solved
```

Once our code is in the desired state, we will be ready to begin placing it back into a long-lived environment on the Puppet Master. Modules should have their code merged back to the master, and changes to the control repository will need to be merged with a longer lived branch.

Merging branches

In our earlier steps, we isolated our working code into a feature-branch and a short-lived, non-production environment. While teams and organizations should select some merging safeguards and strategies, such as peer code reviews and automated testing, this section will focus on the steps required to merge branches into master or long-lived branches in Puppet. Enterprise and open source web-based Git solutions usually contain some extra controls to indicate who can merge into a repository, and to which branches. The general best practice is to allow for a peer review of code, and the reviewer can accept the code into the long-lived branch or master branch. Merging our code via the command line is a simple process, as follows:

1. Switch to the branch that you want to merge to (`git checkout`)
2. Merge another branch into this one (`git merge`)
3. Push the merged branch into upstream repository (`git push`):

   ```
   # Many Enterprise-focused git repositories have built in merge
   features, that ar
   # likely more robust and easier to use than a simple git merge. If
   you have an in
   # house git solution, follow the program documentation on a merge
   request

   # On Module
   # We'll change to target branch, in this case master
   $ git checkout master

   $ git merge feature_branch
   Updating 0b3d899..227a02e
   Fast-forward
    README.md | 1 +
    1 file changed, 1 insertion(+)
    create mode 100644 README.md
   ```

```
# Push the branch to upstream repository so Puppet can find it.
$ git push origin master
```

Merging in the control repository can sometimes be troublesome, due to the Puppetfile being (intentionally) different between versions. Our production-like branches should use Git tags to declare the intended version of the code to be deployed and promoted up the series of environments. Our non-production-like environments are generally pointed to the master branch of each module, providing the latest accepted stable code to the environment for testing and development. Merging is performed in the same way as with a component module; just ensure that you don't overwrite the Puppetfile on a production-like branch with the less controlled Puppetfile in a non-production-like branch. Production branches should refer to Git tags for deploying code.

Git tags and versioning

Git tags are used to create a permanent state of code and separate it from the existing branches. Tags are not intended to be iterated upon, but rather, should be used as a marker in time for the state of the code. This makes tags a perfect fit for the release versioning of Puppet code. We can create tags from any branch, but the master is the most common branch to cut release tags from. We can simply use the git tag command on our module repository to create a snapshot with a semantic version number and push it to the origin repository, to be called on by r10k or Code Manager. The workflow for a Git tag is also short, as follows:

1. Check out the target branch (usually the master) for the tag (git checkout)
2. Version the code (git tag)
3. Push the tag to the remote repository (git push):

```
rary at Ryans-MBP in ~/workspace/packt/module (master)
$ git tag 'v1.4'

$ git tag -l
v1.4

$ git push origin v1.4
```

After our module has been properly versioned, we can edit the production-like Puppetfile to utilize our tag, rather than point to a particular development or master branch:

```
# Production-like branch, tagged with a solid version number
forge https://forge.puppetlabs.com
```

```
mod 'module',
  git => 'git@gitserver.com:puppet/module.git',
  tag => 'v1.4'
```

This is a simple version of the Puppet workflow, but it still leaves room for improvement. Puppet recently released a tool called the PDK, to help facilitate quality Puppet tooling into your workflow.

Using the PDK

A good workflow should provide ease of use, rapid feedback, ease of onboarding, and quality control. The PDK aims to increase productivity across this space. Many tools in the PDK have existed for quite some time, but they were often difficult to use and configure for workstation development.

PDK

Puppet makes the PDK freely available on their website, and it has a release for each major operating system. It uses a fully isolated environment to provide Puppet binaries and RubyGems that make development much simpler. Tools included in the PDK, as of version 1.5.0, are as follows:

- Create new Puppet artifacts:
  - Modules
  - Classes
  - Defined types
  - Tasks
  - Puppet Ruby providers
- PDK validate—simple health checks:
  - Puppet parser validate (Puppet syntax)
  - Puppet lint (Puppet style)
  - Puppet metadata syntax
  - Puppet metadata style
  - RuboCop (Ruby style)
- PDK test unit (Puppet RSpec—unit testing)

Creating new Puppet artifacts

The PDK allows users to create new artifacts, using best practices. Each `pdk new` command builds an artifact already structured for Puppet. These artifacts are intended to conform to Puppet's best practices. If you're testing the PDK in an isolated environment for the first time, starting with a new module is the easiest method.

The pdk new command

The command `pdk new module` brings the user to a prompt, requesting that the user specify the Puppet Forge username, the author's full name, the module license, and the supported operating systems. If you do not have a Forge username or a module license, you can enter in any value. After the prompt, you'll find a new directory that contains code. If you want to send this code to an upstream repository, follow these steps on the command line:

```
# From directory pdk new module was run in, enter the module, create a
# git repository and add all files to staging
$ cd module
$ git init
$ git add .

# Initial Commit is a good common message as a starting point
$ git commit -m 'Initial Commit'

# Add the upstream remote
$ git remote add origin git@gitserver.com:puppet/module.git

# Push to master and begin regular module development workflow
$ git push origin master
```

If you're working with a previously created module, you can use the `pdk convert` command to place any items missing from the template into the existing module. By default, the PDK deploys the templates found at `https://github.com/puppetlabs/pdk-templates`. If you need to change any of the files found here, you can clone a copy of `pdk-templates` from the official repository and send it to a central Git repository. You'll need to use the `pdk convert --template-url <https>` to select the new template and deploy it to the existing module. The `--template-url flag` command will also set the new URL as the default URL on the workstation.

You should feel free to make your own copy of this template, as the one provided by Puppet is fairly extensive and rather opinionated. It even includes some ways to get started with CI/CD systems, such as `gitlab-ci`. Trim the files for systems that you don't use, and make sure that everything provided by the template makes sense for your organization.

The template repository provides three directories and configuration files to the PDK, as follows:

- `moduleroot`: The Ruby templates in this directory will be placed on top of existing files. This is useful when you want to enforce a particular file, like a CI/CD pipeline.
- `moduleroot_init`: The Ruby templates in this directory will not override existing files. This is great for starter files, like module templates.
- `object_templates`: The Ruby templates that determine the output of the file on commands like `pdk new class`.
- `config_defaults.yaml`: This provides defaults and variables to be used for all Ruby templates in the PDK template.

Once you have your new module template, you can begin to create manifests inside of the module for Puppet code with the PDK. From inside of the new module, we can use `pdk new class` to begin making manifests. The command creates manifests according to an autoload layout, so running `pdk new class server::main` would create a file at `manifests/server/main.pp`. The class created with the default template will start as an empty, non-parameterized class, with Puppet string-style documentation at the top of the file. The `pdk new defined_type` command will make a similar file, but will use the defined declaration instead of the class declaration:

```
$ pdk new class config
pdk (INFO): Creating
'/Users/rary/workspace/packt/module/manifests/config.pp' from template.
pdk (INFO): Creating
'/Users/rary/workspace/packt/module/spec/classes/config_spec.rb' from
template

# Sample with folders
$ pdk new class server::main
pdk (INFO): Creating
'/Users/rary/workspace/packt/module/manifests/server/main.pp' from
template.
pdk (INFO): Creating
'/Users/rary/workspace/packt/module/spec/classes/server/main_spec.rb' from
template.
```

The `pdk new task` command will create files in the `tasks` directory, based on the template for use with Puppet tasks. Puppet tasks are a way to automate ad hoc scripts and commands across your infrastructure, using Puppet. `pdk new provider` is an experimental feature for designing new custom Ruby providers to Puppet.

Once the new objects are created and developed against, the PDK will also provide a tool suite for syntax and style, with `pdk validate`.

The pdk validate command

The PDK provides `pdk validate` to check both syntax and style. Syntax checks make sure that your code can compile, and that you're not missing things such as commas or closing braces in manifests or JSON metadata. Syntax checks can also be performed manually on manifests with `puppet parser validate`. Style checking looks at the code to make sure that it adheres to a standard style guide. Puppet-lint is used to provide style checks to Puppet, and all of the rules can be found at `http://puppet-lint.com/`. When a module is healthy, the PDK will return check marks against all tasks:

```
$ pdk validate
pdk (INFO): Running all available validators...
pdk (INFO): Using Ruby 2.4.4
pdk (INFO): Using Puppet 5.5.1
[X] Checking metadata syntax (metadata.json tasks/*.json).
[X] Checking module metadata style (metadata.json).
[X] Checking task metadata style (tasks/*.json).
[X] Checking Puppet manifest syntax (**/**.pp).
[X] Checking Puppet manifest style (**/*.pp).
[X] Checking Ruby code style (**/**.rb).
```

An invalid `metadata.json` will prevent the uploading of modules to the Forge and the running of RSpec tests. This file details the author of the module, and other information, such as dependencies and supported operating systems:

```
#Invalid Metadata.json

$ pdk validate
/opt/puppetlabs/pdk/private/ruby/2.4.4/lib/ruby/gems/2.4.0/gems/pdk-1.5.0/l
ib/pdk/module/metadata.rb:142:in `validate_name': Invalid 'name' field in
metadata.json: Field must be a dash-separated user name and module name.
(ArgumentError)
```

`pdk validate` also runs Puppet parser validation across every manifest in the module. In the following example, a curly brace was forgotten at the end of `init.pp`, and the PDK is informing us that the code will not compile:

```
# Failed Parser Validation
# Can be ran alone with puppet parser validate

$ pdk validate
```

```
pdk (INFO): Running all available validators...
pdk (INFO): Using Ruby 2.4.4
pdk (INFO): Using Puppet 5.5.1
[X] Checking metadata syntax (metadata.json tasks/*.json).
[X] Checking module metadata style (metadata.json).
[X] Checking Puppet manifest syntax (**/**.pp).
[X] Checking Ruby code style (**/**.rb).
info: task-metadata-lint: ./: Target does not contain any files to validate
(tasks/*.json).
Error: puppet-syntax: manifests/init.pp:9:1: Could not parse for
environment production: Syntax error at '}'
```

If the Puppet parser validation passes, `puppet-lint` will run on all manifests. It will print out errors and warnings in the code, based on the Puppet Style Guide. In the following example, we run pdk validate against a manifest has a line that continues beyond 140 characters on line 10 and trailing whitespace after line 9:

```
$ pdk validate
pdk (INFO): Running all available validators...
pdk (INFO): Using Ruby 2.4.4
pdk (INFO): Using Puppet 5.5.1
[X] Checking metadata syntax (metadata.json tasks/*.json).
[X] Checking module metadata style (metadata.json).
[X]Checking Puppet manifest syntax (**/**.pp).
[X] Checking Puppet manifest style (**/*.pp).
[X] Checking Ruby code style (**/**.rb).
info: task-metadata-lint: ./: Target does not contain any files to validate
(tasks/*.json).
warning: puppet-lint: manifests/init.pp:10:140: line has more than 140
characters
error: puppet-lint: manifests/init.pp:9:28: trailing whitespace found
```

In some cases, rather than print out a warning or error, we want to disable it. A list of checks can be found at `http://puppet-lint.com/checks/`, and can be used to disable individual checks. In the following example, notice the comment after the message statement, telling lint to ignore the 140-character limit:

```
# A description of what this class does
#
# @summary A short summary of the purpose of this class
#
# @example
# include module
class module {
```

```
notify {'String-trigger':
    message =>'This is the string that never ends. Yes it goes on and on my
friends. Some developer just started writing without line breaks not
knowing what they do, so this string will go on forever just because...' #
lint:ignore:140chars
    }


}
```

If we have multiple places in a single manifest that we'd like to ignore, we can use the lint block ignore by placing the comment on a line alone and ending it with # lint:endignore. In the following example, we have two large strings that won't be alerted on puppet-lint:

```
class module::strings {

# lint:ignore:140chars
    notify {'Long String A':
        message =>'This is the string that never ends. Yes it goes on and on my
friends. Some developer just started writing without line breaks not
knowing what they do, so this string will go on forever just because this
is the string that never ends...'
    }

    notify {'Long String B':
        message =>'This is another string that never ends. Yes it goes on and
on my friends. Some developer just started writing without line breaks not
knowing what they do, so this string will go on forever just because this
is the string that never ends...'
    }

# lint:endignore


}
```

If you have a check that you'd like to disable, you can also create a puppet-lint.rc file. This file can be placed in /etc for a global config, as .puppet-lint.rc in the home directory for a user config, or at the base of a module, as .puppet-lint.rc. If your team uses local development workstations, consider adding a .puppet-lint.rc to your PDK template, to enforce a standard on each repository:

```
# Permanently ignore ALL 140 character checks
$ cat puppet-lint.rc
--no-140chars-check
```

Finally, any Ruby code will be validated by RuboCop. RuboCop will check the style of all Ruby files in a module. This provides style checking to custom facts, types, providers, and even tasks written in Ruby:

```
$ pdk validate
pdk (INFO): Running all available validators...
pdk (INFO): Using Ruby 2.4.4
pdk (INFO): Using Puppet 5.5.1
[X] Checking metadata syntax (metadata.json tasks/*.json).
[X] Checking module metadata style (metadata.json).
[X] Checking Puppet manifest syntax (**/**.pp).
[X] Checking Puppet manifest style (**/*.pp).
[X] Checking Ruby code style (**/**.rb).
info: task-metadata-lint: ./: Target does not contain any files to validate
(tasks/*.json).
error: rubocop: spec/classes/config_spec.rb:8:38: unexpected token tRCURLY
(Using Ruby 2.1 parser; configure using `TargetRubyVersion` parameter,
under `AllCops`)
```

`pdk validate` provides a quick check of the style and syntax of your code. It does not check the functionality of your code. The PDK also provides a boiler template for RSpec tests out of the box, so that when a new class is created with `pdk new class`, a simple corresponding RSpec test is created along with it.

The pdk test unit command

New manifests built with `pdk new class` are also provided with a default RSpec test. Unit tests are written to ensure that a manifest performs what is expected as it is running. The default unit test provided by Puppet ensures that the code compiles successfully on every operating system listed in the `metadata.json`, with default facts for those operating systems. This can be expanded to create more robust unit tests. In the following example, a check has been added that states that the `init.pp` of the module should provide a file called `/etc/example` that is not provided by the manifest:

```
$ pdk test unit
pdk (INFO): Using Ruby 2.4.4
pdk (INFO): Using Puppet 5.5.1
[X] Preparing to run the unit tests.
[X] Running unit tests.
 Evaluated 45 tests in 2.461011 seconds: 9 failures, 0 pending.
[X] Cleaning up after running unit tests.
failed: rspec: ./spec/classes/module_spec.rb:9: expected that the catalogue
```

```
would contain File[test]
 module on centos-7-x86_64 should contain File[test]
 Failure/Error:

it { is_expected.to compile }
it { is_expected.to contain_file('/etc/example') }
end
end
```

The simple test provided by the default PDK only provides it { is_expected.to compile } as an RSpec test for each module. In the next chapter, we'll expand upon our initial RSpec module, as we cover unit tests and provide some basic code coverage testing to our Puppet modules.

Summary

We started this chapter by detailing what makes for a good workflow. Much of the workflow becomes easier when combined with continuous integration and continuous delivery strategies, which will be covered in the next chapter. We'll expand upon the RSpec tests built by the Puppet PDK, and we'll discuss acceptance test strategies. We'll also cover some new workflows and tools to provide more immediate feedback during the development of Puppet code and manifests.

7
Continuous Integration

Continuous Integration as a practice is ensuring that each time code is committed, it is built and tested the same way consistently. We use Continuous Integration systems to automate this practice, making it practical for use on every commit. Some Continuous Integration pipelines eventually evolve into Continuous Delivery or Continuous Deployment pipelines. The key difference between Continuous Integration and delivery is that delivery ensures that every time code is committed, it is also wrapped up (or packaged) and delivered to the doorstep of the server it needs to run on. Continuous Delivery requires the ability to deploy your entire infrastructure and application consistently with a single orchestration command. Continuous Deployment requires an end-to-end suite of tests for every component in your infrastructure, but is the simple task of automating that single orchestration command when every test passes.

How these systems become useful to the individual application and infrastructure is unique to every company and organization, much like any other business rule. There are some common use cases and business rules that are nearly universal in everyone's Continuous Integration pipelines, and some that teams strive for.

In this chapter, we will do the following:

- Set up a Continuous Integration system (Jenkins) using Puppet
- Create a job for a profile module
- Set up our first test
- Integrate the **Puppet Development Kit (PDK)** test suite
- Write RSPec unit tests
- Set up Puppet integration tests with Test Kitchen

Continuous Integration systems

Our Continuous Integration system is a panel that keeps track of our code repositories. For each of these repositories, you'll find what is commonly referred to as a job. A job is a series of steps, usually written in code, that informs the system of what it should do when a build is triggered through a button or CLI. A build is simply a single instance of that job that is running or has already run. Finally, that build contains log files, key information about the build, and any artifacts (objects) you want the system to store or ship off closer to the endpoint.

We'll build our CI system using Puppet, which will eventually manage our Puppet code. This is a common scenario when you start with CI in an existing environment in an organization.

Puppet Pipelines

Puppet Pipelines is a new product by Puppet. In September of 2017, Puppet acquired Distelli so that they could build the new Puppet Pipelines program. This CI system is still heavily geared toward containers and applications, but work is being done to improve its feature set for Puppet as well. Puppet Pipelines can still be used for a Continuous Integration system for puppet code, but may undergo quite a few changes in the next year around Puppet code. For this chapter, we'll be using a very popular open source Continuous Integration system: Jenkins.

Jenkins

Jenkins is one of the oldest and most common Continuous Integration systems fielded today. It began as Hudson initially, in 2005, and grew into the fork of Jenkins that we see today. Jenkins is both a powerful and complicated system in comparison to most other CI systems due to its highly pluggable nature. There are a plethora of Jenkins plugins designed to add features to the CI system, from source code management, to graphs and viewing, to orchestration and automated testing and linting for nearly every language. With this wide feature set, Jenkins can also often be complicated. Out of the box, Jenkins doesn't do a whole lot outside of running shell commands on the system. In this section, we'll be exploring how to build a bare basic Jenkins setup for our needs, using Puppet, to manage our Puppet code.

Managing Jenkins with Puppet

We're using Puppet to manage the Continuous Integration system, because it's a system. We're using Jenkins to manage our configuration management code, because it's code. This is why we'll build Jenkins with Puppet, and then check our Puppet code into Jenkins.

rtyler/jenkins

We should always seek a forge module when building new software, so I'm going to reach for `rtyler/jenkins` on the forge. This module will cover our basic needs for installing our Jenkins LTS server, installing our Jenkins plugins, and each package we'll need to run our builds.

In larger infrastructures, we wouldn't run builds on our Jenkins server, we'd run it on the Jenkins agents attached to it. Because this setup has no agents, Jenkins will act as our build agent and run the jobs for us. Therefore, we'll need to install Git and the PDK so that it can run commands for us. We use the Git plugin to provide us with a direct connection to our code, and the pipelines plugin gives us a DSL to write our steps in.

We're going to build a new module with the PDK by creating a profile directory, a manifests directory inside of that, and create a `jenkins.pp` in that folder:

```
#profile/manifests/jenkins.pp
class profile::jenkins {

  class { 'jenkins': lts => true }

  package {'git': ensure => latest }

  file {'/tmp/pdk.rpm':
    ensure => file,
    source =>
'https://puppet-pdk.s3.amazonaws.com/pdk/1.7.0.0/repos/el/7/puppet5/x86_64/
pdk-1.7.0.0-1.el7.x86_64.rpm',
  }
```

```
# Install latest PDK directly from Puppet Source
package {'pdk':
  ensure => installed,
  source => '/tmp/pdk.rpm',
  require => File['/tmp/pdk.rpm'],
}


}
```

We're going to install our plugins manually. `rtyler/jenkins` does support plugins for Jenkins, but does not support dependencies. There are quite a few dependencies in these build pipelines, so we're going to manually install the plugins to highlight the two main plugins.

After our profile has been applied to the node, we've got a fresh Jenkins installation with our desired plugins. We can reach our new Jenkins node via the web URL on port `8080`:

Managing our plugins

If you want to Puppetize each plugin, you can use the `jenkins::plugin` resource provided by this Jenkins module. You can find each plugin installed on your Jenkins master in the `/var/lib/jenkins/plugins` file, or in the **Installed plugins** tab of your Jenkins instance.

The resource syntax is as follows:

```
jenkins::plugin {'<plugin': version => 'version' }
```

We're going to grab two key plugins for our CI/CD workflow in this section: Git and Pipeline. We can reach the plugin page by clicking on **Manage Jenkins** on the left-hand side of the screen, and then **Manage Plugins** near the bottom of the menu. There is an ever-growing amount of plugins for Jenkins, and we need to select the appropriate ones:

It can be difficult to locate a plugin by name only, so try using some of the descriptions to locate these within the list.

Once we select these plugins, and click **Download and Install after Restart**, we'll be taken to a page listing all plugins that have an installation pending, in progress, or successful. At the bottom of this page is a checkmark that allows us to restart the server when the full download is complete. Make sure that you check that box:

Pipeline

A suite of plugins that lets you orchestrate automation, simple or complex. See Pipeline as Code with 2.5 Jenkins for more details.

Creating our first build

After our required plugins are installed in Jenkins, we can start putting together our first build. We'll start at the bare minimum for a code repository, and then demonstrate how to have Jenkins read that repository and automatically run a build when new code is checked in.

 This project will need a Git repository available for Jenkins. If you don't have an already accessible Git repository, open up an account on GitHub and use a public repository. We're not writing anything sensitive, so it's okay that the world can see your repository.

Building our profile module

We wrote some code that defined our Jenkins server in the form of a profile at the beginning of this chapter. First, let's inspect the directory structure that we're working with for our already existing code:

```
profile/
└── manifests
        └── jenkins.pp
```

This is a pretty bare minimum profiles module, with a single manifest. We'll turn this simple module into a Git repository first:

```
[rary@workstation ~]# cd profile/
[rary@workstation profile]# git init
Initialized empty Git repository in ~/profile/.git/
```

If we run `git status`, we'll see that the `manifests` directory is checked in. Every file in this repository right now is new, so we'll need to add each file and check them into our first commit, often called the `'initial commit'`:

```
[rary@workstation profile]# git add -A
[rary@workstation profile]# git commit -m 'initial commit'
[master (root-commit) 64f24a1] initial commit
 1 file changed, 19 insertions(+)
 create mode 100644 manifests/jenkins.pp
[root@pe-puppet-master profile]# git status
# On branch master
nothing to commit, working directory clean
```

We're then ready to send off our initial commit to the remote repository:

```
[rary@workstation profile]# git remote add origin
git@github.com:RARYates/cicd-walkthrough-profile.git
[rary@workstation profile]# git push origin master
Counting objects: 4, done.
Delta compression using up to 2 threads.
Compressing objects: 100% (2/2), done.
Writing objects: 100% (4/4), 519 bytes | 0 bytes/s, done.
Total 4 (delta 0), reused 0 (delta 0)
To git@github.com:RARYates/cicd-walkthrough-profile.git
 * [new branch] master -> master
```

Building our Jenkinsfile

The Pipeline plugin we installed on our Jenkins node allows us to declare our pipeline directly in the same repository as our code, as a script called a Jenkinsfile. This Jenkinsfile describes the details of our build steps, which can be automatically read by Jenkins to execute our build. We'll begin with a very simple Jenkinsfile that checks to make sure that all of our manifests pass a puppet parser validate:

```
pipeline {
    agent any

    stages {
        stage('Test') {
            steps {
                sh 'find manifests -name *.pp -exec /usr/local/bin/puppet
parser validate {} +;'
            }
        }
    }
}
```

This Jenkinsfile describes a pipeline that can be run on any agent (we only have one: our Jenkins node). It has stages, but only a single stage named Test, with a single step that runs puppet parser validate on every file ending in .pp (every manifest).

Then, we send this file up to our remote repository so that it can be found by Jenkins through the normal Git workflow we've been using.

Connecting Jenkins to our repository

Now that we have a build declared in our Jenkinsfile, we can build our first job. We'll start by clicking **New Item** in the top left corner, and create a new **Multibranch Pipeline** job called profile:

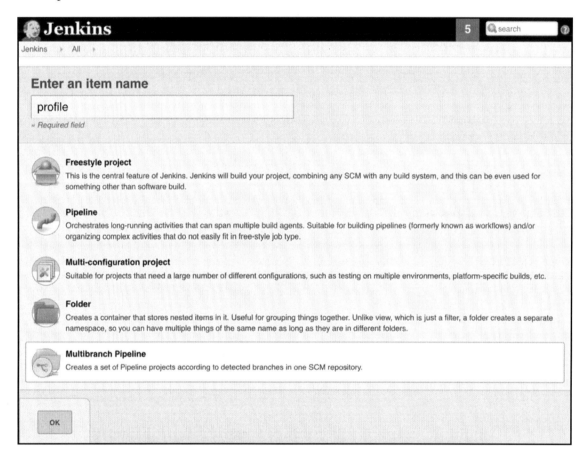

For our build, we'll need to edit the **Branch Sources** by adding the **Project Repository** and set our scan interval to run every minute. This is a public repository for me, so I don't need to attach any credentials. I'll use the default behaviors and property strategy:

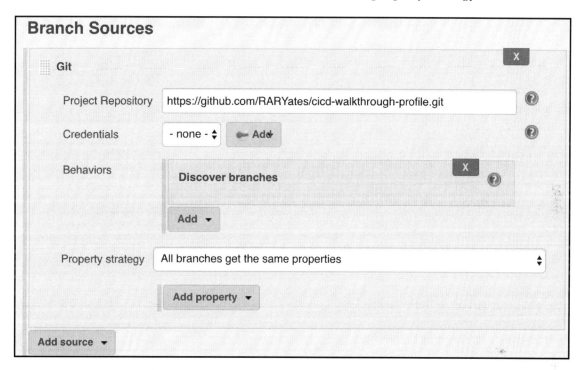

Some hosted Git repositories, such as GitHub Enterprise, allow for the scanning of all repositories in an organization. It can save a lot of time managing Jenkins if all repositories are automatically discovered.

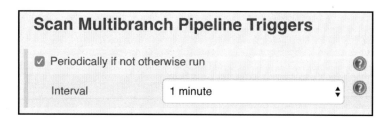

After I click **Scan**, an immediate job will be run to discover branches on that repository. Although this screen looks just like a Jenkins build, its pass or fail status is entirely based on the ability to connect to your Git repository and find a Jenkinsfile on a branch. Let's check on our first build by returning to the home page:

Our splash page has our first build in it! The sun represents a passing build, indicating that each step in our build returned a positive exit status. On the far right of the build is a run build button, which is for if we'd like to run the build again. For now, click on the name profile and enter the details of the build. Because this is a multibranch pipeline, we'll also want to click the master branch to bring us into our status. You'll see that our build has run, and you can inspect each step of the way from this menu.

 To ensure that this exercise does not require us to put our Jenkins somewhere publicly accessible, we'll be using repository polling. While this will work for most, the most effective strategy is really using a Git hook to trigger Jenkins to run after every build.

At this part of the phase, we have a set of commands that can be run on demand. To really make Continuous Integration work, we'll need to have our code test itself. Within our job, we can select **View Configuration** to come to the configuration page. We'll be setting our **Build Triggers** to poll the SCM every minute:

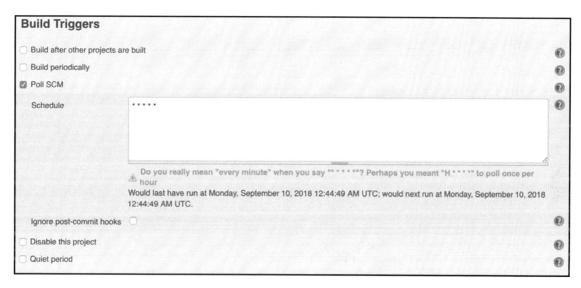

Once we've saved this configuration, Jenkins will automatically check our remote repository for changes every minute. We now have the simplest form of Continuous Integration: code that tests itself on every commit. With such a small amount of code coverage, our Continuous Integration pipeline doesn't provide us with much value, other than alerting us when we've created a malformed manifest.

Integrating the PDK

The Puppet PDK provides us with a framework for repeatable Continuous Integration. We'll be taking our bare bones module and converting it with PDK, and then we will begin by using PDK validate to replace our basic `puppet parser validate` command. Because the PDK is available on our Jenkins master, all PDK commands will also be available for use.

Our first step will be to change branches so that we don't impact the master as we're adding new code:

```
[root@pe-puppet-master profile]# git checkout -b pdk
Switched to a new branch 'pdk'
```

Next, let's convert our existing module with the PDK convert command. We'll be prompted with a series of questions, mostly aimed at publishing modules to the forge. The final question asks which operating system this is relevant to and actually does help form our test bindings, so we'll minimize this to just the targeted operating system: Red Hat-based Linux. Simply run `pdk convert` and follow the prompts.

The default PDK template contains three files not relevant to us: `.gitlab-ci.yml`, `.travis.yml`, and `appveyor.yml`, which are used for other CI systems. We'll then add our new files and commit them into a new code commit:

```
[rary@workstation profile]# rm .gitlab-ci.yml .travis.yml appveyor.yml
rm: remove regular file '.gitlab-ci.yml'? y
rm: remove regular file '.travis.yml'? y
rm: remove regular file 'appveyor.yml'? y
[rary@workstation profile]# git add -A
[rary@workstation profile]# git commit -m 'Initial PDK integration'
[pdk 7eb5009] Initial PDK integration
 10 files changed, 350 insertions(+)
 create mode 100644 .gitignore
 create mode 100644 .pdkignore
 create mode 100644 .rspec
 create mode 100644 .rubocop.yml
 create mode 100644 .yardopts
 create mode 100644 Gemfile
 create mode 100644 Rakefile
 create mode 100644 metadata.json
 create mode 100644 spec/default_facts.yml
 create mode 100644 spec/spec_helper.rb
```

Then, we'll change our Jenkinsfile `Test` stage to use the `pdk validate` utility:

```
pipeline {
  agent any
    stages {
        stage('Test') {
            steps {
                sh '/usr/local/bin/pdk validate'
            }
        }
    }
}
```

We'll push that back up to our remote repository with our Git workflow, and our Jenkins instance will automatically pick up our job on our new PDK branch after sending it remotely with `git push origin pdk`. Back on our **profile** page, we will now see a new branch:

The inside of this PDK branch should appear similar to our previous branch, but we want to inspect the logs of our test. Inside, we'll see that a few `puppet-lint` warnings were triggered, but did not fail the build. Puppet lint warnings by default provide an exit status of `0`, allowing your build to still pass:

```
warning: puppet-lint: manifests/jenkins.pp:1:1: class not documented
warning: puppet-lint: manifests/jenkins.pp:14:12: indentation of => is not
properly aligned (expected in column 13, but found it in column 12)
warning: puppet-lint: manifests/jenkins.pp:15:12: indentation of => is not
properly aligned (expected in column 13, but found it in column 12)
```

I like the Warnings plugin for viewing lint syntax. It shows trends over time, but is by no means necessary for proper Continuous Integration.

Before we do a pull request of this code into master, let's clean up our lint warnings by adding a comment to the top of our manifest, and aligning the arrows within the PDK package:

```
# Jenkins Profile
class profile::jenkins {

  class { 'jenkins': lts => true }

  package {'git': ensure => latest }

  file {'/tmp/pdk.rpm':
    ensure => file,
    source =>
'https://puppet-pdk.s3.amazonaws.com/pdk/1.7.0.0/repos/el/7/puppet5/x86_64/
pdk-1.7.0.0-1.el7.x86_64.rpm',
  }

  # Install latest PDK directly from Puppet Source
  package {'pdk':
    ensure  => installed,
    source  => '/tmp/pdk.rpm',
    require => File['/tmp/pdk.rpm'],
  }

}
```

We can then add these changes and push them back up to our remote repository. Our Jenkins scan will then pick up these changes within a minute and give us the all clear. Once we're happy with these results, you can merge your code with a pull request back at the remote repository, and watch this test run again on our master branch.

Now that we have some basic validation in place, we can start building some basic test coverage to rely on our profiles not losing features over time, or regressing.

Unit testing with Puppet RSpec

Unit testing is testing focused around the smallest unit of code. In the case of Puppet, the smallest functional unit of code is the manifest. RSpec provides us with a unit testing framework for Puppet code, which is fast and effective at checking that our Puppet code is producing the Puppet catalogs we expect. Whatever tests we write in RSpec, we're essentially asking: *would what I want be in the Puppet catalog when I execute this code?*

RSpec as a system is run on the command line, and does not involve a new virtual machine or container. It is now included in the Puppet PDK under the command `pdk test unit`. We're going to look at the files involved in running unit tests, and writing simple unit tests from the templates provided by the PDK.

We're beginning a new feature set, so we'll want to start from master, pull down the remote commits, and start on a new branch:

```
[rary@workstation profile]# git checkout master
Switched to branch 'master'

[rary@workstation profile]# git pull origin master
remote: Counting objects: 1, done.
remote: Total 1 (delta 0), reused 0 (delta 0), pack-reused 0
Unpacking objects: 100% (1/1), done.
From github.com:RARYates/cicd-walkthrough-profile
 * branch master -> FETCH_HEAD
Updating 1b91eec..639f8f6
Fast-forward
  . . .

[rary@workstation profile]# git checkout -b rspec
Switched to a new branch 'rspec'
```

Before we begin with RSpec, we'll want a sample set of files we can work with. At the time of writing this book, there is no command in the PDK to create a unit test without creating a new manifest. To overcome this limitation, we'll simply rename our `jenkins.pp` file, create a new class with the PDK, and place our existing file back in place over it:

```
[rary@workstation profile]# mv manifests/jenkins.pp
manifests/jenkins.pp.bak;pdk new class jenkins;mv manifests/jenkins.pp.bak
manifests/jenkins.pp
pdk (INFO): Creating '/root/profile/manifests/jenkins.pp' from template.
pdk (INFO): Creating '/root/profile/spec/classes/jenkins_spec.rb' from
template.
mv: overwrite 'manifests/jenkins.pp'? y
```

We'll now have our `jenkins_spec.rb` built from template, and will be ready to begin writing unit tests in RSpec.

Relevant RSpec files

With our files in place, let's inspect the most relevant files we'll work with during the testing of classes:

- `.fixtures.yml`
- `spec/classes/jenkins_spec.rb`

 `spec/spec_helper.rb` provides configuration and variables to every test in your suite. We won't be editing it in this example, but know that this is essentially your global configuration file for all of the modules tests.

.fixtures.yml

Our `fixtures` file lets our tests know what dependencies are required for our manifests. It is placed at the base of the repository, as `profile/.fixtures.yml`. For our particular profile, we'll build a fixtures file that contains `rtyler/jenkins` and all of its dependencies in order to support our test:

```
#profile/.fixtures.yml
fixtures:
  repositories:
    jenkins:
      repo: "git://github.com/voxpupuli/puppet-jenkins.git"
      ref: "1.7.0"
    apt: "https://github.com/puppetlabs/puppetlabs-apt"
    stdlib: "https://github.com/puppetlabs/puppetlabs-stdlib"
    java: "https://github.com/puppetlabs/puppetlabs-java"
    zypprepo: "https://github.com/voxpupuli/puppet-zypprepo.git"
    archive: "https://github.com/voxpupuli/puppet-archive.git"
    systemd: "https://github.com/camptocamp/puppet-systemd.git"
    transition: "https://github.com/puppetlabs/puppetlabs-transition.git"
```

We use this file to declare a module in our test, and use a pointer to a repository to find it. In the preceding case, we're grabbing the latest version of each module except Jenkins, which we've pinned at 1.7.0 as we're using in our Puppetfile. Depending on your strategy for code, you may or may not want to tag a specific reference to a version, like I did previously.

Documentation on fixtures can be found in the `spec_helper.rb` GitHub repository at `https://github.com/puppetlabs/puppetlabs_spec_helper#fixtures-examples`.

jenkins_spec.rb

After our fixtures are in place, let's inspect our `jenkins_spec.rb`, as provided by the PDK:

```
# Brings in our Global Configuration from spec/spec_helper.rb
require 'spec_helper'

# Tells RSpec with manifest to check, in this case:
profile/manifests.jenkins.pp
describe 'profile::jenkins' do

# Runs the test once for each operating system listed in metadata.json,
with a suite of default facts
  on_supported_os.each do |os, os_facts|
    context "on #{os}" do
      let(:facts) { os_facts }

# The manifest should compile into a catalog
      it { is_expected.to compile }
    end
  end
end
```

The preceding simple test just ensures that the catalog compiles for each and every operating system listed in `metadata.json`. Normally, we'd run this test and we'd receive a passing status. In this particular case, `rtyler/jenkins` requires us to supply an additional fact of `systemd` that is not available in the base `on_supported_os` function.

Check popular modules on the forge for samples of code, especially in cases where you're testing profiles against existing modules. Often, the upstream module has a fix, like the one we're about to implement.

We'll edit our existing `spec` class to introduce a new fact to our system to support `systemd`:

```
require 'spec_helper'

describe 'profile::jenkins' do
  on_supported_os.each do |os, os_facts|
    context "on #{os}" do

# Add a new ruby variable that returns true when the OS major release
version is 6
    systemd_fact = case os_facts[:operatingsystemmajrelease]
                     when '6'
                       { systemd: false }
                     else
                       { systemd: true }
                     end
# Change our facts to merge in our systemd_fact
      let :facts { os_facts.merge(systemd_fact) }

      it { is_expected.to compile }
    end
  end
end
```

Now, our test will be able to compile, as the upstream Jenkins module will have the `systemd` fact it needs to compile. Let's go ahead and compile our tests:

```
[root@pe-puppet-master profile]# pdk test unit
pdk (INFO): Using Ruby 2.4.4
pdk (INFO): Using Puppet 5.5.2
[✔] Preparing to run the unit tests.
[✔] Running unit tests.
  Evaluated 4 tests in 3.562477833 seconds: 0 failures, 0 pending.
```

You may have noticed that we have four passing tests. Although we wrote just one test, our `on_supported_os` function looked in our `metadata.json` file and provided a test for each listed operating system, all within the Red Hat family.

Extending our Jenkinsfile

We're going to change up our Jenkinsfile to support our new RSpec test. We're going to remove our original `Test` stage and be more clear by creating the `Validate` and `Unit Test` stages. We'll simply incorporate the two as `pdk validate` and `pdk test unit`:

```
pipeline {
    agent any

    stages {
        stage('Validate') {
            steps {
                sh '/usr/local/bin/pdk validate'
            }
        }
        stage ('Unit Test') {
            steps {
                sh '/usr/local/bin/pdk test unit'
            }
        }
    }
}
```

This will change our pipeline to three distinct phases: checkout `SCM`, `Validate`, and `Unit Test`. We'll be able to see where our build passes or fails along each step in Jenkins.

Now that we have a basic framework for our test laid out, let's get our code back to the remote repository:

```
[root@pe-puppet-master profile]# git commit -m 'Initial RSpec Framework'
[rspec 2bc4765] Initial RSpec Framework
 3 files changed, 37 insertions(+), 1 deletion (-)
 create mode 100644 .fixtures.yml
 create mode 100644 spec/classes/jenkins_spec.rb
[root@pe-puppet-master profile]# git push origin rspec
Counting objects: 8, done.
Delta compression using up to 2 threads.
Compressing objects: 100% (5/5), done.
Writing objects: 100% (6/6), 892 bytes | 0 bytes/s, done.
Total 6 (delta 1), reused 0 (delta 0)
remote: Resolving deltas: 100% (1/1), completed with 1 local object.
To git@github.com:RARYates/cicd-walkthrough-profile.git
 * [new branch] rspec -> rspec
```

Back in our Jenkins instance, we can see the new RSpec branch and the new logs for our test. Notice each section, and that we're also seeing our Jenkins instance pass our four RSpec tests.

Extending our test

Now that we can write a test, we'll write one simple test that simply mirrors our manifest. This test will help us prevent regression, as changing an existing value or removing an existing resource will cause the test to fail. If this change is intended, the test must also be changed. Although this intuitively feels like it would slow down development, it saves even more time in integration when you can ensure that no new errors have been introduced.

Here is our RSpec test containing the mirror of our original profile:

```
require 'spec_helper'

describe 'profile::jenkins' do
  on_supported_os.each do |os, os_facts|
    context "on #{os}" do
      systemd_fact = case os_facts[:operatingsystemmajrelease]
                      when '6'
                        { systemd: false }
                      else
                        { systemd: true }
                      end
      let :facts do
        os_facts.merge(systemd_fact)
      end

      ####  NEW CODE  ####

      context 'With Defaults' do
        it do
          # Jenkins must be the LTS
          is_expected.to contain_class('jenkins').with('lts' => 'true')

          # We're unsure if we want latest git, but we want to make sure
it's installed
          is_expected.to contain_package('git')

          # Download this particular version of the PDK
          is_expected.to contain_file('/tmp/pdk.rpm').with('ensure' =>
'file',
                                              'source' =>
'https://puppet-pdk.s3.amazonaws.com/pdk/1.7.0.0/repos/el/7/puppet5/x86_64/
pdk-1.7.0.0-1.el7.x86_64.rpm')

          # Install PDK from Disk. We'll change this test if we place this
in a proper yumrepo one day
          # Also not that that_requires, and  the lack of quotes within the
```

```
File array
        is_expected.to contain_package('pdk').with('ensure'  =>
'installed',
                                        'source'  =>
'/tmp/pdk.rpm').that_requires('File[/tmp/pdk.rpm]')
      end
    end

    ### END NEW CODE ###

    it { is_expected.to compile }
  end
 end
end
```

When we create a commit with this new test, and send it back up to Jenkins, we'll see our build actually perform this test. Up to this point, we've never intentionally broken a test. Let's go ahead and prove our test now. Comment out one resource in your original manifest, or change some configuration before sending this repository back to the remote server. After pushing this, you should be able to see a failed test in Jenkins! Simply uncomment out your resources and push a new commit up to your remote, and you'll see Jenkins pass this build. Once your build is passing, go ahead and merge into master so that we can continue onto our next section of integration testing.

 There is great documentation on writing RSpec tests out there at `http://rspec-puppet.com/`.

Acceptance testing with Test Kitchen

An acceptance test is a test that is performed to validate that requirements are met. While RSpec is a fast way to check that a catalog is compiled the way you expect it to be, it does not actually run the catalog on the system and verify that the expected results can be seen. An acceptance test, in the context of Puppet, is applying your selected manifest to a system and verifying that the system meets the requirements after the catalog is applied, preferably with a method that isn't the Puppet Agent itself.

In this chapter, we're going to build an acceptance test for our Jenkins Profile that ensures that Jenkins is running and that we can reach it on port 8080 so that we can view the web page. This extends beyond the ability of RSpec, as Rspec doesn't actually build a node we can verify on. When we use an acceptance testing harness in Puppet, we also tie it to a hypervisor so that it can manage a node, or **System Under Test** (**SUT**).

Beaker

Puppet provides a perfectly adequate acceptance testing harness in Beaker. Beaker is designed to connect to a hypervisor and spin up nodes as defined in configuration files and apply the Puppet tests. It uses a simple language called Serverspec to define tests. It also has the benefit of checking for idempotence by running a second time. Puppet themselves have also connected it to another application called VMPooler, which preemptively spins up a pool of virtual machines to act as SUTs and replaces themselves when the test is done, providing rapid response time to acceptance tests. If you, as an organization, are far along in your CI/CD process, and require virtual machines, I highly recommend Beaker. For this section, we'll do our acceptance testing in Test Kitchen, simply because I believe it's easier to work with and provides more options for workstation development.

Test Kitchen and kitchen-puppet

Test Kitchen is actually the testing framework built by Chef. It is very simple to use and get started with, and uses a language even easier to work with than Serverspec called Inspec. We'll be extending Test Kitchen to support Puppet using `rubygem kitchen-puppet`, found at `https://github.com/neillturner/kitchen-puppet`. We'll need to prepare our Jenkins node to start taking advantage of Test Kitchen and running another set of validation tests.

Preparing Test Kitchen on our Jenkins node

Test Kitchen directly supports the development activities of our Puppet code. We'll be using a single composite command from Test Kitchen in our CI/CD run: `kitchen test`. Kitchen test is an orchestration of the destroy, create, converge, setup, verify, and commands, taking us through cleaning up, building, applying code, and testing each run. You can run Test Kitchen locally, as well as on our CI/CD system, which is one of the greatest strengths of using kitchen-puppet. We'll be adding a lot of code in this section, from updating our Jenkins Profile to supporting Test Kitchen, to building the test and Test Kitchen configuration.

Jenkins Profile

We'll change up our profile first. In the following example, we'll add the following resources and features:

- Install Docker, if the node is not already a Docker Container
- Install RVM, Ruby 2.4.1 and all RubyGems needed for Kitchen

We have added the preceding resources and features in the following code:

```
# Jenkins Profile
class profile::jenkins {

  class {'jenkins':
    lts => true,
  }

  package {'git': ensure => latest }

  file {'/tmp/pdk.rpm':
    ensure => file,
    source =>
'https://puppet-pdk.s3.amazonaws.com/pdk/1.7.0.0/repos/el/7/puppet5
/x86_64/pdk-1.7.0.0-1.el7.x86_64.rpm',
  }

# Install latest PDK directly from Puppet Source
  package {'pdk':
    ensure => installed,
    source => '/tmp/pdk.rpm',
    require => File['/tmp/pdk.rpm'],
  }

  if $::virtual != 'docker' {
    class {'docker':
      docker_users => ['jenkins']
    }
  }

  include rvm

  rvm::system_user { 'jenkins':}

  rvm_system_ruby {'ruby-2.4.1':
    ensure => 'present',
    default_use => true,
  }

  rvm_gem {['ruby-2.4.1/librarian-puppet',
            'ruby-2.4.1/test-kitchen',
            'ruby-2.4.1/executable-hooks',
            'ruby-2.4.1/kitchen-inspec',
            'ruby-2.4.1/kitchen-puppet',
            'ruby-2.4.1/kitchen-docker']:
    ensure => installed,
    require => Rvm_system_ruby['ruby-2.4.1'],
```

```
            notify => Service['jenkins'],
    }

  }
```

 We'll need to deploy this new profile to our Jenkins node before we continue through the rest of the section. Make sure you deploy this to your Puppet Master before continuing on editing the build. Working with your CI/CD system can sometimes feel like a series of chicken before the egg scenarios. This is normal, but the concepts extend beyond our CI/CD system.

.kitchen.yml

The first file we'll work with is our `.kitchen.yml`. This file determines how Test Kitchen performs the build. This YAML file provides us with the following:

- **Driver**: This is used for running the build in Docker as a privileged user starting with the init process. If you're unfamiliar with working with containers, we're setting it up this way to act more like a traditional VM, and less like a wrapper around an application.
- **Provisioner**: We're setting up Test Kitchen to use the Puppet provisioner with a local manifests and modules path in our build.
- **Verifier**: Use Inspec for testing.
- **Platforms**: We are going to configure our container to use the CentOS SystemD container. We're passing additional commands to ensure that SSH works properly, and that init scripts are available for our Jenkins run.
- **Suites**: This is used for describing each test suite we run. This first one is defined with `jenkins.pp` in our test directory, which is a simple `include` `profile::jenkins`, like we may see in an `example.pp`. Notice our pre-verify stage in this one, giving our Jenkins instance 30 seconds to finish coming up before we test:

```
---
driver:
  name: docker
  privileged: true
  use_sudo: false
  run_command: /usr/sbin/init

provisioner:
  name: puppet_apply
  # Not installing chef since inspec is used for testing
```

```
      require_chef_for_busser: false
      manifests_path: test
      modules_path: test/modules

  verifier:
    name: inspec

  platforms:
  - name: centos
    driver_config:
      image: centos/systemd
      platform: centos
      run_command: /usr/sbin/init
      privileged: true
      provision_command:
        - yum install -y initscripts
        - sed -i 's/UsePAM yes/UsePAM no/g' /etc/ssh/sshd_config
        - systemctl enable sshd.service

  suites:
    - name: default
      provisioner:
        manifest: jenkins.pp
      lifecycle:
        pre_verify:
        - sleep 30
```

`.kitchen.yml` will work for us locally as well, allowing us to run tests and verify them before sending our code up to our remote repository. We can also use `kitchen converge` to build the machine and apply the code if we want to inspect the end-state on our local system.

Puppetfile

The kitchen-puppet gem runs via Puppetfile. Underneath the covers, it's using a tool called librarian-puppet to pull down all modules and dependencies found in the Puppetfile. Librarian and r10k came around the same time, with r10k providing no automatic dependency resolution, preferring explicit naming. Due to our use of Puppet Librarian, we're explicitly adding an exclusion for Java and Apt, which our 2-year old Puppet module locks to old versions. Our Jenkins module works just fine with modern versions of Java and Apt, but this automatic dependency resolution has to be muted so that we do not fail:

```
forge 'https://forge.puppetlabs.com'
mod 'rtyler/jenkins',
   :git => 'https://github.com/voxpupuli/puppet-jenkins.git',
   :ref => 'v1.7.0'
```

```
#mod 'puppetlabs-stdlib'
mod 'darin-zypprepo'
mod 'puppet-archive'
mod 'camptocamp-systemd'
mod 'puppetlabs-transition'
mod 'maestrodev-rvm'
mod 'puppetlabs-docker'

mod 'puppetlabs-java'
mod 'puppetlabs-apt'

exclusion 'puppetlabs-apt'
exclusion 'puppetlabs-java'
```

Jenkinsfile

I'm adding two new objects to our Jenkinsfile: an integration test provided by a shell script, and a post action that tells Jenkins to clean up our workspace. We're using an external script instead of running inline for ease of management, as each `sh` step is an independent shell in Jenkins. Our post cleanup action just makes sure that we don't retain any artifacts from a previous build:

```
pipeline {
    agent any

    stages {
        stage('Validate') {
            steps {
                sh '/usr/local/bin/pdk validate'
            }
        }
        stage ('Unit Test') {
            steps {
                sh '/usr/local/bin/pdk test unit'
            }
        }
        stage ('Integration Test') {
            steps {
                sh './acceptance.sh'
            }
        }
    }
```

```
post {
        always {
            deleteDir()
        }
    }
}
```

acceptance.sh

Our acceptance shell script is relatively small, but allows Jenkins to have a path for this build and sources in RVM prior to running Kitchen Test. We want to make sure that the build stays consistent, so we want to control the environment around the build as well:

```
#profile/acceptance.sh
#!/bin/bash
PATH=$PATH:/usr/local/rvm/gems/ruby-2.4.1/bin/:/usr/local/bin
source /usr/local/rvm/bin/rvm
/usr/local/rvm/gems/ruby-2.4.1/wrappers/kitchen test
```

Test

Our actual test itself is one of the simplest files in our new iteration. We're placing it in the default folder, so it's found by the default suite we mentioned previously. We're building a single control or set of tests, with three tests:

- Ensure that the Jenkins package is installed
- Ensure that the Jenkins service is running
- Ensure that Jenkins can be reached on the localhost at `8080`, and returns a 200 exit status:

```
# profile/integration/default/jenkins_spec.rb
control 'Jenkins Status' do
  describe package('jenkins') do
    it { is_expected.to be_installed }
  end

  describe http('http://localhost:8080', open_timeout: 60, read_timeout:
60) do
    its('status') { is_expected.to cmp 200 }
  end
```

```
describe service('jenkins') do
    it { is_expected.to be_running }
  end
end
```

Performing the test

Now that we have all of the pieces in place, let's go ahead and deploy our code to our repository, and let Jenkins run the job. If you haven't already run our new Jenkins Profile, you'll need to make sure it's deployed to your master and that your Jenkins node has already converged on it. Once we push our test to the CI/CD system, it will read our code and begin the test. Of particular note, this test will take significantly longer than the tests we've written previously, as the container will need to be downloaded, built, spun up, converged, and tested, compared to our PDK commands that simply checked syntax or compiled a quick catalog.

We've built a lot of files during this chapter, so let's take a quick look at just the files we've managed, ignoring anything automatically built by software:

```
rary at Ryans-MacBook-Pro-3 in ~/workspace/packt
$ tree cicd-walkthrough-profile
cicd-walkthrough-profile
├── Jenkinsfile # Test to be Performed
├── Puppetfile # Dependencies for Kitchen Tests
├── acceptance.sh # Command to run Test Kitchen for Jenkins
├── manifests
│   └── jenkins.pp # Jenkins Profile
├── spec
│   ├── classes
│   │   └── jenkins_spec.rb # Our Inspec test for the Kitchen Phase
└── test
    ├── integration
    │   └── default
    │       └── jenkins_spec.rb # Our RSpec Test, checking the Catalog
    └── jenkins.pp # Our example manifest that applies the Profile for
Kitchen

13 directories, 18 files
```

Summary

In this chapter, we focused on building out a CI System (Jenkins) and performing a validation check, a unit test, and an acceptance test. CI/CD is a continual journey, and there is always room for improvement in our workflows. Continuous Integration provides us with a valuable safety net for development, allowing us to develop without worrying about feature loss or regression.

Where are some places to go to from here? Integrate your Git system closer to Jenkins by using Git hooks to deploy code, and providing a status back before a pull request is added. You can also add notifications to developers, alerting them when their tests have gone from passing to failing. If you find some of these warnings to be too much, tune the system providing the warning to avoid some of these errors. Everyone has a different CI/CD journey, so explore for yourself and figure out what works for you!

The next chapter covers Puppet Tasks and Puppet Discovery. Puppet Tasks allows us to run ad-hoc commands and use them as building blocks for imperative scripts. We'll be building a task to inspect log files and planning to build an aggregated log file for our Puppet Master. Puppet Discovery allows us to inspect our existing infrastructure and determine ground truth on packages, services, users, and various other components of a virtual machine or container.

8
Extending Puppet with Tasks and Discovery

Since the launch of Puppet 5, three new services have been announced by Puppet: Tasks, Discovery, and Pipelines. Puppet Tasks provides us an imperative solution for automating ad hoc tasks. Puppet Discovery allows us to discover the state of infrastructure. Puppet Pipelines, which will be discussed briefly in the next chapter, covers application-level CI/CD.

In this chapter, we'll investigate and use Puppet Tasks to help manage a web server. We'll walk through some best practices and appropriate times for using Puppet Tasks. We'll then dive into Puppet Discovery and inspect our infrastructure. We'll use Puppet Discovery to make intelligent decisions on what to automate in our infrastructure.

Puppet Tasks

Puppet is designed to provide continual enforcement of an end-state on nodes in an infrastructure. While Puppet can cover most infrastructure tasks, some things are better left to ad hoc tasks. Puppet Tasks are on-demand actions that can be run on nodes and containers. You write tasks in a similar way to scripts, and they can be written in any language that's available on the target node. When deciding on the right tool for the job, between a task or a Puppet manifest, I stick to a simple thought process: is this something I want permanently, or a single one-off action?

Let's think about some things in a normal workplace that would be permanent, or stateful. The physical address of where I work and the building, rooms, and furniture are examples of physical things I'd want permanently enforced. Things like weekly meetings or the daily scrum would also be something to continually enforce, as a business rule. All of these things have components, from the brick and mortar to the time and place of the weekly scrum. If we could manage the real world with our IT tools, Puppet would be the perfect tool to describe our office and business rules, which we expect to stay constant.

In the same context, an impromptu meeting or after-work function would consist of a series of tasks, performed once, but mostly in the same manner every time (with variables). If a customer orders something, we'd use a task to deliver the request. If the request was custom, we'd instead use a series of tasks to build the composite whole. These are the things we do consistently, but with variations and at unknown points in time. An external event or person drives the creation of this work, but we try to repeat things in an automated way to save time and increase consistency.

The chief difference between Tasks and Puppet for management is imperative and declarative models. In this section, we'll be setting up Bolt (the technology that powers tasks), building a web server with Puppet, and then deploying our websites on demand with Bolt.

Bolt

Bolt is the primary driver for Puppet Tasks, and is an open source project written in Ruby for remotely executing scripts of any language, on systems over SSH and WinRM. You can write your tasks in any language supported by the end host, such as PowerShell and Bash on Windows and Linux, or Ruby and Python if interpreters are available. Bolt was designed as an agentless system to distribute scripts and execute remote commands over standard protocols, using SSH public key encryption or a username and password. There is also a built-in command-line tool for building inventory files over PuppetDB queries. Bolt also supports task plans, packaged in forge modules, which chain multiple tasks together, providing more complex tasks.

Installing Bolt

Bolt can be installed via a number of methods, all described at `https://puppet.com/docs/bolt/0.x/bolt_installing.html`:

- A downloadable package from `http://downloads.puppet.com/`
- A public Chocolatey package
- OSX Homebrew installation
- Linux native package repositories
- Rubygems

 Bolt works remotely over standard connection protocols. Try installing it and using it on your workstation, instead of the Puppet Master, during this lesson.

On my MacBook, I'll install Bolt using Homebrew:

```
rary at Ryans-MacBook-Pro in ~/workspace/packt
$ brew cask install puppetlabs/puppet/puppet-bolt
==> Tapping puppetlabs/puppet
Cloning into '/usr/local/Homebrew/Library/Taps/puppetlabs/homebrew-
puppet'...
remote: Counting objects: 15, done.
remote: Compressing objects: 100% (14/14), done.
remote: Total 15 (delta 1), reused 8 (delta 1), pack-reused 0
Unpacking objects: 100% (15/15), done.
Tapped 3 casks (49 files, 54.9KB).
==> Satisfying dependencies
==> Downloading
https://downloads.puppet.com/mac/puppet5/10.13/x86_64/puppet-bolt-0.22.0-1.
osx10.13.dmg
########################################################################
100.0%
==> Verifying SHA-256 checksum for Cask 'puppet-bolt'.
==> Installing Cask puppet-bolt
==> Running installer for puppet-bolt; your password may be necessary.
==> Package installers may write to any location; options such as --appdir
are ignored.
Password:
installer: Package name is puppet-bolt
installer: Installing at base path /
installer: The install was successful.
puppet-bolt was successfully installed!
```

I'll then close my Terminal, and reopen it and verify that the `bolt` command is in my path:

```
$ bolt
Usage: bolt <subcommand> <action> [options]

Available subcommands:
  bolt command run <command> Run a command remotely
  bolt file upload <src> <dest> Upload a local file
  bolt script run <script> Upload a local script and run it remotely
  bolt task show Show list of available tasks
  bolt task show <task> Show documentation for task
  bolt task run <task> [params] Run a Puppet task
  bolt plan show Show list of available plans
  bolt plan show <plan> Show details for plan
  bolt plan run <plan> [params] Run a Puppet task plan
  bolt puppetfile install Install modules from a Puppetfile into a Boltdir

Run `bolt <subcommand> --help` to view specific examples.
```

Managing nodes

In Bolt, we have to explicitly list the nodes that we want to manage. We can do this via the `--nodes` command flag, or by providing an inventory file. An inventory file is a YAML file that contains groups of nodes, with configuration options already set. By default, an `inventory` file placed at `~/.puppetlabs/bolt/inventory.yaml` will be used by Bolt. For this section, we'll only be targeting our Puppet Master, so I'll ensure that it is in the `inventory` file:

```
# ~/.puppetlabs/bolt/inventory.yaml
---
groups:
  - name: puppetserver
    nodes:
    - pe-puppet-master.puppet.net
    config:
      transport: ssh
      ssh:
        user: root
```

Before I can run Bolt to that server, I'm going to need to ensure that my SSH key is available as the root user on that system. I'll use the `ssh-copy-id` utility to transfer this from my UNIX-based system to the root user:

```
rary at Ryans-MacBook in ~/workspace/packt
$ ssh-copy-id root@pe-puppet-master.puppet.net

/usr/bin/ssh-copy-id: INFO: attempting to log in with the new key(s), to
filter out any that are already installed
/usr/bin/ssh-copy-id: INFO: 1 key(s) remain to be installed -- if you are
prompted now it is to install the new keys
root@pe-puppet-master.puppet.net's password:

Number of key(s) added: 1

Now try logging into the machine, with: "ssh 'root@pe-puppet-
master.puppet.net'"
and check to make sure that only the key(s) you wanted were added.
```

Ad hoc commands

At the very basic core of Puppet Bolt, we issue remote commands, send scripts, and run scripts. Bolt provides three simple commands to do just that: `bolt command run`, `bolt file upload`, and `bolt script run`. To test our SSH key from earlier, let's run a simple command using `bolt command run`:

```
rary at Ryans-MacBook-Pro-3 in ~/workspace/packt/bolt
$ bolt command run "echo 'Hello World'" --nodes puppetserver --no-host-key-
check
Started on puppetserver.puppet.net...
Finished on puppetserver.puppet.net:
  STDOUT:
    Hello World
Successful on 1 node: pe-puppet-master.puppet.net
Ran on 1 node in 0.40 seconds
```

For simple one-off tasks, running the `bolt` command can be a great way to inspect a system. When we have a larger list of instructions to send, we'll want to write a script and run it remotely. Here is a simple script that returns users and all open ports:

```
#./inspect.sh

#!/bin/bash

echo 'Users:'
cat /etc/passwd | cut -f 1 -d ':'
echo 'Ports:'
netstat -tulpn
```

When we run this script via `bolt script run`, we get the following:

```
$ bolt script run inspect.sh --nodes puppetserver --no-host-key-check
Started on puppetserver.puppet.net...
Finished on puppetserver.puppet.net:
  STDOUT:
    Users:
    root
    ...
    vboxadd
    vagrant
    Ports:
    Active Internet connections (only servers)
    Proto Recv-Q Send-Q Local Address Foreign Address State PID/Program
name
      tcp 0 0 0.0.0.0:22 0.0.0.0:* LISTEN 1258/sshd
    ...
Successful on 1 node: puppetserver.puppet.net
Ran on 1 node in 0.85 seconds
```

Finally, if I wanted to make this script available on the Puppet Server for a local user, I could send it over with `bolt script upload`:

```
rary at Ryans-MacBook in ~/workspace/packt/bolt
$ bolt file upload inspect.sh /tmp/inspect.sh --nodes puppetserver --no-
```

```
host-key-check
Started on puppetserver.puppet.net...
Finished on puppetserver.puppet.net:
  Uploaded 'inspect.sh' to 'puppetserver.puppet.net:/tmp/inspect.sh'
Successful on 1 node: puppetserver.puppet.net
Ran on 1 node in 0.66 seconds
```

Bolt tasks

Bolt tasks allow us to write and extend a script with additional metadata parameters. These parameters can be provided on execution by environment variables, PowerShell named arguments, or as JSON input in more advanced cases. Bolt tasks are similar to resources in Puppet, allowing us to parameterize an action and use a command in a repeatable way. We'll be writing a simple task that allows us to inspect certain log files on the Puppet Master by name. This task will be part of a logs module, named `puppetserver`.

task.json

This JSON parameter file is an optional component for tasks and allows the passing of parameters as environment variables to our scripts. We can use this file to also limit user input as well, leaving a small number of options available for our users if necessary. In the following example, our script will accept a log and store the parameter. The log parameter will only allow three choices, which determine where to find the log file the user is searching for. The store parameter will be off by default, but will allow us to aggregate logs for the plan we'll build in the next section:

```
#logs/tasks/puppetserver.json
{
  "puppet_task_version": 1,
  "supports_noop": false,
  "description": "Retrieve a log file from the puppetserver",
  "parameters": {
    "log": {
      "description": "The Puppetserver log you want to read",
      "type": "Enum[console,puppetdb,puppetserver]"
    },
    "store": {
      "description": "Store logfile in /tmp/puppetlog.log",
      "type": "Optional[Boolean]"
    }
  }
}
```

The parameters use the same data types as Puppet. You can use any data type available to Puppet as a data type for Puppet tasks.

Task

Our task will be a simple shell script that reads a named file based on our input parameters, makes a decision on whether or not to store the output, and then returns the output as JSON to Bolt. It's important that our return comes back as JSON so that it can be picked up by Bolt. In more complex use cases, we could even use this JSON to pass key value pairs to a follow-on task in plans, which we'll cover in the next section.

A task can be written in any language available to the system. This example will use Bash, as nearly every administrator has worked with it. If you haven't tried writing scripts in Python, Ruby, Golang, or any other scripting language outside of shell, give it a shot. These tasks actually become easier to write in these more advanced languages.

There are a few things worth noting in our shell script:

- Values returned from our JSON parameters file become environment variables, and start with `PT_`. Our script refers to `$PT_log` and `$PT_store` to check the values that will be sent over the command line.
- We're using a case statement to map `$PT_log` to a log file. This use is similar to a selector statement in Puppet.
- If `$PT_store` is true, we'll build a log file that can be appended to.
- The log is printed out in the final line as JSON so that Puppet Tasks knows it is a valid output to the command line:

```
# logs/tasks/puppetserver.sh
#!/bin/sh

# Map $PT_log to a $logfile variable
case "$PT_log" in
  'console') logfile='/var/log/puppetlabs/console-services/console-services.log' ;;
  'puppetdb') logfile='/var/log/puppetlabs/puppetdb/puppetdb.log' ;;
  'puppetserver')
logfile='/var/log/puppetlabs/puppetserver/puppetserver.log' ;;
esac

# Variable that stores all the text from inside the logfile
log=`cat $logfile`
```

```
# If store is true, build a header and then print out $log
if [ $PT_store == 'true' ]
then
  echo "${PT_log}\r=============" >> /tmp/puppetlog.log
  echo $log >> /tmp/puppetlog.log
fi

# print out the key value of "<chosen log>":"all log contents" in JSON to
be
# read by the Bolt interpreter
echo -e "{'${PT_log}':'$log'}"
```

Let's double check that the files we've written are in the proper location before we run our command:

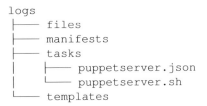

```
logs
├── files
├── manifests
├── tasks
│   ├── puppetserver.json
│   └── puppetserver.sh
└── templates
```

We can then run our command on the command line. We've added some parameters that help along the way:

- `nodes`: This determines which nodes based on our inventory file to run on.
- `modulepath`: Where to look for modules. Because we're working on this module directly, we've just set the modulepath to the directory above the module.
- `--no-host-key-check`: You may not need this, but to ease troubleshooting of SSH in this section, we'll use this flag.
- `log=puppetdb`: This is the parameter which we wrote in our JSON file. It will be transformed into `$PT_log` and used in our shell script:

```
$ bolt task run logs::puppetserver --nodes puppetserver --modulepath ..
log=puppetdb --no-host-key-check

Started on pe-puppet-master.puppet.net...
Finished on pe-puppet-master.puppet.net:
  {'puppetdb':'2018-09-23T00:20:55.115Z INFO [p.p.command]
[8-1537662054876] [212 ms] 'replace facts' command processed for pe-puppet-
master
  2018-09-23T00:21:12.077Z INFO [p.p.command] [9-1537662071679] [370 ms]
'store report' puppet v5.5.2 command processed for pe-puppet-master
  2018-09-23T00:21:53.936Z INFO [p.p.c.services] Starting sweep of stale
nodes (threshold: 7 days)
```

```
...'}
    {
    }
Successful on 1 node: pe-puppet-master.puppet.net
Ran on 1 node in 0.89 seconds
```

Try the command out for yourself. It will return a different log file for each command, and if you pass `store=true`, it will even start appending this log to a file in `/tmp` named `puppetlog.log`.

Bolt plans

If Puppet tasks are our imperative resources, Puppet plans are our Puppet manifests. Here, we combine multiple tasks and commands to form an orchestrated plan. These plans are written in the same DSL as Puppet code, although at the time of writing this book, only puppet functions can be used, and not many objects like resources or class are included.

In our sample plan, we're going to introduce two parameters:

- `$enterprise`: This is used to determine if `pe-console-services` should be checked in the plan (it is possible to use facts from the target or PuppetDB as well)
- `$servers`: This is a list of servers that's passed as a comma-separated list

Our task will clean up any existing stored logs and build a fresh set. This script will run the log scraper task we built in the last section for each section, and aggregate all the logs together. Enterprise, as an optional flag, will determine if `pe-console-services.log` is included as well. After we've built the log, we'll simply read the log file and ensure that it is returned to the command line with the `return` function. Finally, we'll clean up after ourselves and clean the aggregated log we just built in `/tmp`:

```
# logs/plans/puppetserver.pp
plan logs::puppetserver (
  Boolean $enterprise,
  TargetSpec $servers,
) {

  run_command('rm -f /tmp/puppetlog.log', $servers)
  run_task('logs::puppetserver', $servers, log => 'puppetserver', store =>
true)
  run_task('logs::puppetserver', $servers, log => 'puppetdb', store =>
true)

  if $enterprise == true {
```

```
      run_task('logs::puppetserver', $servers, log => 'console', store =>
  true)
    }

    return run_command('cat /tmp/puppetlog.log', $servers)
    run_command('rm -f /tmp/puppetlog.log', $servers)

  }
```

Once we've built our plan, we can run `bolt plan run`, passing our `modulepath` and parameters:

```
rary at Ryans-MacBook-Pro-3 in ~/workspace/packt/logs
$ bolt plan run logs::puppetserver --modulepath .. --no-host-key-check
enterprise=false servers=root@pe-puppet-master
Starting: plan logs::puppetserver
Starting: command 'rm -f /tmp/puppetlog.log' on root@pe-puppet-master
Finished: command 'rm -f /tmp/puppetlog.log' with 0 failures in 0.38 sec
Starting: task logs::puppetserver on root@pe-puppet-master
Finished: task logs::puppetserver with 0 failures in 0.39 sec
Starting: task logs::puppetserver on root@pe-puppet-master
Finished: task logs::puppetserver with 0 failures in 0.45 sec
Starting: command 'cat /tmp/puppetlog.log' on root@pe-puppet-master
Finished: command 'cat /tmp/puppetlog.log' with 0 failures in 0.15 sec
Finished: plan logs::puppetserver in 1.39 sec
[
  {
    "node": "root@pe-puppet-master",
    "status": "success",
    "result": {
      "stdout": "puppetserver\n============\n2018-09-23T00:20:54.905Z INFO
[qtp417202273-69] [puppetserver] Puppet 'replace_facts' command for pe-
puppet-master submitted to PuppetDB with UUID fc691079-
debf-4c99-896b-3244f353a753\n2018-09-23T00:20:55.268Z ERROR
[qtp417202273-69] [puppetserver] Puppet Could not find node statement with
name 'default' or 'pe-puppet-master' on node pe-puppet-master\n ...",
      "stderr": "",
      "exit_code": 0
    }
  }
]
```

You may notice that the log comes back as a big JSON object, with no line breaks represented. If you want to view this aggregated log file for yourself, try running the following command and inspecting the new `puppetlog.log` file:

```
$ rm -f *.log;bolt plan run logs::puppetserver --modulepath .. --no-host-
key-check enterprise=false servers=root@pe-puppet-master > compressed.log;
```

```
head -n 6 compressed.log | tail -n 1 | awk '{gsub("\\\\n","\n")};1' >
puppetlog.log
```

Puppet Enterprise Task Management

Bolt is a fully-featured open source product. It does not need Puppet Enterprise to work well in your environment. That being said, the console for Puppet Enterprise ties in very nicely with Bolt. There is a single tasks page on the left-hand side of the console that will take you to the main tasks page. Once you enter, you'll be greeted with the **Run a task** page, which provides you with a few convenient features if you're sharing yours tasks in your organization.

 This section is only relevant for Puppet Enterprise users. This module will need to be in `/etc/puppetlabs/code/environments/production/modules` via r10k or manual placement to be read by the Puppet Enterprise console.

The first main feature is the ability to directly view the supporting JSON parameters file before running the task. Notice that our description and optional parameters are represented in tasks when we add `logs::puppetserver,` making documentation for other users convenient:

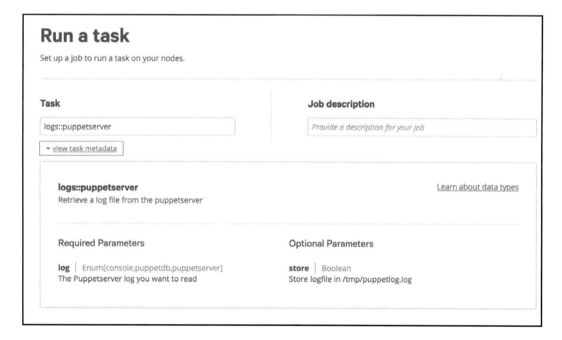

Every parameter is also represented as a drop-down menu. Because we selected **Enum[console,puppetdb,puppetserver]** as our type in `puppetserver.json`, those are the only options available to the users in the console. Store is also a true or false only value drop-down, thanks to our Boolean selection:

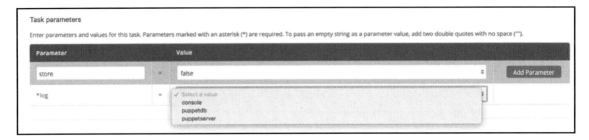

Once we run the job, we'll get back a cleaned up version of the logs that we've selected. If you're in a large organization, you could put this task into the inventory and allow administrators to remotely view log files on demand without ever needing to log into the server or manage the code:

This task was meant to be a simple example. With complicated tasks and plans, you can orchestrate automation of any kind and in any language across your infrastructure, using just SSH or WinRM. Our tasks have the ability to import and export JSON variables, allowing us to build more complex dependencies between tasks. Puppet Tasks is still relatively new to the Puppet ecosystem, but is a promising new addition, allowing for the rapid sharing of administration automation tasks within an organization.

Puppet Discovery

Puppet Discovery is a new product by Puppet. Puppet Discovery is a standalone containerized application built to discover information about containers and virtual machines in real-time. This platform is designed to have an inventory of all IT resources, discover details about each resource, and take action on those machines. Although still in the early phases of development, I expect to see tighter integration between Discovery, Puppet Tasks, and the greater Puppet ecosystem.

Puppet Discovery is generally safe to install and use to inspect a production-level system. Puppet Discovery does do an active scan of all sources, and may trigger security warnings in your organization. Make sure that you coordinate with a security team if you decide to use Puppet Discovery against corporate resources.

In this section, we'll be installing Puppet Discovery and viewing what is available to us. We'll start by installing the system, followed by adding an IP CIDR block of our infrastructure machine, and then connect to our machines using credentials. Then we'll explore Puppet Discovery to view details of individual nodes and packages across our infrastructure.

This may trigger security alerts in production if security isn't notified.

Installing Discovery

Puppet Discovery is not a **Free and Open Source Software** (**FOSS**). We'll need a license from Puppet, which can be obtained at `licenses.puppet.com`. Select an available Puppet Discovery license to get started and then download it to the target machine you'll run Puppet Discovery on. This JSON file will be used in the installation of our Puppet Discovery application.

 You'll need Docker available on the machine. In order to install Puppet Discovery, you'll need to have Docker on the host.

Preparing Puppet Discovery

Download Puppet Discovery for your operating system at `https://puppet.com/download-puppet-discovery`. This section will help us put the binary in our path and set up Puppet Discovery for the first time.

After we've downloaded Puppet Discovery, we'll want to move the binary into our path. On most Unix-based operating systems, `/usr/local/bin` is in your path. We need to place our binary in our path, make it executable, and ensure we can run it as the local user:

 If `/usr/local/bin` is not in your path, you can see which directories are in your path by using `echo $PATH` on your system. This will come back as a list separated by colons.

```
rary at Ryans-MacBook-Pro in ~/workspace
$ mv ~/Downloads/puppet-discovery /usr/local/bin

rary at Ryans-MacBook-Pro in ~/workspace
$ chmod a+x /usr/local/bin/puppet-discovery

rary at Ryans-MacBook-Pro in ~/workspace
$ puppet-discovery
A discovery application for cloud-native infrastructure

  Find more information at https://puppet.com/products/puppet-discovery

Usage:
  puppet-discovery [command]

  . . .
```

Once we've verified that the binary works, we'll run `puppet-discovery start` to start the service. We'll be prompted to provide a license key, read the EULA (which will pop up in a browser), and generate an administrative password:

```
rary at Ryans-MacBook-Pro in ~
$ puppet-discovery start
Please enter the path to your Puppet Discovery license: Documents/License-
puppet-discovery-trial-2018-10-23.puppet_discovery.json

By continuing with installation, you agree to terms outlined in the Puppet
Discovery End User License Agreement located here: /Users/rary/.puppet-
discovery/data/puppet-discovery-eula-1537730629.html

Do you agree? [y/n]: y

****************************************************************************
* NOTE: If you forget your password you lose all of your discovery data *
****************************************************************************

Password requirements:
* Password must have at least 6 characters
* Password must use at least 3 of the 4 character types: lowercase letters,
uppercase letters, numbers, symbols
* Password cannot be the same as current password

Please create an admin password: **************
Verify by entering the same password again: **************

Puppet Discovery: started 15s
[===================================================================] 100%
Puppet Discovery: pulled [8/8] 1m3s
[===================================================================] 100%
Opening Puppet Discovery at https://localhost:8443 ...
```

Once we've finished this step, Puppet Discovery will be running on port 8443 on our target machine in a Docker container.

At the time of writing this book, the license prompt uses a relative path not an absolute path, so ensure you're running this command from somewhere you can find that JSON file.

Managing sources

Our initial login won't take us to our splash screen until we've provided a basic list of target machines and credentials to Puppet Discovery. Puppet Discovery has the ability to tie into an entire Amazon Web Services, Google Compute Platform, Microsoft Azure, or VMWare VSphere account and perform automatic discovery of available resources. We can also provide a direct list of IP addresses if no API-driven platform is available.

In this section, we'll be adding a CIDR block of IP addresses to Discovery, which will be available to all users regardless of platform and hypervisor.

Adding sources by IP address

If you're using a cloud provider to test this setup, go ahead and use the cloud provider instead. The rest of this section will not be reliant on the methodology that we use to connect to machines.

During the writing of this book, several nodes have been created in my Puppet Infrastructure so that we can inspect them. I've used Vagrant and VirtualBox as my platform, and I will be using my local network of 10.20.1.0/24 to discover all of my Puppet infrastructure. When selecting the IP address you will use to demonstrate this section, make sure that the machine you've installed Docker on has the ability to find the nodes over the network provided:

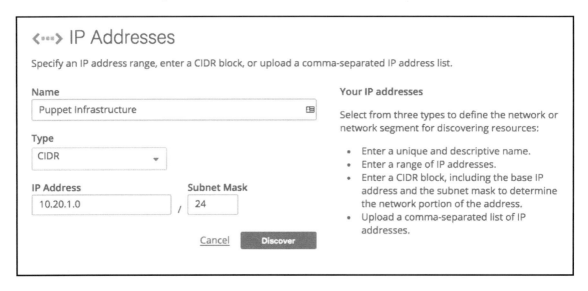

Managing credentials

After our first list of nodes to discover, Puppet Discovery will automatically take us to a splash page, allowing us to select an authentication method. At the time of writing this book, three methods are available: an SSH Private Key, an SSH Credential, and a WinRM Credential. SSH Private Keys are generally the most secure method available, but if SSH keys are not available on the remote systems, a username and password is taken via SSH Credential for Linux or WinRM Credential for Windows.

In this section, we'll be using an SSH key to provide connections to the machines we discovered in the previous step.

SSH key file

If you're using vagrant for testing this, rather than a cloud provider, I'm simply using the default insecure keys provided by vagrant. This key can always be found at `https://github.com/hashicorp/vagrant/tree/master/keys`.

When adding credentials, we're also scoping our credentials. In an SSH private key credential, you begin by selecting the PEM file you wish to apply from your local hard drive. We have three available RBAC options:

- **Discover data on hosts**: Should this key be used to discover information?
- **Run tasks on target hosts**: Should this key be able to run and execute tasks?
- **Escalate privileges to root**: Should this user become the root user for discovery and tasks?

Finally, we have a username and passphrase. Our username is the user we want to connect as to our remote machines. As my machines are all in vagrant, vagrant is also the user I'll be connecting with. The passphrase is used to decrypt the SSH key, and is optional if your key doesn't have a passphrase like mine:

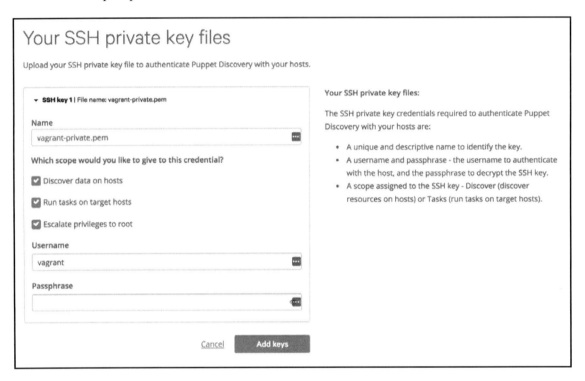

Once we've set up our first set of hosts and credentials, we'll be ready to use Puppet Discovery.

Discovering

It may take some time for Puppet Discovery to collect all the information on your infrastructure. Additionally, browser caching can prevent population of this page after discovery. You may need to wait and clear your cache before you see any data populate on the dashboard.

Our splash page now displays all the hosts, packages, and containers that can be found against all of the sources we've provided and all authentication methods we've entered. This dashboard is interactive, and clicking any box will take you into a view, displaying all nodes that represent the information on the dashboard:

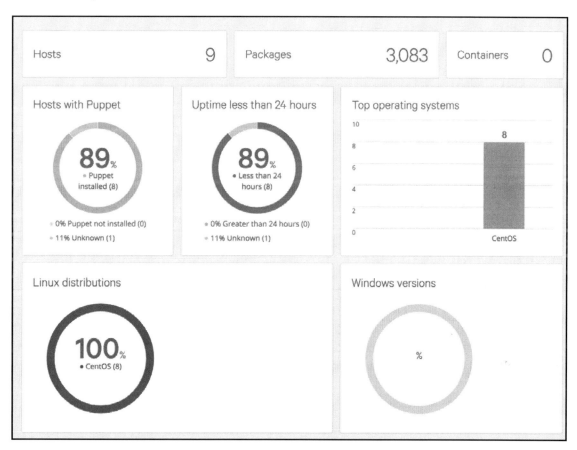

If you're curious about the process used to discover these nodes, you can click the **Previous Events** icon in the top-left corner of Discovery and view the log for the discovery.

Viewing the Discovery

In my original sample, I provided the `10.20.1.0/24` CIDR block to scan. Puppet Discovery attempted a connection to the entire IP range using my provided credentials and returned all my nodes. You may had noticed that I have one failed node, which is actually my gateway and cannot be logged into using my credentials:

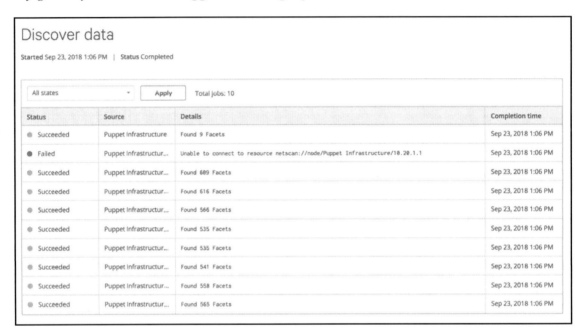

Discovering hosts

Back on the dashboard, let's go ahead and select **Hosts** to view a list of all hosts, not narrowed down to specific information. We'll see some basic information displayed about all of these hosts, from the operating system to the uptime of the machine itself:

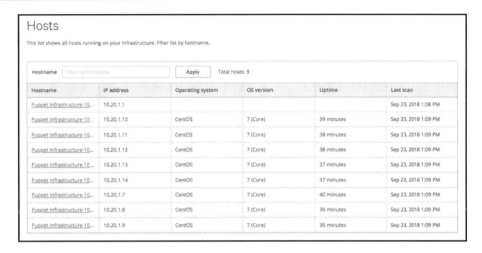

If we select the hyperlink for any individual node, we'll get a much more useful list of objects to work with, which provides us with detailed information about each host. Each tab will present us with different information:

- **Attributes**: The primary attributes used by Puppet Discovery itself, including hostname, DNS name, and operating system details
- **Services**: All services on the node, and their current state (running, stopped)
- **Users**: All users on the system, and their home directory
- **Groups**: All groups available on the system
- **Packages**: Each package on the system, their version, and the method used to install them
- **Tags**: Any tags listed by the cloud provider
- **Containers**: Any containers running on the host system

Discovering packages

We can inspect packages as a whole in Puppet Discovery. When you select packages from the dashboard, you'll be taken to a page that lists all packages, their version, package manager, and, most importantly, the number of instances they're running on. We can use this information to see if software has been universally installed on our infrastructure, or to track versioning across infrastructure. This information is particularly helpful in security remediation when attempting to determine vulnerable systems in the infrastructure:

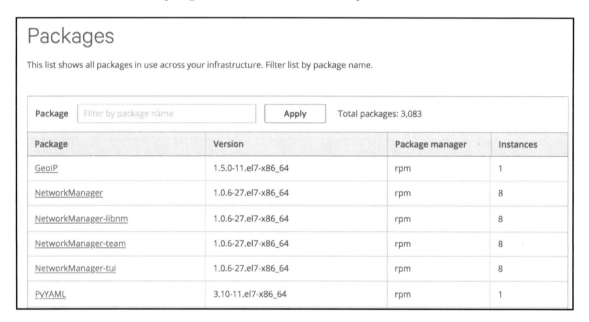

Acting

Puppet Discovery also allows us to take a very limited set of actions against our infrastructure today: installing Puppet agents and managing services. In the future, Puppet Discovery may include the ability to federate tasks over your infrastructure as well. You can access these actions by selecting the **Act +** icon in the top bar of Puppet Discovery. You'll be redirected to the **Select a task** page:

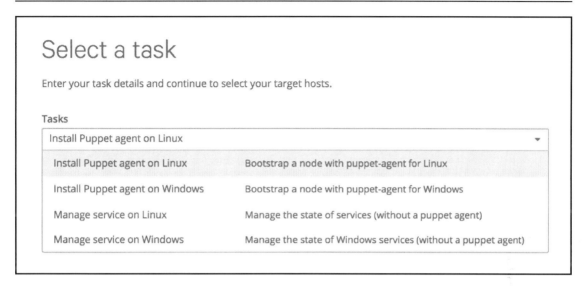

Installing agents

Installing agents using Puppet Discovery is one of the easiest ways to install Puppet agents throughout your infrastructure. You're currently able to provide the following parameters and apply the tasks to a list of hosts:

- `master`: Which Puppet Master to use. This is the only non-optional parameter.
- `cacert_content`: Expected CA certificate the Master should return.
- `certname`: Certname of agent.
- `environment`: Environment the node should run in.
- `dns_alt_names`: DNS alternate names baked into the agent certificate.
- `custom_attributes`: Any custom CSR attributes.
- `extension_request`: Any specific extension requests (such as `pp_role`) to add to the certificate.

Managing services

Managing services is also available in Puppet Discovery, and gives us only two fields to use: **Action** and **Name**. Use these two fields to find a service on the machine and start, stop, or restart any services on the node. This is a convenient agent-free way to do some basic management of your infrastructure before introducing Puppet on each node.

Uses for Discovery

Discovery is still pretty new to the Puppet ecosystem. It is meant to be the first thing installed before determining how you want to proceed with your greater Puppet infrastructure rollout. That being said, Puppet Discovery has a few key uses:

- Determining what you already have in your environment
- Ensuring that security patches are properly installed on target machines
- Inspecting resources at a higher level, rather than executing on them

Summary

In this chapter, we took a look at Puppet Tasks and Puppet Discovery. Bolt and Puppet Tasks allow us to perform remote ad hoc commands on target machines. We can parameterize these ad hoc commands and build tasks that are highly shareable actions in our organization. We can even chain together these tasks as Puppet Plans to build more complex actions that we can share across our infrastructure. We inspected Puppet Discovery, installed it on our local system, and viewed the existing infrastructure. We learned how to view and deploy agents, as well as manage services with Puppet Discovery.

We will cover virtual and exported resources in Puppet in the next chapter.

9
Exported Resources

Exported resources provide a way for a system to declare a resource, but not necessarily realize it. They are designed to allow nodes to publish information about themselves to a central database (PuppetDB), so that another node can collect the Puppet resource and realize it on the system. Exported resources primarily provide a way to create an infrastructure that is aware of other infrastructures in your environment. They provide the most value for an infrastructure that must eventually converge with information from an infrastructure that has been dynamically created by an automated process.

The following topics will be covered in this chapter:

- Virtual and exported resources
- Some use cases

Virtual and exported resources

To understand exported resources, it first helps to understand virtual resources. Virtual resources declare a state that could be made available, but will not be enforced until declared with the `realize` function. These resources are designed to allow you to prepublish a resource, but only enforce it if other conditions are met. Virtual resources help overcome the single declaration challenge that can emerge in Puppet code if you have multiple manifests that need to generate the same resource—you may need to include more than one of these manifests on a single node. If multiple modules need to manage the same file, consider virtualizing the resource, and making that resource available from multiple modules.

Virtual resources

A common use example of virtual resources is the use of special access administrative users. With a robust security policy, you may not want any single user having administrative access to all systems in an infrastructure. You'd then want to declare the administrative user as a virtual resource and allow profiles to realize those users where appropriate. In the following example, I'll add myself to a Linux system as an administrative user, and then realize the resource in multiple manifests, not causing resource conflict but allowing me to place myself surgically on the appropriate systems.

First, I need to declare myself and possibly other users as a virtual resource:

```
# modules/admins/manifests/infrastructure.pp
# This manifest declares the virtual resource for my administrative user
class admins::infrastructure {
  @user {'rrussellyates':
    ensure => present,
    comment => 'Ryan Russell-Yates',
    groups => ['wheel']
  }
}
```

I want to use the `realize` function in multiple profiles to call the user object from the catalog, and ensure it is on the system. Notice the use of the capital letter in the reference: `User['rrussellyates']`. This object already exists in the catalog, so I'm calling an object that already exists. I'll want to make sure that I include the manifest this is declared in so that the virtual user is already in the catalog and realized by the profile:

```
# modules/profile/manifests/monitoring_support.pp
# Assume I'm a member of a monitoring team, that monitors critical
applications
class profile::monitoring_support {
  include admins::infrastructure
  include profile::nagios
  include profile::monitoring_baseline

  realize User['rrussellyates']
}

# modules/profile/manifests/team/baseline.pp
# This profile combines our multiple required classes for the application
class profile::my_app
 {

  include admins::infrastructure
  include security
```

```
    include ntp
    include dns

    realize User['rrussellyates']
}
```

Now, my production-level application requires two manifests that call me as an administrative user. Because this is a virtual resource that has only been declared once, both manifests can call the user independently or together without conflict:

```
# The role for our production application with special SLA monitoring
# Notice that both my_app and monitoring support require me as an
administrative
# user. A development version of the application needs my support, as well
as
# anything with a production-level SLA for monitoring. If I attempted to
declare
# myself as a resource in both of these profiles, we'd have a duplicate
resource
# declaration.
class role::production_app {
  include profile::my_app
  include profile::monitoring_support
}
```

We'll then apply this role to our node, using our `site.pp`:

```
# site.pp

node 'appserver' {
  include role::production_app
}
```

When we run this on our system, this administrative user will be realized with no duplicate resource declaration errors, even though the user is realized in both profiles. We can successfully call this user from multiple places, without resource conflicts:

```
[root@wordpress vagrant]# puppet agent -t
Info: Using configured environment 'production'
Info: Retrieving pluginfacts
Info: Retrieving plugin
Info: Retrieving locales
Info: Loading facts
Info: Caching catalog for wordpress
Info: Applying configuration version '1529120853'
Notice: /Stage[main]/Admins::Infrastructure/User[rrussellyates]/ensure:
created
Notice: Applied catalog in 0.10 seconds
```

Tags

Not all virtual resources are independent from each other. Sometimes, we want to generate a collection of resources that we can realize together as a group. Puppet provides a metaparameter called a tag that allows us to categorize resources together. Tags allow us to run a subset of Puppet code using `puppet agent -t --tags <tag>`. They provide a user-specific marking of a resource in order to build a collection of similar objects. Tags are an array, so you can apply more than one tag to a resource, but still call them separately. Virtual resources with tags can be called with a resource collector, sometimes called the *spaceship operator*. The simple format for calling resources by a tag is `Resource <| |>`. Inside of the two pipes, you can search the catalog for any parameter or metaparameter.

By using tags, we could call that administrative user with `User <| tag == 'monitoring_admin' |>`. This allows us to bundle resources and call them as a group, rather than as an individual pocket. Let's take the preceding example and expand it to use a tag-based system:

```
class admins::infrastructure {
  @user {'rrussellyates':
    ensure  => present,
    comment => 'Ryan Russell-Yates',
    groups  => ['wheel'],
    tag     => ['infrastructure_admin','monitoring_support'],
  }
  @user {'jsouthgate':
    ensure  => present,
    comment => 'Jason Southgate',
    groups  => ['wheel'],
    tag     => ['infrastructure_admin'],
  }
  @user {'chuck':
    ensure  => present,
    comment => 'Our Intern',
    groups  => ['wheel'],
    tag     => ['monitoring_support'],
  }
}
```

Now, we've tagged `chuck` as a member of monitoring support, Jason as a member of infrastructure administrators, and myself as a member of both teams. My manifest would then call users of a group, rather than the users individually:

```
class profile::my_app {
  include admins::infrastructure
  include security
```

```
  include ntp
  include dns

  # This line calls in all Monitoring Support and Infrastructure Admin
users.
  User <| tag == 'monitoring_support' or tag == 'infrastructure_admin' |>
}
```

After we change our profile to use both tags, the two additional users will be added: jsouthgate and chuck. The administrative user russellyates was already on the system, so he was not created again:

```
[root@wordpress vagrant]# puppet agent -t
Info: Using configured environment 'production'
Info: Retrieving pluginfacts
Info: Retrieving plugin
Info: Retrieving locales
Info: Loading facts
Info: Caching catalog for wordpress
Info: Applying configuration version '1529120940'
Notice: /Stage[main]/Admins::Infrastructure/User[jsouthgate]/ensure:
created
Notice: /Stage[main]/Admins::Infrastructure/User[chuck]/ensure: created
Notice: Applied catalog in 0.11 seconds
```

Exported resources

Virtual resources allow us to stage resources to be used by the node they were created on. Expanding on this, exported resources allow a node to create a virtual resource and share it with other nodes in the infrastructure. Exported resources are a useful way to design automated systems that need information from other automated systems. In implementation, you can think of an exported resource as virtualized and announced. The resource is not realized on the system (although it could be), and it is instead shared with the rest of the infrastructure. This allows us to build systems that manage things based on knowing the states of other nodes in the infrastructure.

Declaring an exported resource is done in the same way as a virtual resource, except we use two @ symbols instead of one:

```
class profile::fillsuptmp
{
  # Exported Resource. Virtual and Shared
  # Notice that only the @@ is different!
  @@file {
"/tmp/${::fqdn}":
```

```
        ensure  => present,
        content => $::ipaddress,
        tag     => ['Fillsuptmp']
    }
}
```

Although we wouldn't want to use this particular example, we could realize this resource on the local system using file <| |> and receive just the local resource. By adding an additional set of brackets, <<| |>>, our infrastructure would take this file as described by every node in the infrastructure. The following example shows how to retrieve our resources from an exported catalog:

```
class profile::filltmp {
# This simple declaration will call our file from above and place one from
# each machine on the system. Notice the title containing $::fqdn, so a new
# file in /tmp will be created with the FQDN of each machine known to
PuppetDB.
  include profile::fillsuptmp

  File <<| tag == 'Fillsuptmp' |>>
}
```

We'll add this profile to our site.pp outside of a node definition so that it is utilized by all nodes:

```
# site.pp

include profile::filltmp
```

When we run the agent, we will see a file being placed in /tmp for each node in the infrastructure. For each node that checks into the master, all other nodes will also gain a new file:

```
[root@wordpress vagrant]# puppet agent -t
Info: Using configured environment 'production'
Info: Retrieving pluginfacts
Info: Retrieving plugin
Info: Retrieving locales
Info: Loading facts
Info: Caching catalog for wordpress
Info: Applying configuration version '1529121275'
Notice: /Stage[main]/Profile::Fillsuptmp/File[/tmp/wordpress]/ensure:
defined content as '{md5}c679836c51e9e0e92191c7d2d38f5fe5'
Notice: /Stage[main]/Profile::Filltmp/File[/tmp/pe-puppet-master]/ensure:
defined content as '{md5}c679836c51e9e0e92191c7d2d38f5fe5'
Notice: Applied catalog in 0.10 seconds
```

Exported resources are collected out of the storage of catalogs last reported to PuppetDB. If a node has a change in the catalog, and the exported resource is no longer available in the last run, it will not be available for resource collection.

One thing to take note of with exported resources: Your node that realizes these resources will *eventually* converge to the intended state of the infrastructure. Until a node reports this resource to the Puppet Master, your node will be unaware of the existence of the node. Let's use a scenario where you have a new node that you've classified with an external resource in the catalog. Until that node checks into the master for the first time, that resource will not populate into PuppetDB. Even after it checks into PuppetDB, the node realizing the resource must also run another `puppet agent run`. This means that, on a node that has just run Puppet with the default timer of 30 minutes, it may take 30 minutes to report its exported resource to the Puppet Master. Then, your node collecting these resources may take up to another 30 minutes to check in with the master and receive these changes. Exported resources are not immediate, but your infrastructure will eventually converge around the new information provided to PuppetDB.

The built-in default for a Puppet agent is a 30-minute timer to check in with the Puppet Master. If you have a simply configured machine that should find this information faster, such as a load balancer, consider having it check into the master more often. A load balancer that checks in every 5 minutes should report the node as online shortly after its initial configuration via Puppet.

Use cases

Exported resources are best used delicately within an infrastructure. We'll go over a few use cases, and talk about similar applications that may use this information as we go. We'll use Forge modules where they make sense, but we'll also build some custom exported resources so that a functional sample is available. In this section, we'll be discussing a few examples of exported resources:

- A dynamic `/etc/hosts` file
- Adding a node to an `haproxy` load balancer
- Building an external database on a database server for an application server
- Custom configuration files using the `concat` and `File_line` Puppet resources

Hosts file

This first sample is easy to understand and interpret, but definitely should not be used in place of a true **Domain Name Server** (**DNS**). A few years ago, I had a customer that was using a public cloud, but it had been acquired by a very large company, which had a team dedicated to managing corporate DNS. The turnaround for a DNS record was often 4 days, while many of the applications they launched had a lifetime of only a few days before being replaced with a new node. The solution had some issues for resolution if node networking information changed for a period of time, but it was an effective short-term solution until the policies around DNS were relaxed for the customer.

In the following example, we'll use a single profile that exports the FQDN and IP address of every system classified by `profile::etchosts`, which is to be consumed and actioned on by every node (including the originator) in the environment:

```
class profile::etchosts {
# A host record is made containing the FQDN and IP Address of the
classified node
  @@host {$::fqdn:
    ensure => present,
    ip      => $::ipaddress,
    tag     => ['shoddy_dns'], }
# The classified node collects every shoddy_dns host entry, including its
own,
# and adds it to the nodes host file. This even works across environments,
as
# we haven't isolated it to a single environment.
  Host <<| tag == 'shoddy_dns' |>>
}
```

If we wanted to ensure that we only collect host entries for hosts in the same Puppet environment, we can simply change our manifest to read `Host <<| tag == 'shoddy_dns'` **and** `environment == $environment |>>`.

This manifest contains both the exported resource and the resource collection call. Any node we include this on will both report its host record and retrieve all host records (including its own). Because we want to apply this code to all nodes in our infrastructure, we will place it outside of any node definition in `site.pp`, causing it to apply to all nodes in the infrastructure:

```
# site.pp
include profile::etchosts
# Provided so nodes don't fail to classify anything
node default { }
```

When we run our agent, we retrieve each host entry individually and place it in
/etc/hosts. In the following example, I run this catalog against my Puppet Master. The
Puppet Master retrieves each host entry found in PuppetDB and places it in /etc/hosts.
The nodes reported are haproxy, appserver, and mysql. These nodes will be used for the
rest of the examples in this chapter:

```
[root@pe-puppet-master vagrant]# puppet agent -t
Info: Using configured environment 'production'
Info: Retrieving pluginfacts
Info: Retrieving plugin
Info: Retrieving locales
Info: Loading facts
Info: Caching catalog for pe-puppet-master
Info: Applying configuration version '1529033713'
Notice: /Stage[main]/Profile::Etchosts/Host[mysql]/ensure: created
Info: Computing checksum on file /etc/hosts
Notice: /Stage[main]/Profile::Etchosts/Host[appserver]/ensure: created
Notice: /Stage[main]/Profile::Etchosts/Host[haproxy]/ensure: created
Notice: Applied catalog in 14.07 seconds

[root@pe-puppet-master vagrant]# cat /etc/hosts
# HEADER: This file was autogenerated at 2018-06-15 03:36:02 +0000
# HEADER: by puppet. While it can still be managed manually, it
# HEADER: is definitely not recommended.
127.0.0.1 localhost
10.20.1.3 pe-puppet-master
10.20.1.6 mysql
10.20.1.5 appserver
10.20.1.4 haproxy
```

As noted previously, this should not be seen as a replacement for a true
DNS. It is a simple and functional sample of how to build and use a
Puppet exported resource.

Load balancing

A load balancer is a common system that uses the exported resources pattern in Puppet.
Load balancers are used to forward traffic across multiple nodes, providing both high
availability through redundancy and performance via horizontal scaling. Load balancers
like HAProxy also allow for the design of applications that forward a user to data centers
more local to them for performance.

The load balancer itself will receive a traditional configuration, while every member of the balancer will export a resource to be consumed by the load balancer. The load balancer then uses each entry from each exported resource to build a combined configuration file.

 The following sample uses `puppetlabs-haproxy` (for more information visit `https://forge.puppet.com/puppetlabs/haproxy`) from the Puppet Forge. HAProxy is a free and open source load balancer that can be used without a license at home. There are other modules available for a few other load balancers on the Forge, and users are free to create their own custom modules for solutions in the Enterprise.

We'll need to create two profiles to support this use case: one for the load balancer and one for the balancer member. The balancer member profile is a simple exported resource that declares the listener service it will use, and reports its hostname, IP address, and available ports to the HAProxy. The `loadbalancer` profile will configure a very simple default `loadbalancer`, a listening service to provide forwarding on, and most importantly collect all configurations from exported resources:

```
class profile::balancermember {
  @@haproxy::balancermember { 'haproxy':
    listening_service => 'myapp',
    ports             => ['80','443'],
    server_names      => $::hostname,
    ipaddresses       => $::ipaddress,
    options           => 'check',
  }
}
class profile::loadbalancer {
  include haproxy

  haproxy::listen {'myapp':
    ipaddress => $::ipaddress,
    ports => ['80','443']
  }

  Haproxy::Balancermember <<| listening_service == 'myapp' |>>
}
```

We'll want then to place these profiles on two separate hosts. In the following example, I'm placing the `balancermember` profile on the `appserver`, and the `loadbalancer` profile on the `haproxy`. We'll continue expanding on our `site.pp` from before, adding code as we go along:

```
#site.pp
include profile::etchosts
```

```
node 'haproxy' {
  include profile::loadbalancer
}

node 'appserver' {
  include profile::balancermember
}

# Provided so nodes don't fail to classify anything
node default { }
```

In the following sample, the load balancer had already been configured as a load balancer but had no balancer members to forward to. The appserver had also completed a run and reported its exported haproxy configuration to PuppetDB. Finally, the HAProxy server collects and realizes that resource and places it as a line in its configuration files, enabling the forwarding of traffic to the appserver from the haproxy:

```
root@haproxy vagrant]# puppet agent -t
Info: Using configured environment 'production'
Info: Retrieving pluginfacts
Info: Retrieving plugin
Info: Retrieving locales
Info: Loading facts
Info: Caching catalog for haproxy
Info: Applying configuration version '1529036882'
Notice:
/Stage[main]/Haproxy/Haproxy::Instance[haproxy]/Haproxy::Config[haproxy]/Co
ncat[/etc/haproxy/haproxy.cfg]/File[/etc/haproxy/haproxy.cfg]/content:
--- /etc/haproxy/haproxy.cfg 2018-06-15 04:27:25.398339144 +0000
+++ /tmp/puppet-file20180615-17937-6bt84x 2018-06-15 04:28:05.100339144
+0000
@@ -27,3 +27,5 @@
 bind 10.0.2.15:443
 balance roundrobin
 option tcplog
+ server appserver 10.0.2.15:80 check
+ server appserver 10.0.2.15:443 check

Info: Computing checksum on file /etc/haproxy/haproxy.cfg
Info:
/Stage[main]/Haproxy/Haproxy::Instance[haproxy]/Haproxy::Config[haproxy]/Co
ncat[/etc/haproxy/haproxy.cfg]/File[/etc/haproxy/haproxy.cfg]: Filebucketed
/etc/haproxy/haproxy.cfg to puppet with sum
dd6721741c30fbed64eccf693e92fdf4
Notice:
/Stage[main]/Haproxy/Haproxy::Instance[haproxy]/Haproxy::Config[haproxy]/Co
ncat[/etc/haproxy/haproxy.cfg]/File[/etc/haproxy/haproxy.cfg]/content:
```

```
content changed '{md5}dd6721741c30fbed64eccf693e92fdf4' to
'{md5}b819a3af31da2d0e2310fd7d521cbc76'
Info: Haproxy::Config[haproxy]: Scheduling refresh of
Haproxy::Service[haproxy]
Info: Haproxy::Service[haproxy]: Scheduling refresh of Service[haproxy]
Notice:
/Stage[main]/Haproxy/Haproxy::Instance[haproxy]/Haproxy::Service[haproxy]/S
ervice[haproxy]: Triggered 'refresh' from 1 event
Notice: Applied catalog in 0.20 seconds
```

This module uses a `Concat` fragment to build an entire file. If a node does not report their `haproxy::balancermember` exported resource on a run, it will be removed from the `loadbalancer` realizing these resources on the next run.

When a user requests port 80 (`http`) or port 443 (`https`) from the HAProxy server, it will automatically retrieve and forward traffic from our `appserver`. If we had multiple app servers, it would even split the load between the two, allowing for horizontal scaling.

Database connections

Many applications require databases to store information between sessions. In many large organizations, it is common to centralize these databases and point applications to them externally. The following example will consist of two profiles: one for the database and one for the application seeking to use the database.

The following sample uses `puppetlabs-mysql` from the Puppet Forge. MySQL is a free and open source SQL database that can be used without a license at home. There are other modules available for other databases, such as SQL Server, OracleDB, Kafka, and MongoDB. These modules can be used in a familiar fashion to provide exported resources to an external database.

In the following example, the `appserver::database` profile provides a very simple installation of MySQL. It also retrieves all `mysql::db` resources tagged `ourapp`, and realizes them on the central server. The `appserver` profile accepts a parameter for the password that could be supplied via `hiera` or encrypted using `eyaml`. Using this password, it will export a database resource to be collected and realized on the database server. Other configurations could be made to an application on this server to ensure it uses the database provided by this exported resource:

```
class profile::appserver (
  $db_pass = lookup('dbpass')
```

```
) {
  @@mysql::db { "appdb_${fqdn}":
    user     => 'appuser',
    password => $db_pass,
    host     => $::fqdn,
    grant    => ['SELECT', 'UPDATE', 'CREATE'],
    tag      => ourapp,
  }
}

class profile::appserver::database {
  class {'::mysql::server':
    root_password => 'suP3rP@ssw0rd!',
  }

  Mysql::Db <<| tag == 'ourapp' |>>
}
```

We'll go ahead and insert these profiles into the node definition for our `appserver` and a new node definition for `mysql`. This configuration will ensure that our `appserver` has a relevant database on the `mysql` server, and that its application is forwarded properly through the `haproxy`. Notice the passing of the password on the `appserver` node:

```
#site.pp

include profile::etchosts

node 'haproxy' {
  include profile::loadbalancer
}
node 'appserver' {
  include profile::balancermember
  class {'profile::appserver': db_pass => 'suP3rP@ssw0rd!' }
}
node 'mysql' {
  include profile::appserver::database
}
# Provided so nodes don't fail to classify anything
node default { }
```

When applied to a previously configured database server, with a freshly exported resource from our `appserver`, a new database, database user, and set of permissions has been created on the DB Server:

```
[root@mysql vagrant]# puppet agent -t
Info: Using configured environment 'production'
Info: Retrieving pluginfacts
```

```
Info: Retrieving plugin
Info: Retrieving locales
Info: Loading facts
Info: Caching catalog for mysql
Info: Applying configuration version '1529037526'
Notice:
/Stage[main]/Profile::Appserver::Database/Mysql::Db[appdb_appserver]/Mysql_
database[appdb_appserver]/ensure: created
Notice:
/Stage[main]/Profile::Appserver::Database/Mysql::Db[appdb_appserver]/Mysql_
user[appuser@appserver]/ensure: created
Notice:
/Stage[main]/Profile::Appserver::Database/Mysql::Db[appdb_appserver]/Mysql_
grant[appuser@appserver/appdb_appserver.*]/ensure: created
Notice: Applied catalog in 0.34 seconds
```

One flaw with this system is the up to 30-minute gap between the appserver being launched and the database being realized on the system. In the next chapter, we'll also be discussing application orchestration, which helps solve this problem by linking nodes together and orchestrating the agent runs. If you have time to let the infrastructure converge, this exported resource can work for databases and applications alone.

Concat, file lines, and you!

The previous samples relied on existing resources such as the host, or existing forge modules such as haproxy and mysql. In some cases, we'll need to build custom configuration files on systems using exported resources. We'll go over samples using both concat and file_line. concat to declare the entire contents of a file, using a list of ordered strings. File line is part of puppetlabs-stdlib (for more information visit https://forge.puppet.com/puppetlabs/stdlib) and it places lines that are not present into an existing file, and can also be used to match an existing line using regex.

Concat – the hammer

We'll be building a file called /tmp/hammer.conf that is comprised of a header section and a variable number of sections provided by exported resources. This class was designed to be used on all machines in an infrastructure, but could easily be turned into a single server configuration file by splitting the exported resource into a separate profile from the concat resource and the header concat::fragment.

The following sample uses `puppetlabs-concat` from the Puppet Forge.(For more information visit `https://forge.puppet.com/puppetlabs/concat`). The `concat` module allows us to declare a file, made from pieces or fragments, and order the creation of a single file on a system. This allows us to define one or more headers and footers, while leaving room for dynamic lines to be added into the file.

In the following example, we're building a manifest that builds `hammer.conf`. The `concat` resource gives each fragment a location to build on. The hammer time `concat::fragment` is used to manage the header, as noted by order `01` in the parameters. Each machine will export a `concat` fragment detailing an FQDN, IP address, operating system, and version as a line in the file in order to simulate a global configuration file or inventory file. Finally, each machine will realize all of these exported fragments using the resource collector for `concat` fragments:

```
class files::hammer {

  $osname = fact('os.name')
  $osrelease = fact('os.release')

  concat {'/tmp/hammer.conf':
    ensure => present,
  }

  concat::fragment {'Hammer Time':
    target => '/tmp/hammer.conf',
    content => "This file is managed by Puppet.It will be overwritten",
    order => '01',
  }

  @@concat::fragment {"${::fqdn}-hammer":
    target => '/tmp/hammer.conf',
    content => "${::fqdn} - ${::ipaddress} - ${osname} ${osrelease}",
    order => '02',
    tag => 'hammer',
  }

  Concat::Fragment <<| tag == 'hammer' |>>

}
```

We'll add `files::hammer` outside of any node definitions so that this inventory file is created on all of the machines in our infrastructure:

```
include profile::etchosts
include files::hammer
```

```
node 'haproxy' {
  include profile::loadbalancer
}

node 'appserver' {
  include profile::balancermember
  class {'profile::appserver': db_pass => 'suP3rP@sswOrd!' }
}

node 'mysql' {
  include profile::appserver::database
}

# Provided so nodes don't fail to classify anything
node default { }
```

When this is run on our `mysql` node as the final node in the infrastructure,
`/tmp/hammer.conf` is created and contains Facter facts provided by each node in the
infrastructure:

```
root@mysql vagrant]# puppet agent -t
Info: Using configured environment 'production'
Info: Retrieving pluginfacts
Info: Retrieving plugin
Info: Retrieving locales
Info: Loading facts
Info: Caching catalog for mysql
Info: Applying configuration version '1529040374'
Notice:
/Stage[main]/Files::Hammer/Concat[/tmp/hammer.conf]/File[/tmp/hammer.conf]/
ensure: defined content as '{md5}f3f0d7ff5de10058846333e97950a7b9'
Notice: Applied catalog in 0.33 seconds

# /tmp/hammer.conf
This file is managed by Puppet. It will be overwritten
haproxy - 10.0.2.15 - CentOS 7
mysql - 10.0.2.15 - CentOS 7
pe-puppet-master - 10.0.2.15 - CentOS 7
appserver - 10.0.2.15 - CentOS 7
```

Most configuration files should be built this way, and be holistically managed by Puppet.
In a case where the entirety of a file is not managed, we can use `file_line` provided by
`stdlib` in its place.

file_line – the scalpel

In this exercise, we'll be using a Puppet file resource to build a file, but only if it's not already present in the system. Then, we'll use file lines to insert values we want into the file, which are collected from exported resources across all systems.

 The following sample uses `puppetlabs-stdlib` (for more information visit `https://forge.puppet.com/puppetlabs/stdlib`) from the Puppet Forge. `stdlib` contains a large number of functions to use in manifests, as well as the resource `file_line`. `file_line` allows a line to be individually managed inside of a file, and can also be used to provide regex matching when you want to use it as a find-and-replace to the unmanaged file. If targeting INI files, consider using `puppetlabs-inifile` instead.(For more information visit `https://forge.puppet.com/puppetlabs/inifile`).

In this example, we will first build a file called `/tmp/scalpel.conf`. We'll ensure that this file is present and has ownership by root. We will set the replace flag to alert Puppet not to replace the content of this file if it's already present on the system, ensuring that any content already found in this file is not overwritten. A default will be provided by the content line if the file is not currently on the system. We'll then build an exported `file_line` to simulate a line of configuration with a match statement to ensure that we replace misconfigured lines rather than create new ones. Finally, we'll realize all of these resources on every node that this is classified on:

```
class files::scalpel {

  $arch = fact('os.architecture')
  file {'/tmp/scalpel.conf':
    ensure => file,
    owner => 'root',
    group => 'root',
    content => 'This file is editable, with individually managed
settings!',
    replace => false,
  }
  @@file_line {"$::fqdn - setting":
    path => '/tmp/scalpel.conf',
    line => "${::fqdn}: $arch - ${::kernel} - Virtual: ${::is_virtual}",
    match => "^${::fqdn}:",
    require => File['/tmp/scalpel.conf'],
    tag => 'scalpel',
  }
  File_line <<| tag == 'scalpel' |>>
}
```

The scalpel configuration file is designed to be used on each machine in the infrastructure, so it is also placed outside of a node definition in the `site.pp`:

```
include profile::etchosts

include files::scalpel

node 'haproxy' {
  include profile::loadbalancer
}

node 'appserver' {
  include profile::balancermember
  class {'profile::appserver': db_pass => 'suP3rP@ssw0rd!' }
}

node 'mysql' {
  include profile::appserver::database
}

# Provided so nodes don't fail to classify anything
node default { }
```

Finally, our node picks up the configuration change, and creates the file. Notice that the file is created, and then the file lines are inserted thanks to the require parameter we used in our exported `file_line` resource:

```
[root@haproxy vagrant]# puppet agent -t
Info: Using configured environment 'production'
Info: Retrieving pluginfacts
Info: Retrieving plugin
Info: Retrieving locales
Info: Loading facts
Info: Caching catalog for haproxy
Info: Applying configuration version '1529041736'
Notice: /Stage[main]/Files::Scalpel/File[/tmp/scalpel.conf]/ensure: defined
content as '{md5}2d3ebc675ea9c8c43677c9513f820db0'
Notice: /Stage[main]/Files::Scalpel/File_line[haproxy - setting]/ensure:
created
Notice: /Stage[main]/Files::Scalpel/File_line[mysql - setting]/ensure:
created
Notice: /Stage[main]/Files::Scalpel/File_line[appserver - setting]/ensure:
created
Notice: /Stage[main]/Files::Scalpel/File_line[pe-puppet-master -
setting]/ensure: created
Notice: Applied catalog in 0.18 seconds

# /tmp/scalpel.conf
```

```
This file is editable, with individually managed settings!
haproxy: x86_64 - Linux - Virtual: true
mysql: x86_64 - Linux - Virtual: true
appserver: x86_64 - Linux - Virtual: true
pe-puppet-master: x86_64 - Linux - Virtual: true
```

Unlike our `concat` example, this file remains editable outside of Puppet, except for the individual lines managed by the manifest. In the following sample, I've edited the file to have comments at the top and changed the `haproxy`'s virtual setting to false:

```
# Our comments now stay in this file, because we're not managing
# The whole file, just individual lines. This methodology can
# come in useful once in a great while. This is still configuration
# drift, so make sure to use it sparingly!
This file is editable, with individually managed settings!
haproxy: x86_64 - Linux - Virtual: false
mysql: x86_64 - Linux - Virtual: true
appserver: x86_64 - Linux - Virtual: true
pe-puppet-master: x86_64 - Linux - Virtual: true
```

When the agent is run again, the `haproxy` line is corrected, but our comments stay at the top of the file. Users could even add their own configuration lines to this file, and as long as that configuration is not reported by Puppet exported resources, it would remain in the configuration file:

```
[root@haproxy vagrant]# puppet agent -t
Info: Using configured environment 'production'
Info: Retrieving pluginfacts
Info: Retrieving plugin
Info: Retrieving locales
Info: Loading facts
Info: Caching catalog for haproxy
Info: Applying configuration version '1529042980'
Notice: /Stage[main]/Files::Scalpel/File_line[haproxy - setting]/ensure:
created
Notice: Applied catalog in 0.15 seconds

# Our comments now stay in this file, because we're not managing
# The whole file, just individual lines. This methodology can
# come in useful once in a great while. This is still configuration
# drift, so make sure to use it sparingly!

This file is editable, with individually managed settings!
haproxy: x86_64 - Linux - Virtual: true
mysql: x86_64 - Linux - Virtual: true
appserver: x86_64 - Linux - Virtual: true
pe-puppet-master: x86_64 - Linux - Virtual: true
```

This methodology does allow for a lot of configuration drift in an infrastructure. If your team is acting to provide controlled self-service resources, this is an effective way to allow your customers to modify configuration files, except for settings specifically managed by your infrastructure team.

Summary

In this chapter, we talked about virtual and exported resources. Virtual resources allow us to describe what a resource should be, and realize it under other conditions. Exported resources allow us to announce our virtual resources to other nodes in the infrastructure by using PuppetDB. We examined writing a virtual resource for administrative users and placed a file in /tmp for all other nodes in our infrastructure using exported resources. We then explored using exported resources to create an /etc/hosts file, a load balancer, a database, and an example of building a custom configuration file with concat and file_line.

When we applied these exported resources across our systems, we noticed that the main limitation of these resources is timing. Our infrastructure will eventually converge, but it does not happen in an orchestrated and timely fashion. Our next chapter will be on application orchestration, which allows us to tie a multitier application together and orchestrate the order Puppet runs in on those nodes.

10
Application Orchestration

Application orchestration provides a few key features for the Puppet language. Application orchestration extends the concept of exported resources to a more targeted application, allowing the sharing of configuration items between nodes. Additionally, this feature provides a way to order Puppet runs to ensure that dependency nodes have finished building or converging prior to the nodes that require them. Application orchestration allows us to entangle multiple nodes together in an ordered run. Most importantly, configuration updates are not randomly applied on check-in, but are applied in a particular, ordered pattern.

 Application Orchestration only works in Puppet Enterprise. Puppet open source users can use the language constructs, but ordered runs are provided by Puppet Enterprise.

Application orchestration has three new language constructs we'll need to use to create ordered runs that share information automatically with each other:

- **Application definitions**: An end-to-end description of a collection of components describing an entire application stack
- **Application components**: An individual component of an entire application stack
- **Service resources**: Resources designed to share information across application components

Application definition

Application definitions look a lot like a defined resource, but are also similar to a traditional Puppet profile. They describe a collection of components that make an entire system, but unlike profiles, are not tied down to a single node. These application definitions describe a configured state of one or more nodes, broken down by application components.

Application definitions will resemble defined types, with a few key differences:

- They are titled `application` instead of `define`.
- Each resource must be name spaced within the module:

```
# Application used instead of 'class' or 'define'
application 'example' (
  $var,
) {

# app1 exports its database configuration items
  example::app1 {
    config => $var,
    export => Database['app1'],
  }

# app2 both imports the previous database and exports its own type:
Application
  example::app2 {
    config  => $var,
    consume => Database['app1'],
    export  => Application['app1'],
  }
```

What is important to note is that each resource in this application can be tied to an entirely different node with our site definition. We can also use our site definitions to pass in those shared configuration items, represented by $var in the preceding code:

```
#/etc/puppetlabs/code/environments/production/manifests/site.pp
site {
  example {'app1':
    var => 'config',
    nodes => {
      Node['database'] => [ Example::App1['app']],
      Node['app']      => [ Example::App2['app']],
    }
  }
}
```

Inside of the node's hash, notice that the `Node` object and `Example::App<X>` objects are capitalized.

Application components

Application components provide the individual pieces of the multi-node application. They are most often defined types (for reusability), but can also consist of classes or even native resources, such as files, in very simple cases. Application components are created by the `export`, `consume`, or `require` metaparameters that are used in an application declaration.

Application components are written as general classes or defined types. They follow the same autoload format as all other Puppet code. The manifest for `example::app2` would still be located at `manifests/example/app2.pp`. Application components can explicitly list the values they export and consume in their individual manifests by placing an additional statement at the bottom of the manifests:

```
class example::app2 (
# $db_host is provided by the consume of the Database
  $db_host,
) {
# Any resources, defined types or class calls in a regular manifest would
be placed here.
}
# Note that the consume is outside of the class declaration
Example::App2 consumes Database {
  db_host => $host,
}
# Note that the produces is outside of both the class declaration, and
above consume
Example::App2 produces Http {
  host => $::fqdn,
  port => '80',
}
```

In the preceding sample, `$db_host` is a value that could be passed to any resource in the manifest. Rather than passing it via Hiera or Puppet DSL, we instead consume that value from the `host` parameter provided by another application. We also export the node's own FQDN and hostname, so that follow-on applications can use those values to point at the web service created by `example::app2`. `Database` and `Http` are both service resources, describing information that's shared between applications.

Service resources

Service resources are environment-wide information pools filled and viewed by application components. Service resources work like exported resources, providing information about other nodes from PuppetDB. The uniqueness of service resources is found in their building of dependencies between nodes. Service resources are declared as Puppet types, written in Ruby. Providers are optional, and allow for exported resource availability tests.

Service resource types provide a framework of information that can be stored and transported via application orchestration's `consume` and `export` metaparameters. The type is required for a service resource, and declares the structure of the information using Ruby code. They are always stored in modules at `lib/puppet/type/<resource>.rb`, and will be sent to all nodes in an environment when deployed, but will not be actioned upon by nodes not using the resource. The following sample type could encompass the database resource exported by `app1` and consumed by `app2`:

```
#lib/puppet/type/database.rb

# Notice the :is_capability => true. This property creates this type as an
# environment-wide service, to be produced and consumed.
Puppet::Type.newtype :database, :is_capability => true do
  newparam :host
end
```

This simple example provides us with a way to export information about a database, specifically the `host` parameter. This can be filled with the `export` parameter, and read with the `consume` parameter.

Modeling applications

For the rest of this chapter, we'll be focusing on building a simple and a more complex example of an orchestrated application. Our first phase will be to create a single database and a single webserver.

Application and database

In our first example, we'll export information from a database on one node, and retrieve it on a WordPress instance. This simple example will allow us to deploy nodes in pairs, and ensure that the database is built before the web application that relies on it.

Dependencies

Before we begin writing our code, we'll want to check the Forge for relevant supported or open source modules. WordPress requires an SQL server and a web host, which we'll provide via Apache HTTPD. Before we begin, we'll want to install the following modules from the Forge:

- `puppetlabs-mysql`
- `puppetlabs-apache`
- `hunner-wordpress`

```
[root@pe-puppet-master myapp]# puppet module install puppetlabs-mysql
Notice: Preparing to install into
/etc/puppetlabs/code/environments/production/modules ...
Notice: Downloading from https://forgeapi.puppet.com ...
Notice: Installing -- do not interrupt ...
/etc/puppetlabs/code/environments/production/modules
└─┬ puppetlabs-mysql (v5.4.0)
  ├── puppet-staging (v3.2.0)
  ├── puppetlabs-stdlib (v4.25.1)
  └── puppetlabs-translate (v1.1.0)
[root@pe-puppet-master myapp]# puppet module install puppetlabs-apache
Notice: Preparing to install into
/etc/puppetlabs/code/environments/production/modules ...
Notice: Downloading from https://forgeapi.puppet.com ...
Notice: Installing -- do not interrupt ...
/etc/puppetlabs/code/environments/production/modules
└─┬ puppetlabs-apache (v3.1.0)
  ├── puppetlabs-concat (v4.2.1)
  └── puppetlabs-stdlib (v4.25.1)
[root@pe-puppet-master myapp]# puppet module install hunner-wordpress
Notice: Preparing to install into
/etc/puppetlabs/code/environments/production/modules ...
Notice: Downloading from https://forgeapi.puppet.com ...
Notice: Installing -- do not interrupt ...
/etc/puppetlabs/code/environments/production/modules
└─┬ hunner-wordpress (v1.0.0)
  ├── puppetlabs-concat (v4.2.1)
  ├── puppetlabs-mysql (v5.4.0)
  └── puppetlabs-stdlib (v4.25.1)
```

Build

We'll write our code from the top down. It helps to think about the end state of the code as we're learning it, and learn the pieces that enable it along the way.

Node declaration

Our first piece will be the node declaration. This will go in our `site.pp`, and each application will go under a specific site call. In the following sample, notice the following:

- All apps are declared in the top-level `site{}` declaration.
- `myapp {'myapp': }` is just one possible app that can go in `site.pp`. We could have another beneath it called `myapp.{'myapp2': }` is inside of the site, and has a second standalone instance of this application.
- `Node['<nodename>']` and `Myapp::<app>` are capitalized.
- I can still use the `site.pp` for other things, as indicated by the classification of the Puppet Master, as follows:

```
site {
  myapp { 'myapp':
      nodes => {
         Node['mysql'] => [ Myapp::Db['myapp']],
         Node['appserver'] => [ Myapp::Web['myapp']],
         Node['haproxy'] => [ Myapp::Lb['myapp']],
      }
   }
}

node 'puppetmaster' {
   include role::puppetmaster
}

# To keep the sample simple, firewalls have been disabled on all
machines.
service {'firewalld': ensure => stopped }
service {'iptables':  ensure => stopped }
```

This particular configuration will ensure that the `mysql` node gets the database, `appserver` will get WordPress, and HAProxy will get the load balancer configuration.

Application declaration

In the previous example, we called a resource called `myapp` just under the `site{}` declaration. This manifest, located in the `myapp` module at `manifests/init.pp`, declares the application, describes some overridable parameters, and orchestrates applications using the `export` and `consume` metaparameters. Notice the following:

- On the first line, the application `myapp` is used in place of a class or define.
- `myapp::db` exports to the SQL resource.

- myapp::web consumes the SQL resource.
- myapp::db will run before myapp::web, because myapp::web has a dependency via consume.
- We use the $name variable so that each component receives myapp as a name, taken from myapp {'myapp':}:

```
application myapp (
   $dbuser = 'wordpress',
   $dbpass = 'w0rdpr3ss!',
   $webpath = '/var/www/wordpress',
   $vhost = 'appserver',
) {
   myapp::db { $name:
      dbuser => $dbuser,
      dbpass => $dbpass,
      export => Sql[$name],
   }
   myapp::web { $name:
      webpath => $webpath,
      consume => Sql[$name],
      vhost => $vhost,
   }
}
```

DB service resource

We'll build our own custom DB type for this simple use case. It will allow us to pass values from our database to our WordPress application. This simple example ensures that the type is named db, marks it as a service resource, and provides five available parameters to the database service resource. This file is placed in lib/puppet/type/db.rb:

```
# lib/puppet/type/db.rb
# Adding :is_capability to the custom type marks the resources as service
resources
Puppet::Type.newtype :db, :is_capability => true do
   newparam :name, :is_namevar => true
   newparam :user
   newparam :password
   newparam :port
   newparam :host
end
```

Application components

Our `myapp` defined type will make use of the `db` resource we created in the previous section, passing four values to PuppetDB, directly from `myapp::db`. We'll use this manifest to build a MySQL server, and provide information to our WordPress instance on another node. Notice the following in the example:

- A regular defined type, with standard Puppet DSL. We build a server and a database to support the app.
- `$host` is not used in the manifest, but is passed along to the produced `Db` resource.
- `Myapp::Db produces Db` is placed directly after the define, in the same manifest:

```
define myapp::db (
  $dbuser,
  $dbpass,
  $host = $::fqdn,
){

  class {'::mysql::server':
    root_password => 'Sup3rp@ssword!',
    override_options => {
      'mysqld' => {
        'bind-address' => '0.0.0.0'
      }
    }
  }

  mysql::db { $name:
    user => $dbuser,
    password => $dbpass,
    host => '%',
    grant => ['ALL PRIVILEGES'],
  }
}
Myapp::Db produces Db {
  dbuser => $dbuser,
  dbpass => $dbpass,
  dbhost => $host,
  dbname => $name,
}
```

Myapp::Web is a defined type meant to consume the Db produced by Myapp::Db. It installs the required packages, installs Apache, builds a vhost, and deploys WordPress to the docroot of the vhost. Notice the following:

- $vhost and $webpath were provided by application myapp.
- $dbuser, $dbpass, $dbhost, and $dbname are provided by the consumes Db {}.
- Because our manifest uses the values dbpass, dbhost, dbuser and dbname, our mappings don't need to be declared. The following example will directly declare variables:

```
define myapp::web (
  $webpath,
  $vhost,
  $dbuser,
  $dbpass,
  $dbhost,
  $dbname,
  ) {

    package {['php',
             'mysql',
             'php-mysql',
             'php-gd'
            ]:
      ensure => installed,
    }

    class {'apache':
      default_vhost => false
    }

    include ::apache::mod::php

    apache::vhost { $vhost:
      port => '80',
      docroot => $webpath,
      require => File[$webpath],
    }

    file { $webpath:
      ensure => directory,
      owner => 'apache',
      group => 'apache',
      require => Package['httpd'],
    }
```

```
class { '::wordpress':
    db_user => $dbuser,
    db_password => $dbpass,
    db_host => $dbhost,
    db_name => $dbname,
    create_db => false,
    create_db_user => false,
    install_dir => $webpath,
    wp_owner => 'apache',
    wp_group => 'apache',
  }
}
Myapp::Web consumes Db { }
```

We can use the preceding collection of code to order and deploy our multitier application. Our current module should resemble the following:

```
myapp
├── lib
│   └── puppet
│       └── type
│           ├── sql.rb
├── manifests
    ├── db.pp
    ├── init.pp
    └── web.pp
```

We can then use the puppet app and puppet job commands to deploy our application.

Deploy

To view applications listed in our site.pp, we can use the command puppet app show. This command reads our main manifest, and lists all applications and their components. In the following example, from the preceding code, we're deploying Myapp::Db to mysql and Myapp::Web to appserver:

You may receive a message when running this lab: *Application management is disabled. To enable it, set `app-management: true` in the orchestrator service config.* To fix this, you can log into the Puppet Enterprise console, enter the Puppet Master configuration and change the value of puppet_enterprise::profile::master::app-management to true.

```
[root@pe-puppet-master manifests]# puppet app show
Myapp[myapp]
    Myapp::Db[myapp] => mysql
      + produces Sql[myapp]
    Myapp::Web[myapp] => appserver
        consumes Sql[myapp]
```

To simulate a deployment, we can use the `puppet job plan` command. We give it both an `application` and `environment` flag to let application orchestrator know which version of `site.pp` to use. This command primarily shows ordering, and you can see in the following results that `mysql` will be configured before `appserver`:

```
[root@pe-puppet-master manifests]# puppet job plan --application Myapp --
environment production

+--------------------+------------+
| Environment | production |
| Target | Myapp |
| Concurrency Limit | None |
| Nodes | 2 |
+--------------------+------------+

Application instances: 1
  - Myapp[myapp]

Node run order (nodes in level 0 run before their dependent nodes in level
1, etc.):
0 -----------------------------------------------------------------
mysql
    Myapp[myapp] - Myapp::Db[myapp]

1 -----------------------------------------------------------------
appserver
    Myapp[myapp] - Myapp::Web[myapp]

Use `puppet job run --application 'Myapp' --environment production` to
create and run a job like this.
Node catalogs may have changed since this plan was generated.
```

By switching from `puppet job plan` to `puppet job show`, we actually deploy our code in an ordered fashion. The run first takes place on the `mysql` server, which produces information that will be consumed by the `appserver` node. This run ensures that the necessary components are fully deployed before attempting to deploy applications that depend on them:

```
Use `puppet job run --application 'Myapp' --environment production` to
create and run a job like this.
```

```
Node catalogs may have changed since this plan was generated.
[root@pe-puppet-master manifests]# puppet job run --application 'Myapp' --
environment production
Starting deployment ...


+-------------------+------------+
| Job ID | 8 |
| Environment | production |
| Target | Myapp |
| Concurrency Limit | None |
| Nodes | 2 |
+-------------------+------------+


Application instances: 1
  - Myapp[myapp]

Node run order (nodes in level 0 run before their dependent nodes in level
1, etc.):
0 -----------------------------------------------------------------------
mysql
    Myapp[myapp] - Myapp::Db[myapp]


1 -----------------------------------------------------------------------
appserver
    Myapp[myapp] - Myapp::Web[myapp]


New job created: 8
Started puppet run on mysql ...
Finished puppet run on mysql - Success!
    Resource events: 0 failed 4 changed 32 unchanged 0 skipped 0 noop
    Report: https://pe-puppet-master/#/run/jobs/8/nodes/mysql/report
Started puppet run on appserver ...
Finished puppet run on appserver - Success!
    Resource events: 0 failed 3 changed 130 unchanged 0 skipped 0 noop
    Report: https://pe-puppet-master/#/run/jobs/8/nodes/appserver/report

Success! 2/2 runs succeeded.
```

We've now deployed a very simple ordered application. Our database will be fully up and running before the configuration of our wordpress server. In the next example, we'll allow for multiple wordpress servers and multiple load balancers to provide scaling to our application.

Adding a load balancer and providing horizontal scaling

In many cases, we want our applications to scale horizontally. Building more nodes allows us to serve more customers. This will be a complete rewrite of the previous application, also incorporating `puppetlabs/app_modeling` from the Forge.

Dependencies

To provide new capabilities, we'll need to grab the `puppetlabs-haproxy` module and the `puppetlabs/app_modeling` module from the Forge. If you're using a `Puppetfile`, simply add them to the `Puppetfile`. In the following example, I am manually installing these dependencies on an existing master:

```
[root@pe-puppet-master myapp]# puppet module install puppetlabs-haproxy
Notice: Preparing to install into
/etc/puppetlabs/code/environments/production/modules ...
Notice: Downloading from https://forgeapi.puppet.com ...
Notice: Installing -- do not interrupt ...
/etc/puppetlabs/code/environments/production/modules
└─┬ puppetlabs-haproxy (v2.1.0)
  ├── puppetlabs-concat (v4.2.1)
  └── puppetlabs-stdlib (v4.25.1)
[root@pe-puppet-master myapp]# puppet module install
puppetlabs/app_modeling
Notice: Preparing to install into
/etc/puppetlabs/code/environments/production/modules ...
Notice: Downloading from https://forgeapi.puppet.com ...
Notice: Installing -- do not interrupt ...
/etc/puppetlabs/code/environments/production/modules
└─┬ puppetlabs-app_modeling (v0.2.0)
  └── puppetlabs-stdlib (v4.25.1)
```

We now have the capability to build `haproxy` nodes and new app orchestration features via `app_modeling`.

Build

We'll begin at the `site.pp` again, and model our application from the endpoint. I have added two additional service lines that ensure that firewalls are disabled for the purpose of this lesson. We could consider using `puppetlabs/firewall` to manage our firewall as well, and even produce and consume FQDNs for our firewall. In the following sample, you will notice a few things:

- We're passing a `dbpass` variable to the application. This could be stored in Hiera and encrypted with EYAML.
- We have two `wordpress` nodes and two `haproxy` nodes that each have their own unique name in the `appserver`:

```
# For the purposes of this demo, the next two lines can be used to ensure
firewalls
# are off for all CentOS nodes.

service {'iptables': ensure => stopped }
service {'firewalld': ensure => stopped }

site {
  myapp { 'myapp':
    dbpass => 'rarypass',
    nodes => {
      Node['mysql']       => [ Myapp::Db['myapp']],
      Node['wordpress']   => [ Myapp::Web['myapp-1']],
      Node['wordpress-2'] => [ Myapp::Web['myapp-2']],
      Node['haproxy']     => [ Myapp::Lb['myapp-1']],
      Node['haproxy-2']   => [ Myapp::Lb['myapp-2']],
    }
  }
}
```

After our application is declared, we can model our `init.pp` to declare the entire application. There is a lot going on in this application, so note the following:

- Five variables are made available, and the db variables are used in both the DB and the App.
- `Myapp::Db` produces a database.
- `Myapp::Web` consumes a database and produces an HTTP service resource.
- We use the `collect_component_titles` function from `puppetlabs/app_modeling` to provide an array that we can iterate over. We're collecting the nodes via `$nodes` that are attached to `Myapp::Web` and `Myapp::Lb`. These values are named `allwebs` and `alllbs`.

- We use a map function from `puppetlabs/stdlib` against `$allwebs`. In this map function, we turn each node name into the value `Http["web-${wordpress_name}"]`, where `$wordpress_name` is the name of each node attached to the `Myapp::Web` application. We use this value as our export on each `MyApp::Web` declaration.

- We provide the value of `$http (Http["web-${wordpress_name}"])` back to the array of `$https`, so that we can use these values on the load balancer.

- Our load balancer uses an each statement in place of a map statement, because we don't need to transform any of this data:

```
application myapp (
  $dbuser   = 'wordpress',
  $dbpass   = 'w0rdpr3ss!',
  $dbname   = 'wordpress',
  $webpath  = '/var/www/wordpress',
  $webport  = '80'
) {

  myapp::db { $name:
    dbuser => $dbuser,
    dbpass => $dbpass,
    dbname => $dbname,
    export => Database["db-${name}"],
  }

  # This section can be confusing, but here is essentially what's
  going on
  # $allwebs is an array full of every node assigned to Myapp::Web in
  our application
  # $https takes that $allwebs array of every node, creates a service
  resource,
  # adds myapp::web to each node providing values for that service
  resource, and then
  # returns all transformed service resource names back to the array.

  # We're transforming each node listed in our site.pp into an array
  of Http[<nodename>]
  # resource calls. And on each node we'll apply our defined type
  inside of the
  # same map.

  $allwebs = collect_component_titles($nodes, Myapp::Web)

  $https = $allwebs.map |$wordpress_name| {

    $http = Http["web-${wordpress_name}"]
```

```
myapp::web { "$wordpress_name":
  dbuser  => $dbuser,
  dbpass  => $dbpass,
  dbname  => $dbname,
  webport => $webport,
  webpath => $webpath,
  consume => Database["db-${name}"],
  export  => $http,
}

$http


}


# We'll use an each statement here instead of a map, because we
don't need
# any Load balancer values returned. They're the end of the chain.
Our each
# statement covers each node, and $https from before is used to add
nodes
# to the load balancer

$alllbs = collect_component_titles($nodes, Myapp::Lb)

$alllbs.each |$load_balancer| {

  myapp::lb { "${load_balancer}":
    balancermembers => $https,
    require => $https,
    port => '80',
    balance_mode => 'roundrobin',
  }


}


}
```

Our `myapp::db` produces a MySQL server, and a single database meant to serve our application. We use the values of `dbuser`, `dbpass`, and `dbname` from our application at `init.pp`. Pay special attention to the produces line, using the `app_modeling` service resource for databases at the bottom of the manifest:

- Produces a host from the FQDN of the machine to be consumed by the web application.

- Produces a port which is not used by our web manifest, but provides an availability test to our application orchestration nodes. The application orchestration for the web will not trigger until the node can reach a database at the FQDN on port 3306. Without this declaration, it will default to 5432, which is the default port of a postgres server:

```
define myapp::db (
  $dbuser,
  $dbpass,
  $dbname,
){

  class {'::mysql::server':
    root_password => 'Sup3rp@ssword!',
    override_options => {
      'mysqld' => {
        'bind-address' => '0.0.0.0'
      }
    }
  }

  mysql::db { $dbname:
    user => $dbuser,
    password => $dbpass,
    host => '%',
    grant => ['ALL'],
  }
}
# This produces line is producing 2 values: host and port. We'll
use host directly
# on Myapp::Web, but the port designator is used to pass the
Resource Type test for
# Database using puppetlabs/app_modeling. Without the port, the
test will fail to find
# the upstream Database and won't finish the agent run.
Myapp::Db produces Database {
  host => $::fqdn,
  port => '3306',

}
```

Our `Myapp::Web` call will make use of five variables from our initial application, but receive its database host from the consumed resources. Pay attention to the following:

- The value for `$dbhost` is filled by consuming the database. At the bottom, we explicitly map the value of `$dbhost` to the consumed `$host` value in the `Myapp::Web` **consumes** `Myapp::Db`.

- We pass $dbhost, provided by the consume to class wordpress, providing an automatic connection to a remote DB.
- Myapp::Web produces an HTTP resource that provides host, port, IP, and status codes. We'll use the host, port, and IP for our load balancer, but the status_codes is another availability test to ensure that the website served by the haproxy is up with a status code of 302 or 200:

```
define myapp::web (
    $webpath,
    $webport,
    $dbuser,
    $dbpass,
    $dbhost,
    $dbname,
    ) {

    package {['php','mysql','php-mysql','php-gd']:
      ensure => installed,
    }

    class {'apache':
      default_vhost => false
    }

    include ::apache::mod::php

    apache::vhost { $::fqdn:
      port => $webport,
      docroot => $webpath,
      require => [File[$webpath]],
    }

    file { $webpath:
      ensure => directory,
      owner => 'apache',
      group => 'apache',
      require => Package['httpd'],
    }

    class { '::wordpress':
      db_user => $dbuser,
      db_password => $dbpass,
      db_host => $dbhost,
      db_name => $dbname,
      create_db => false,
      create_db_user => false,
      install_dir => $webpath,
```

```
                wp_owner => 'apache',
                wp_group => 'apache',
              }
            }
        Myapp::Web consumes Database {
          dbhost => $host,
        }
        Myapp::Web produces Http {
          host => $::clientcert,
          port => $webport,
          ip => $::networking['interfaces']['enp0s8']['ip'],
          # Like the port parameter in the Database provider, we'll need to
        send the status_codes
          # flag to the Http provider to ensure we don't only accept a 302
        status code.
          # A new wordpress application sends status code 200, so we'll let
        it through as well.
          status_codes => ['302','200'],
        }
```

Myapp::Lb doesn't actually consume or export any resources. We build a
haproxy::listen service, and then for every balancermember, we import the
aforementioned values. In our application declaration, we ran each statement against every
member of the $https array, and the following code transforms that data into a relevant
load balancer. We take the host, port, and IP produced from every myapp::web, and add it
as a member to our haproxy::listen:

```
define myapp::lb (
  $balancermembers,
  String $ipaddress = '0.0.0.0',
  String $balance_mode = 'roundrobin',
  String $port = '80',
) {

  include haproxy

  haproxy::listen {"wordpress-${name}":
    collect_exported => false,
    ipaddress => $::networking['interfaces']['enp0s8']['ip'],
    mode => 'http',
    options => {
      'balance' => $balance_mode,
    },
    ports => $port,
  }

  $balancermembers.each |$member| {
```

```
        haproxy::balancermember { $member['host']:
          listening_service => "wordpress-${name}",
          server_names => $member['host'],
          ipaddresses => $member['ip'],
          ports => $member['port'],
        }
      }

    }
```

Deploy

Deploying our new applications uses the same commands as before. We'll use `puppet app show` to provide a list of nodes with ordering. You'll see that our single DB produces a database; each webapp uses that database and produces an HTTP service resource, which is finally consumed by each load balancer:

```
[root@pe-puppet-master manifests]# puppet app show
Myapp[myapp]
    Myapp::Db[myapp] => mysql
      + produces Database[db-myapp]
    Myapp::Web[myapp-1] => appserver
      + produces Http[web-myapp-1]
        consumes Database[db-myapp]
    Myapp::Web[myapp-2] => appserver2
      + produces Http[web-myapp-2]
        consumes Database[db-myapp]
    Myapp::Lb[myapp-1] => haproxy
        consumes Http[web-myapp-1]
        consumes Http[web-myapp-2]
    Myapp::Lb[myapp-2] => haproxy2
        consumes Http[web-myapp-1]
        consumes Http[web-myapp-2]
```

Before we launch our application, we can run a `puppet job plan` to get an idea of what ordering will look like during our run:

```
[root@pe-puppet-master manifests]# puppet job plan --application Myapp --
environment production

+-------------------+-----------+
| Environment | production |
| Target | Myapp |
| Concurrency Limit | None |
| Nodes | 5 |
+-------------------+-----------+
```

```
Application instances: 1
  - Myapp[myapp]

Node run order (nodes in level 0 run before their dependent nodes in level
1, etc.):
0 ----------------------------------------------------------------
mysql
    Myapp[myapp] - Myapp::Db[myapp]

1 ----------------------------------------------------------------
wordpress
    Myapp[myapp] - Myapp::Web[myapp-1]
wordpress2
    Myapp[myapp] - Myapp::Web[myapp-2]

2 ----------------------------------------------------------------
haproxy
    Myapp[myapp] - Myapp::Lb[myapp-1]
haproxy2
    Myapp[myapp] - Myapp::Lb[myapp-2]

Use `puppet job run --application 'Myapp' --environment production` to
create and run a job like this
```

Finally, we run our application and see MySQL configured first, then our `wordpress`
instances, followed by the load balancers. Thanks to the service resources provided
by `puppetlabs/app_modeling`, we also know that our database is actively seen before the
`wordpress` servers, and that our `wordpress` servers are producing 302 status codes prior
to the load balancers being configured:

```
[root@pe-puppet-master production]# puppet job run --application Myapp --
environment production --verbose
Starting deployment ...

+-------------------+------------+
| Job ID | 42 |
| Environment | production |
| Target | Myapp |
| Concurrency Limit | None |
| Nodes | 5 |
+-------------------+------------+

Application instances: 1
  - Myapp[myapp]

Node run order (nodes in level 0 run before their dependent nodes in level
1, etc.):
```

```
0 ------------------------------------------------------------------------
mysql
 Myapp[myapp] - Myapp::Db[myapp]


1 ------------------------------------------------------------------------
wordpress
 Myapp[myapp] - Myapp::Web[myapp-1]
wordpress-2
 Myapp[myapp] - Myapp::Web[myapp-2]


2 ------------------------------------------------------------------------
haproxy
 Myapp[myapp] - Myapp::Lb[myapp-1]
haproxy-2
    Myapp[myapp] - Myapp::Lb[myapp-2]


New job created: 42
Started puppet run on mysql ...
Finished puppet run on mysql - Success!
    Resource events: 0 failed 9 changed 27 unchanged 0 skipped 0 noop
    Report: https://pe-puppet-master/#/run/jobs/42/nodes/mysql/report
Started puppet run on wordpress-2 ...
Started puppet run on wordpress ...
Finished puppet run on wordpress-2 - Success!
    Resource events: 0 failed 81 changed 66 unchanged 0 skipped 0 noop
    Report: https://pe-puppet-master/#/run/jobs/42/nodes/wordpress-2/report
Finished puppet run on wordpress - Success!
    Resource events: 0 failed 81 changed 66 unchanged 0 skipped 0 noop
    Report: https://pe-puppet-master/#/run/jobs/42/nodes/wordpress/report
Started puppet run on haproxy-2 ...
Started puppet run on haproxy ...
Finished puppet run on haproxy - Success!
    Resource events: 0 failed 4 changed 30 unchanged 0 skipped 0 noop
    Report: https://pe-puppet-master/#/run/jobs/42/nodes/haproxy/report
Finished puppet run on haproxy-2 - Success!
    Resource events: 0 failed 4 changed 30 unchanged 0 skipped 0 noop
    Report: https://pe-puppet-master/#/run/jobs/42/nodes/haproxy-2/report

Success! 5/5 runs succeeded.
Duration: 58 sec
```

Summary

In this chapter, we learned how to order our applications using application orchestration. This builds upon the fundamental knowledge we learned when writing Puppet code, and even when using exported resources. As we build more applications and objects to configure, we'll need to make sure that our Puppet Master is available to service all these nodes.

In the next chapter, we'll discuss scaling Puppet Enterprise both horizontally and vertically.

11
Scaling Puppet

Puppet is built to centrally manage all servers in an organization. In some organizations, the total node count may be in the hundreds. Other organizations have thousands or even tens of thousands of servers. For a smaller set of servers, we can configure a single monolithic Puppet Master (Puppetserver, PuppetDB or PE Console) on one server. Once we reach a certain size, we can export the components of Puppet Enterprise into separate servers. With even larger server sizes, we can begin to scale each component individually. This chapter will cover models of installing Puppet Enterprise, scaling to three servers, and finally load balancing multiple puppet components to support very large installations of Puppet.

When supporting a smaller subset of servers, the first stage is to optimize our settings on a monolithic master.

This chapter will primarily cover scaling Puppet Enterprise. Open source techniques will also be discussed in the context of this scaling, but full implementation methods will be left up to individual users of Puppet open source.

Inspection

Before we begin scaling our services, lets understand how to collect and understand metrics on those systems. A dashboard is included for both PuppetDB and the Puppet Enterprise console. We can use these dashboards to inspect the metrics of our system and identify problems along the way. As an environment grows, we want to ensure we have enough system resources available to Puppet to ensure that catalogs can be compiled and served to agents. A separate dashboard is provided for both PuppetDB and Puppetserver.

Puppetserver

Puppetserver is the primary driver behind Puppet and is the only required component in open source Puppet. The Puppetserver developer dashboard is used to track the Puppet Master's ability to serve catalogs to agents. The primary area of tracking on this dashboard focuses on Puppetserver's JRubies. JRubies on the Puppetserver are simply small ruby instances contained in the **Java Virtual Machine (JVM)**, dedicated to compiling catalogs for agents.

 You can reach the Puppetserver developer dashboard at `https://<puppetserver>:8140/puppet/experimental/dashboard.html`.

The dashboard contains a few live metrics about the Puppetserver, broken down into current metrics and average metrics:

- **Free JRubies**: The number of available JRuby instances to serve Puppet catalogs
- **Requested JRubies**: How many JRubies have been requested by agents
- **JRuby Borrow Time**: The amount of time in milliseconds the Puppetserver holds for a single request from an agent
- **JRuby Wait Time**: How long an agent has to wait on average for a JRuby
- **JVM Heap Memory Used**: The amount of system memory the JVM containing the JRubies is consuming
- **CPU Usage**: The CPU used by the Puppetserver
- **GC CPU Usage**: The amount of CPU used by **Garbage Collection (GC)** on the Puppetserver

We can inspect this data to get quite a bit of information about the primary job of the Puppetserver, which is to compile and serve catalogs. One of the first key components to look at is **JRuby Wait Time**. Are our nodes often waiting in line to receive catalogs? If we find the wait time increasing, we'll need more total JRubies available to serve the agents. This can also be indicated by a low average free JRubies count, or a high current requested JRubies status. We can also inspect the **JRuby Borrow Time** to get an idea of how big our catalogs are and how much time each node expects to be able to talk to the Puppetserver. Finally, we have some metrics to let us know if we've allocated enough memory and CPU to the Puppetserver.

We can also get some useful data about our API usage on **Top 10 Requests**, letting us know which APIs are being used most heavily in our infrastructure. **Top 10 Functions** help to identify which Puppet functions are being used most heavily on the master, and our **Top 10 Resources** can help us understand our most used code in an environment.

PuppetDB dashboard

PuppetDB has it's own dashboard, designed to show what's going on in the server. It is primarily aimed at making sense of the data that PuppetDB stores. It covers some performance metrics, like the JVM Heap, and also a quick active and inactive node count. The following information is available on PuppetDB:

- **JVM Heap**: Total memory heap size of database
- **Active and inactive nodes**: Nodes with information inside of PuppetDB
- **Resources**: Total resources seen in PuppetDB
- **Resource Duplication**: Total resources that are a duplicate that PuppetDB can serve (higher is better)
- **Catalog Duplication**: Total catalogs that are a duplicate that PuppetDB can serve (higher is better)
- **Command Queue**: Number of commands waiting to be run
- **Command Processing**: How long commands take to execute against the database
- **Processed**: Number of queries processed since startup
- **Retried**: Number of queries that had to be run more than once
- **Discard**: Number of queries that did not return a value
- **Rejected**: Number of queries that were rejected
- **Enqueuing**: Average amount of time spent waiting to write to the database
- **Command Persistence**: The time it takes to move data from memory to disk
- **Collection Queries**: Collection query service time in seconds
- **DB Compaction**: Round trip time for database compaction
- **DLO Size on Disk**: Dynamic large object size on disk
- **Discarded Messages**: Messages that did not enter PuppetDB
- **Sync Duration**: Amount of time it takes to sync data between databases
- **Last Synced**: How many seconds since the last database sync

By default, PuppetDB runs the PuppetDB Dashboard on port `8080`, but restricts this to localhost. We can reach this locally on our machine by forwarding the web port onto our workstation. The command `ssh -L 8080:localhost:8080 <user>@<puppetdb-server>` will allow you reach the PuppetDB dashboard at `http://localhost:8080` on the same workstation the command was run on.

JVM Heap bytes	107M	
Active Nodes in the population	1	
Inactive Nodes in the population	5	
Resources in the population	2282	
Resource duplication % of resources stored	14.4%	
Catalog duplication % of catalogs encountered	66.7%	
Command Queue depth	0	
Command Processing sec/command	0.417	
Command Processing command/sec	7.62m	
Processed since startup	9	
Retried since startup	0	
Discarded since startup	0	
Rejected since startup	0	
Enqueueing service time seconds	0.0147	
Command Persistence Message persistence time milliseconds	7.6m	
Collection Queries service time seconds	?	
DB Compaction round trip time seconds	0.0700	
DLO Size on Disk bytes	?	
Discarded Messages to be reviewed	?	
Sync Duration seconds	0.00	
Last Synced seconds ago	?	

We can use this information to check the status of our PuppetDB server. We want to see a high resource duplication and catalog duplication, which speeds up our overall runs of Puppet using PuppetDB. Our JVM heap can let us know how we're doing on memory usage. Active and inactive nodes help us understand what's being stored in PuppetDB, and what is on it's way out. Most other data is metrics surrounding the database itself, letting us know the health of the PostgreSQL server. Once we understand some simple live metrics, we can start looking at tuning our environment.

Tuning

Before moving into horizontal scaling of services, we should optimize the workload we have. The best horizontal scaling is scaling you don't need to do. Don't build more puppet component nodes until you can't support your workload with a single large monolithic instance. Adding more resources to Puppet allows it to serve more agents. There is no hard and fast rule on how many agents can be served by a monolithic Puppet Master, even with additional compile masters. The size of Puppet catalogs differs for every organization and is the primary unknown variable for most organizations.

 If you just need some simple settings to get started, Puppet keeps a list of standard recommended settings for small monolithic masters and monolithic masters with additional compile masters at: `https://puppet.com/docs/pe/latest/tuning_monolithic.html`.

Puppetserver tuning

The Puppetserver generates catalogs for each of our agents, using the code placed in our environments and served via JRubies. We'll be configuring the JVM and implementing our changes in Puppet in both an Enterprise and open source installation.

Puppetserver's primary job in our infrastructure is handling agent requests and returning a catalog. In older versions of Puppet, the RubyGem Passenger was commonly used to concurrently serve requests to multiple agents. Today Puppet runs multiple JRuby instances on the Puppetserver to handle concurrent requests. While Ruby itself runs with the operating system's native compiler, JRuby runs Ruby in an isolated JVM instance. These JRubies allow for better scaling with Puppet, providing multiple concurrent and thread-safe runs of Puppet. Each JRuby can serve one agent at a time, and Puppet will queue agents until a JRuby is available.

Every JVM (containing JRuby instances) has a minimum and maximum heap size. The maximum heap size determines how much memory a JVM can consume before garbage collection begins. Garbage collection is simply the process of clearing data from memory, starting from the oldest data to the newest. The minimum heap size ensures that new JVMs are started with enough memory allocated to run the application. If the JRuby can not allocate enough memory to the Puppet instance, it will trigger an OutOfMemory error and shut down the Puppetserver. We generally set our Java maximum heap size (sometimes referred to as -Xmx) and our minimum heap size (-Xms) to the same value, so that new JRubies start with the memory they need. We can also set the maximum number of JRuby instances using the max-active-instances. Puppet generally recommends this number be close to the number of CPUs available to the Puppetserver.

Puppet Enterprise implementation

In Puppet Enterprise, we can configure our Java settings in Puppet with the following settings in Hiera:

```
puppet_enterprise::profile::master::java_args:
  Xmx: 512m
  Xms: 512m
```

Open source implementation

In open source, we need to manage our settings with our own module. Luckily, camptocamp/puppetserver provides exactly what we need! We can use this module to create a profile that applies to our Puppetservers:

```
class profile::puppetserver {

  class { 'puppetserver':
    config => {
      'java_args'     => {
        'xms'         => '4g',
        'xmx'         => '6g',
        'maxpermsize' => '512m',
      },
    }
  }

}
```

In an open source installation, the ulimits required for each component in larger installations may not be present. You can follow the instructions at `https://puppet.com/docs/pe/latest/config_ulimit.html` if your master is serving an immense number of nodes and is unable to open more files on the Linux operating system.

PuppetDB tuning

PuppetDB is installed on a PostgreSQL instance, and can generally be managed the same as any PostgreSQL server. We do have a few configuration options that can help tune your PostgreSQL PuppetDB instance to your environment:

- Deactivate and purge nodes
- Tune max heap size
- Tune threads

Deactivating and purging nodes

PuppetDB keeps records on every node that checks into your Puppet Enterprise installation. In an environment where nodes often come and go, such as an immutable infrastructure, lots of data can pile up about nodes that impact the performance of the database and infrastructure. By default, Puppet will expire nodes that have not checked in for seven days, and will cease exporting objects from the catalog. This setting can be managed with the `node-ttl` setting underneath the `[database]` section of `puppet.conf`. An additional setting, `node-purge-ttl`, lets the database know when to drop records for a node. By default, 14 days is the purge time for Puppet Enterprise. We can also perform these tasks manually with `puppet node deactivate` and `puppet node purge`.

We can manage the default settings using `puppetlabs/inifile` as shown below:

```
# This profile will clean out nodes much more aggressively, deactivating
nodes not seen for 2 days, and purging nodes not seen for 4.

class profile::puppetdb {

  ini_setting { 'Node TTL':
    ensure  => present,
    path    => '/etc/puppetlabs/puppet/puppet.conf',
    section => 'database',
    setting => 'node-ttl',
    value   => '2d',
  }
```

```
ini_setting { 'Node Purge TTL':
  ensure  => present,
  path    => '/etc/puppetlabs/puppet/puppet.conf',
  section => 'database',
  setting => 'node-purge-ttl',
  value   => '4d',
}

}
```

Managing the heap size

The maximum heap size of our PuppetDB will depend on the total number of nodes checking into the system, the frequency of the Puppet runs, and the amount of resources managed by Puppet. The easiest way to determine heap size needs is to estimate or use defaults, and monitor the performance dashboard. If your database triggers an OutOfMemory exception, just provide a larger memory allocation and restart the service. If the JVM heap metric often gets close to maximum, you'll need to increase the max heap size using Java args, managed by the PostgreSQL init script. PuppetDB will begin handling requests from the same point in the queue as when the service died. In an open source installation, this file will be named puppetdb, and will be named pe-puppetdb in a Puppet Enterprise installation. On an Enterprise Linux distribution (such as Red Hat), these files will be located in /etc/sysconfig. Debian based systems such as Ubuntu will place this file in /etc/default.

In a Puppet Enterprise installation, we can set our heap size using the following Hiera values:

```
puppet_enterprise::profile::puppetdb::java_args:
  Xms: 1024m
  Xmx: 1024m
```

In an open source installation, preferably using puppet/puppetdb from the forge, we can simply set the Java args via the puppetdb class:

```
class profile::puppetdb {

  class {'puppetdb':
    java_args => {
      '-Xmx' => '1024m',
      '-Xms' => '1024m',
    },
  }

}
```

Tuning CPU threads

Tuning CPU threads for PuppetDB is not always a simple case of *add more and it will perform better*. CPUs on the PuppetDB are in use for the PostgreSQL instance, the **Message Queue (MQ)** and web server provided by PuppetDB. If your server does have CPUs to spare, consider adding more CPU threads to process more messages at a time. If increasing the number of CPUs to PuppetDB is actually decreasing throughput, instead make sure more CPU resources are available for the MQ and web server. The setting for CPU threads is also found in `puppet.conf`, under the `[command-processing]` section.

On a Puppet Enterprise installation, we'll find this setting managed by Hiera:

```
puppet_enterprise::puppetdb::command_processing_threads: 2
```

In an open source installation, we will again use `puppetlabs/puppetdb` to manage this setting:

```
class profile::puppetdb {

  class {'puppetdb':
    command_threads => '2',
  }

}
```

Automatically determining settings

Now that we've seen some of the settings, we can look at some tools to help us deliver a decent baseline using our hardware. To begin with, we'll be looking at automatically tuning our full Puppet Enterprise installation and using PGTune to tune our PuppetDB instance.

Puppet Enterprise

Before we inspect and tune our system, we will find a set of recommended settings based on the hardware available. Thomas Kishel at Puppet has designed a Puppet Face that queries PuppetDB for Puppet Enterprise Infrastructure. This command inspects available resources on the system and provides a sane default for the following Puppet Enterprise installations:

- Monolithic infrastructure
- Monolithic with compile masters
- Monolithic with external PostgreSQL

- Monolithic with compile masters with external PostgreSQL
- Monolithic with HA
- Monolithic with compile masters with HA
- Split infrastructure
- Split with compile masters
- Split with external PostgreSQL
- Split with compile masters with external PostgreSQL

To get started with `tkishel/pe_tune`, we'll want to clone the Git repository onto our Puppet Enterprise on our primary master, and make the `tune.rb` script executable:

```
git clone https://github.com/tkishel/pe_tune.git
chmod +x ./pe_tune/lib/puppet_x/puppetlabs/tune.rb
```

When we have the binary cloned and executable, we'll want to run `tune.rb` to get information back about our system and return sane Puppet Enterprise settings in Hiera:

```
[root@pe-puppet-master ~]# ./pe_tune/lib/puppet_x/puppetlabs/tune.rb
### Puppet Infrastructure Summary: Found a Monolithic Infrastructure

## Found: 4 CPU(s) / 9839 MB RAM for Primary Master pe-puppet-master
## Specify the following optimized settings in Hiera in nodes/pe-puppet-
master.yaml


---
puppet_enterprise::profile::database::shared_buffers: 3072MB
puppet_enterprise::puppetdb::command_processing_threads: 2
puppet_enterprise::master::puppetserver::jruby_max_active_instances: 2
puppet_enterprise::master::puppetserver::reserved_code_cache: 1024m
puppet_enterprise::profile::master::java_args:
  Xms: 2048m
  Xmx: 2048m
puppet_enterprise::profile::puppetdb::java_args:
  Xms: 1024m
  Xmx: 1024m
puppet_enterprise::profile::console::java_args:
  Xms: 768m
  Xmx: 768m
puppet_enterprise::profile::orchestrator::java_args:
  Xms: 768m
  Xmx: 768m


## CPU Summary: Total/Used/Free: 4/4/0 for pe-puppet-master
## RAM Summary: Total/Used/Free: 9839/8704/1135 for pe-puppet-master
## JVM Summary: Using 768 MB per Puppet Server JRuby for pe-puppet-master
```

We can then place these values in Hiera anywhere that the Puppet Enterprise installation would be able to pick them up. I recommend `common.yaml`, unless you have a Hiera layer specifically set aside for Puppet settings.

> This script will fail to run by default on infrastructure hosts with less than 4 CPUs or 8 GB of RAM. You can run the command with the `--force` flag to get results, even on nodes that are smaller than the recommended 4 CPUs and 8GB of memory.

PuppetDB – PostgreSQL with PGTune

When in doubt about how to tune a PostgreSQL server, try PGTune. This project will read your current `postgresql.conf` and output a new one with tuning settings designed for the machine it's running on. As an important side note, this will not take into account the necessary memory for the message queue or the web server, so leaving a small amount of extra resources by slightly tuning down these settings can help with performance.

> Please note that PGTune assumes the only purpose of the node it is running on is to serve a Postgres server. These settings will be difficult to use on a single monolithic master, and `tkishel/pe_tune` will be a much more useful tool for configuring these servers.

We'll want to begin by cloning and entering the current PGTune project:

```
git clone https://github.com/gregs1104/pgtune.git
Cloning into 'pgtune'...
remote: Counting objects: 112, done.
remote: Total 112 (delta 0), reused 0 (delta 0), pack-reused 112
Receiving objects: 100% (112/112), 66.21 KiB | 0 bytes/s, done.
Resolving deltas: 100% (63/63), done.
cd pgtune
```

Then we run PGTune against our Puppet Enterprise `postgresql.conf`:

```
./pgtune -i /opt/puppetlabs/server/data/postgresql/9.6/data/postgresql.conf
#-----------------------------------------------------------------------
----
# pgtune for version 8.4 run on 2018-08-19
# Based on 3882384 KB RAM, platform Linux, 100 clients and mixed workload
#-----------------------------------------------------------------------
----

default_statistics_target = 100
maintenance_work_mem = 224MB
checkpoint_completion_target = 0.9
```

```
effective_cache_size = 2816MB
work_mem = 18MB
wal_buffers = 16MB
checkpoint_segments = 32
shared_buffers = 896MB
max_connections = 100
```

These settings come back in a form for manually managing a `postgresql.conf`. Let's translate these values into Puppet Enterprise Hiera settings that can be placed in `common.yaml` to drive our PuppetDB:

```
---
puppet_enterprise::profile::database::maintenance_work_mem: 224MB
puppet_enterprise::profile::database::checking_completion_target = 0.9
puppet_enterprise::profile::database::effective_cache_size: 2816MB
puppet_enterprise::profile::database::work_mem: 18MB
puppet_enterprise::profile::database::wal_buffers: 16MB
puppet_enterprise::profile::database::checkpoint_segments: 32
puppet_enterprise::profile::database::shared_buffers: 896MB

# PgTune recommends just 100 max_connections, but Puppet Enterprise
# generally recommends a higher amount due to the number of nodes that
# can connect to the system. I'll tune it for that purpose.
puppet_enterprise::profile::database::max_connections: 400
```

When using open source, we'll instead want to lean on the `puppetlabs/postgresql` module that is a dependency of `puppetlabs/puppetdb`. Each value we want to set is an individual resource, and can be represented in Hiera at the PuppetDB level. I would not recommend putting these particular settings in `common.yaml` if you have other PostgreSQL servers in your environment:

```
---
postgresql::server::config_entries:
  maintenance_work_mem: 224MB
  checkpoint_completion_target: 0.9
  effective_cache_size: 2816MB
  work_mem: 18MB
  wal_buffers: 16MB
  checkpoint_segments: 32
  shared_buffers: 896MB
  max_connections: 400
```

Understanding these key concepts allows us to configure our individual nodes to maximize performance. For many users, this will be enough to run Puppet in their environment. For more extreme cases, we can turn to horizontal scaling, allowing more copies of our Puppetservers and PuppetDBs to support more agents.

Horizontal scaling

When a single monolithic master can no longer serve our environment, we split our master into distinct components: console, Puppetserver and PuppetDB. This allows us to serve more clients with a smaller footprint. In an ever growing environment, even this setup may not be able to cover your needs for all agents.

In this section, we'll be discussing the scaling of Puppetserver, PuppetDB and our certificate authority to serve more agents. With concepts of vertical tuning and horizontal scaling, we can serve a very large installation of nodes, up to the tens of thousands of individual servers on a single setup.

Puppetserver

Generally, the first component that is required to scale in any Puppet setup is the Puppetserver. The Puppetserver does the bulk of the work in Puppet, compiling catalogs to agents. In this section, we're going to explore some of the theory behind how many agents a Puppetserver can support, how to create new Puppetservers, and some load balancing strategies around your Puppet Masters. We'll be viewing this from the lens of open source and Enterprise.

Estimating the number of agents a Puppetserver supports

Puppet has a mathematics equation for estimating how many nodes a Puppetserver can support. This equation is an estimate and should not replace actual benchmarks, as things such as catalog compile size often shift over time.

The estimation of Puppetservers is represented as $j = ns/mr$. In this equation, we see the following values:

- j: JRuby instances per master
- m: Number of compile masters (Puppetservers)
- n: Number of nodes served by the master
- s: Catalog compile size in seconds
- r: Run interval in seconds

Using this equation, let's post a simple metric to work with: how many nodes can a single Puppetserver with one JRuby instance serve, with an average catalog compile time of 10 seconds and a default run interval of 30 minutes? Our equation looks like this: $1 = n10 / 1*1800$. We can simplify this to $1 = n10 / 1800$. We can multiple both sides of our equation to get $1800 = n10$. Simplifying by dividing both sides by 10 gives us $n = 180$.

A single master, with one JRuby instance, with a run interval of 30 minutes and catalog compile time of 10 seconds can serve 180 agents. If we want to serve more agents, we have the following options:

- Increase the number of JRuby instances per master
- Increase the number of compile masters
- Decrease run interval
- Decrease catalog compilation times with more efficient code

Just increasing this tiny server to a server with 8 CPUs, and setting the `jruby_max_active_instances` setting to 8 would allow us to serve 1,440 agents on this server. Adding two more compile masters with the same number of CPUs would get us to 4,320 agents to serve. We can continually add more Puppetservers to this until we have the ability to serve all the nodes in our infrastructure.

Adding new compile masters

In a Puppet Enterprise installation, bringing on new compile masters is very easy. Simply add a new node to the PE Master **Classification** group underneath the PE Infrastructure:

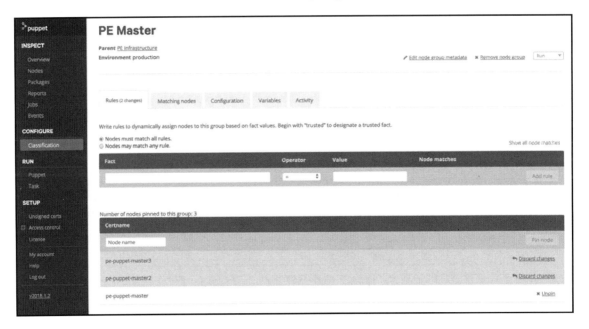

These nodes will receive the same configuration as the Primary Master, including code manager configuration and necessary connections to PuppetDB. There are no hidden tricks to managing additional compile masters in Puppet Enterprise. Classify and add them to a load balancer.

In open source, we need to ensure each Puppet Master is configured to use PuppetDB. Luckily, `puppetlabs/puppetdb` provides that connection for us:

```
class profile::puppetserver {
  class { 'puppetdb::master::config':
    puppetdb_server => <hostname of PuppetDB>,
  }
}
```

We'll still need to make sure this open source installation has the ability to retrieve code. r10k does not federate across servers, unlike Code Manager, so you'll need to determine a strategy for deploying code out to these masters. One easy method of managing this is included in the `puppet/r10k module`! Not only can the `puppet/r10k` module configure r10k in the same way across each Puppetserver, but a new Puppet task is available for deploying code in that module. This can be run from the command line, or preferably from a CI/CD server on commit:

```
$ puppet task run r10k::deploy environment=production -n puppet-
master1,puppet-master2,puppet-master3
```

Load balancing

When we have multiple Puppetservers, it's important we decide how agents determine which server to connect to. We'll be inspecting a simple strategy of placing Puppetservers closest to the nodes they serve, as well as load balancing strategies that cover larger infrastructure needs. These two methods can be combined if there is a security requirement for isolated masters and a technical requirement for more catalog compilation from additional Puppetservers.

Simple setup – direct connection

One of the simplest setups many organizations use is to isolate data centers and provide a Puppetserver for each data center. Some organizations have data centers across the world, whether in the cloud in regions, or on site in various locations. Providing a compile master to these individual data centers is a fairly simple task and only requires a few things:

- The agent is aware of compile master FQDN and has network connectivity to it
- Compile master has connectivity back to the primary master, sometimes called **Master of Masters**

In this setup, during provisioning an agent would reach out to the local compile master for it's agent installation. On a Puppet Enterprise installation, the agent can simply run `curl -k https://<compile_master>:8140/packages/current/install.bash` command during provisioning, and it will retrieve an agent thanks to the `pe_repo` classification found in the PE Master node group. This agent will not need network connectivity to PuppetDB, the Primary Master, or the PE console, as information will be handled by the compile master in the middle.

The following infographic from Puppet shows the necessary firewall connections required for each component in a large environment installation of Puppet Enterprise:

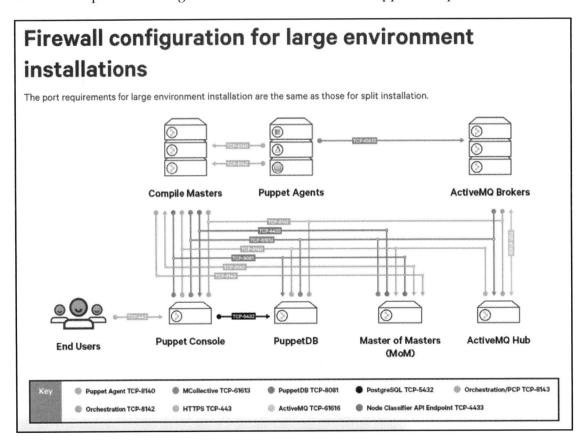

These same ports remain true in an open source installation, although the node classifier API endpoint will not be available from the Puppet console.

If a single data center grows so large that it needs multiple compile masters, or we want to centralize our compile masters for every data center, we'll instead need to focus on load balancing. Everything in this section still applies in a load balanced cluster, but there are a few new pieces to work with behind a load balancer.

Load balancing

In very large environments, we may worry about having enough resources to serve all of our agents. We start building more compile masters and our agents need to connect to them. There are only a few key additional concerns when placing our compile masters behind a load balancer: certificate management and load balancing strategy.

Puppet builds trusted SSL connections between agents and masters at compile time using self-signed certificates. The FQDN of both the master and the agent are recorded in their respective certs by default. During each connection, the agent inspects the certificate to ensure that the requested domain name is in the certificate. If our agent uses DNS or a VIP from load balancing to connect to a master at `puppet.example.com`, and the certificate does not contain that name explicitly, the agent will reject the connection. We want to identify a common name for our pool of compile masters (often just a shortname, such as `puppet`), and embed that into the certificate. We can include multiple DNS alt names in the `puppet.conf` in the main section on each compile master:

```
[main]
dns_alt_names = puppet,puppet-portland
...
```

When we connect to the Puppet Master for the first time, these `dns_alt_names` will be embedded into our certificate. For Enterprise users, this certificate will not show up in the Puppet Enterprise console, so that no one can accidentally approve DNS alt names from the GUI. You'll need to log in to the Puppet Master and run `puppet cert sign <name> --allow-dns-alt-names` to sign the certificate, and accept it with alternate names. If you have already built this compile master and need to regenerate the certificates, you can run `puppet cert clean <name>` on the Master of Masters, and remove the SSL directory with `sudo rm -r $(puppet master --configprint ssldir)` on the compile master prior to running the agent again.

> It is generally considered safe to remove the SSL directory on any agent, including compile masters. Running this on the Master of Masters, which acts as the centralized Certificate Authority, on the other hand, will cause all SSL connections and all Puppet runs to stop in the environment. If you do this, you'll need to rebuild your certificate authority on the Master of Masters. Directions can be found at: `https://docs.puppet.com/puppet/4.4/ssl_regenerate_certificates.html`.

Your agents should now be referring to all compile masters by their common DNS alt name. You'll need to decide a load balancing strategy: using DNS round robin, DNS SRV records, or a dedicated load balancer. Major DNS providers provide a mechanism for DNS round robin and SRV records, and you should consult their documentation. We'll walk through a sample of setting up HAProxy as a software load balancer for our compile masters, as if they were all in a single pool. We'll be using puppetlabs/haproxy and the usage sample on the forge to build a HAProxy instance for multiple compile masters. We could use our exported resources sample from Chapter 9, *Exported Resources*, but we'll use a simple example as we don't often add Puppet Masters to our load balancer:

```
class puppet::proxy {

  include ::haproxy

  haproxy::listen { 'puppetmaster':
    collect_exported => false,
    ipaddress        => $::ipaddress,
    ports            => '8140',
  }

  haproxy::balancermember { 'master00':
    listening_service => 'puppetmaster',
    server_names      => 'master00.packt.com',
    ipaddresses       => '10.10.10.100',
    ports             => '8140',
    options           => 'check',
  }
  haproxy::balancermember { 'master01':
    listening_service => 'puppetmaster',
    server_names      => 'master01.packt.com',
    ipaddresses       => '10.10.10.101',
    ports             => '8140',
    options           => 'check',
  }
}
```

Using this configuration, our HAProxy will be able to serve requests to all agents requesting a connection to a compile master.

Certificate authority

In a Puppet Enterprise installation, the certificate authority portion of compile masters is fairly easy to solve. Puppet Enterprise uses separate node groups for a CA and compile master. By adding additional compile masters to the PE Master classification group, each master is configured to use the centralized certificate authority on the Master of Masters.

In Puppet open source, we'll need to disable the certificate authority on each of our compile masters using Trapperkeeper. You can simply open `/etc/puppetlabs/puppetserver/services.d/ca.cfg` and comment out the line `puppetlabs.services.ca.certificate-authority-service/certificate-authority-service` and uncomment `#puppetlabs.services.ca.certificate-authority-disabled-service/certificate-authority-disabled-service`. Finally, you'll need each agent in your infrastructure (including the compile masters) to add the `ca_server` setting into the `[main]` section of the `puppet.conf`, pointing at the Master of Masters. Note that this requires network connectivity over the CA port to the Master of Masters, which by default is `8140`, but can be toggled with the `ca_port` setting.

The final goal of this setup is that each compile master has a DNS alt name, and every agent is connecting to the master via that DNS alt name, while using the Master of Master as the certificate authority for all nodes.

PuppetDB

Scaling PuppetDB is generally scaling PostgreSQL. A single PuppetDB can cover a large number of nodes and compile masters, but should you need to scale PuppetDB, consult PostgreSQL documentation and organizational database guidance. Known methodologies of scaling PostgreSQL that work with Puppet include:

- High availability setups
- Load balancing
- Database replication
- Database clustering
- Connection pooling

Summary

In this chapter, we talked about scaling Puppet. We started by learning how to monitor the components inside Puppet and how to tune individual Puppet components. We then discussed horizontal scaling, adding more compile masters to serve more agents. We discussed how to load balance our Puppetservers behind a HAProxy and discussed that PuppetDB can be scaled like any PostgreSQL database.

In our next chapter, we'll look at troubleshooting Puppet Enterprise. Learning to read and understand the errors you may see in Puppet will teach you to be a better practitioner, and allow you to really understand the Puppet system.

Troubleshooting and Profiling 12

Sometimes, our Puppet infrastructure and code don't seem like they're cooperating with us. In this chapter, we'll focus on troubleshooting some common issues.

The main topics that we'll cover in this chapter are as follows:

- Puppet infrastructure component errors
- Common catalog compilation errors
- Logging

Although this is not always the most exciting topic, knowing how to work with these issues is the key to success with any system and language, including Puppet. Before we dive into our code, we'll make sure that our Puppet infrastructure is ready to go.

Common component errors

This section will be all about a healthy Puppet installation. We'll primarily focus on the common issues that we see on agents, and what they may mean for your Puppet system. We'll tackle this for the times that we most commonly see errors: while writing, testing, and deploying code to our servers. We will be troubleshooting primarily from the perspective of the Puppet agent, so you will see the most common issues that team members encounter while working on a Puppet deployment.

Puppet agents and Puppetserver

All of the nodes in a Puppet infrastructure contain a Puppet agent. In a split installation, each component checks in with a Puppetserver, just like any other node managed in the infrastructure. In a monolithic installation, the Puppet agent checks in with itself. Every other node managed by Puppet must use the agent to retrieve a configuration. Because the agent is everywhere, understanding some of the common errors with the agent will be universally useful for troubleshooting. Some of the common causes of a malfunctioning agent are as follows:

- Certificate reuse
- Wrong user context when connecting to the master
- Network connectivity
- DNS alternate name

Waiting on certificate signing

One of the simplest errors that you will see when running the agent for the first time is a message stating, `failed to retrieve certificate and waitforcert is disabled`:

```
Exiting; failed to retrieve certificate and waitforcert is disabled
```

This particular message is easy to fix. Our agent is informing us that it has not received a signed certificate back from the master. We can solve this problem by simply logging in to the Puppet Master as the root user and signing our certificate. We can view any pending certificates on our Puppet Master with the command `puppet cert list`, as follows:

```
[root@wordpress puppetlabs]# puppet agent -t
Exiting; no certificate found and waitforcert is disabled
```

In the preceding code, we can see that our `wordpress` node hasn't been signed, and we can simply approve this node for use with `puppet cert sign`:

```
[root@pe-puppet-master ~]# puppet cert list
  "wordpress" (SHA256)
F4:9E:56:9E:07:3F:66:B3:B4:CE:81:9E:1E:ED:FC:43:B9:A2:CC:88:78:8D:C5:30:CA:
B0:B7:6D:0F:77:86:20

[root@pe-puppet-master ~]# puppet cert sign wordpress
Signing Certificate Request for:
  "wordpress" (SHA256)
F4:9E:56:9E:07:3F:66:B3:B4:CE:81:9E:1E:ED:FC:43:B9:A2:CC:88:78:8D:C5:30:CA:
```

```
B0:B7:6D:0F:77:86:20
Notice: Signed certificate request for wordpress
Notice: Removing file Puppet::SSL::CertificateRequest wordpress at
'/etc/puppetlabs/puppet/ssl/ca/requests/wordpress.pem'
```

If we're not auto-signing our certificates through our `autosign.conf` or using an ENC that provides automatic signing for us, we'll always need to remember to sign certificates for new nodes.

Certificate reuse

Sometimes, we spin up a new node by using a `cert` name previously known to the Puppet Master, especially in immutable infrastructures. Our Puppet infrastructure is designed with certificate security in mind, so having a new node with a name already known by the Puppet Master will present a message like the following:

```
[root@wordpress puppet]# puppet agent -t
Error: Could not request certificate: The certificate retrieved from the
master does not match the agent's private key. Did you forget to run as
root?
Certificate fingerprint:
88:7F:B2:88:15:20:0A:55:3F:DE:2A:36:2C:B1:52:50:F1:77:96:EA:79:75:A1:00:B9:
D6:3E:0B:93:45:D8:1C
To fix this, remove the certificate from both the master and the agent and
then start a puppet run, which will automatically regenerate a certificate.
On the master:
  puppet cert clean wordpress
On the agent:
  1a. On most platforms: find /etc/puppetlabs/puppet/ssl -name
wordpress.pem -delete
  1b. On Windows: del "\etc\puppetlabs\puppet\ssl\certs\wordpress.pem" /f
  2. puppet agent -t

Exiting; failed to retrieve certificate and waitforcert is disabled
```

The simple fix for this error is to simply clean the certificate on our Puppet Master before running the agent again, and also signing the certificate again, as follows:

```
[root@pe-puppet-master manifests]# puppet cert clean wordpress
Notice: Revoked certificate with serial 18
Notice: Removing file Puppet::SSL::Certificate wordpress at
'/etc/puppetlabs/puppet/ssl/ca/signed/wordpress.pem'
Notice: Removing file Puppet::SSL::Certificate wordpress at
'/etc/puppetlabs/puppet/ssl/certs/wordpress.pem'
```

Additionally, Puppet will not let us rerun the agent until we delete the certificate that was recently generated. The message provided by the error provides the best command to remove the certificate, so it can be regenerated on our agents: `find /etc/puppetlabs/puppet/ssl -name <fqdn>.pem -delete`. On most agents, it is actually safer to delete the entire SSL directory, with `rm -rf /etc/puppetlabs/puppet/ssl`.

> Deleting the SSL directory on the Puppet Master will delete the entire certificate chain, causing a need for a whole new set of certificates. This problem was more difficult to resolve in older versions of Puppet; we can now resolve it by following the directions at `https://puppet.com/docs/puppet/latest/ssl_regenerate_certificates.html`. Ensure that you don't accidentally delete the SSL certificates on the master, rather than the agent.

Preventing this error is as simple as running `puppet cert clean <nodename>` on the Puppet Master, after decommissioning any node attached to the Puppet Master.

Wrong Puppet user

When we're writing code, we often log in to a test machine to run our agent manually and get a sense of what's going on. We rarely log in directly as the root, and it's easy to forget to switch our user to root. This problem can be particularly frustrating, because it appears as a certificate error. Our individual user generates a new certificate, and cannot connect to the Master using the SSL error. The key difference that you'll notice in the error log is the recommendation to remove the local certificate.

This happens primarily when doing testing and running the agent as the wrong user on a Puppet agent. Take note of the generating new key, and the user context user in line 1, and in the certificate clean message:In the following example, notice a new SSL key being generated, and that I'm running this command as my own users instead of root:

```
[rary@wordpress ~]$ puppet agent -t
Info: Creating a new SSL key for wordpress
Info: Caching certificate for ca
Info: Caching certificate for wordpress
Error: Could not request certificate: The certificate retrieved from the
master does not match the agent's private key. Did you forget to run as
root?
Certificate fingerprint:
0C:10:48:BB:F9:F4:12:4A:66:52:FD:BB:33:DF:54:67:98:B4:D1:01:96:DE:6B:A4:D1:
29:19:3C:C8:83:15:8C
To fix this, remove the certificate from both the master and the agent and
```

then start a puppet run, which will automatically regenerate a certificate.
On the master:
  puppet cert clean wordpress
On the agent:
  1a. On most platforms: find /home/rary/.puppetlabs/etc/puppet/ssl -name
wordpress.packt.com.pem -delete
  1b. On Windows: del
"\home\rary\.puppetlabs\etc\puppet\ssl\certs\wordpress.packt.com.pem" /f
  2. puppet agent -t

Exiting; failed to retrieve certificate and waitforcert is disabled

Network connectivity

Network connectivity issues can be pretty noisy in Puppet. The agent in the following code sample does not have the ability to talk to the master, due to either a bad networking route or a firewall stopping traffic to our Puppet Master. In the following example, a firewall is blocking the agent from connecting to the master:

```
[root@wordpress ~]# puppet agent -t
Warning: Unable to fetch my node definition, but the agent run will
continue:
Warning: Failed to open TCP connection to pe-puppet-master:8140 (No route
to host - connect(2) for "pe-puppet-master" port 8140)
Info: Retrieving pluginfacts
Error: /File[/opt/puppetlabs/puppet/cache/facts.d]: Failed to generate
additional resources using 'eval_generate': Failed to open TCP connection
to pe-puppet-master:8140 (No route to host - connect(2) for "pe-puppet-
master" port 8140)
Error: /File[/opt/puppetlabs/puppet/cache/facts.d]: Could not evaluate:
Could not retrieve file metadata for puppet:///pluginfacts: Failed to open
TCP connection to pe-puppet-master:8140 (No route to host - connect(2) for
"pe-puppet-master" port 8140)
Info: Retrieving plugin
Error: /File[/opt/puppetlabs/puppet/cache/lib]: Failed to generate
additional resources using 'eval_generate': Failed to open TCP connection
to pe-puppet-master:8140 (No route to host - connect(2) for "pe-puppet-
master" port 8140)
Error: /File[/opt/puppetlabs/puppet/cache/lib]: Could not evaluate: Could
not retrieve file metadata for puppet:///plugins: Failed to open TCP
connection to pe-puppet-master:8140 (No route to host - connect(2) for "pe-
puppet-master" port 8140)
Info: Loading facts
Error: Could not retrieve catalog from remote server: Failed to open TCP
connection to pe-puppet-master:8140 (No route to host - connect(2) for "pe-
puppet-master" port 8140)
```

```
Warning: Not using cache on failed catalog
Error: Could not retrieve catalog; skipping run
Error: Could not send report: Failed to open TCP connection to pe-puppet-
master:8140 (No route to host - connect(2) for "pe-puppet-master" port
8140)
```

You may notice recurring themes in the preceding examples: No route to host and Failed to open TCP Connection. Each component of our catalog compilation will individually print a message back, alerting us to a connection failure. When we see no route to the host, we know that a firewall is between our agent and master, or that there is no network route to the host. This can also be caused by an improper DNS or /etc/hosts entry on the agent attempting to connect to the master.

DNS alt name

DNS alt names are very convenient in larger Puppet infrastructures. They allow us to effectively nickname our servers individually, or as a group. A common DNS alt name might be puppet, so that you can use a load balancer to serve all of your individual Puppetservers.

In the following example, we're trying to connect to our Puppetserver using the name alt-name.puppet.net, which was never baked in to the certificate on the original signing of our Puppet server:

```
[root@wordpress puppet]# puppet agent -t --server=alt-name.puppet.net
Warning: Unable to fetch my node definition, but the agent run will
continue:
Warning: SSL_connect returned=1 errno=0 state=error: certificate verify
failed: [ok for /CN=pe-puppet-master]
Info: Retrieving pluginfacts
Error: /File[/opt/puppetlabs/puppet/cache/facts.d]: Failed to generate
additional resources using 'eval_generate': SSL_connect returned=1 errno=0
state=error: certificate verify failed: [ok for /CN=pe-puppet-master]
Error: /File[/opt/puppetlabs/puppet/cache/facts.d]: Could not evaluate:
Could not retrieve file metadata for puppet:///pluginfacts: SSL_connect
returned=1 errno=0 state=error: certificate verify failed: [ok for /CN=pe-
puppet-master]
Info: Retrieving plugin
Error: /File[/opt/puppetlabs/puppet/cache/lib]: Failed to generate
additional resources using 'eval_generate': SSL_connect returned=1 errno=0
state=error: certificate verify failed: [ok for /CN=pe-puppet-master]
Error: /File[/opt/puppetlabs/puppet/cache/lib]: Could not evaluate: Could
not retrieve file metadata for puppet:///plugins: SSL_connect returned=1
errno=0 state=error: certificate verify failed: [ok for /CN=pe-puppet-
master]
```

```
Info: Loading facts
Error: Could not retrieve catalog from remote server: SSL_connect
returned=1 errno=0 state=error: certificate verify failed: [ok for /CN=pe-
puppet-master]
Warning: Not using cache on failed catalog
Error: Could not retrieve catalog; skipping run
Error: Could not send report: SSL_connect returned=1 errno=0 state=error:
certificate verify failed: [ok for /CN=pe-puppet-master]
```

There are two possible fixes for this: either set your agent to call the master by a known DNS name, or rebuild the certificate on your Puppetserver with the new DNS alt name. This can be done by removing the SSL cert with `find /etc/puppetlabs/puppet/ssl -name <fqdn>.pem -delete` on the offending master, and running `puppet agent -t --dns-alt-names=<name1>,<name2>,<etc>` on the master, connecting to the master of masters, and building a new certificate. This certificate has to be signed via the command line on the CA (usually the Master of Masters), and cannot be signed in the PE console, due to the DNS alt names.

Date and time

Time is an important factor in maintaining integrity between SSL connections. `puppetlabs/ntp` is usually the module most curated by Puppet, due to the fact that Puppet needs an accurate date and time on each node during a transaction. If you receive a message stating that the certificate revocation list (CRL) is not yet valid on your runs, ensure that NTP is properly configured across your nodes:

```
[root@wordpress puppet]# puppet agent -t
Warning: Unable to fetch my node definition, but the agent run will
continue:
Warning: SSL_connect returned=1 errno=0 state=error: certificate verify
failed: [CRL is not yet valid for /CN=Puppet Enterprise CA generated on pe-
puppet-master at +2018-06-15 02:28:12 +0000]
Info: Retrieving pluginfacts
Error: /File[/opt/puppetlabs/puppet/cache/facts.d]: Failed to generate
additional resources using 'eval_generate': SSL_connect returned=1 errno=0
state=error: certificate verify failed: [CRL is not yet valid for
/CN=Puppet Enterprise CA generated on pe-puppet-master at +2018-06-15
02:28:12 +0000]
Error: /File[/opt/puppetlabs/puppet/cache/facts.d]: Could not evaluate:
Could not retrieve file metadata for puppet:///pluginfacts: SSL_connect
returned=1 errno=0 state=error: certificate verify failed: [CRL is not yet
valid for /CN=Puppet Enterprise CA generated on pe-puppet-master at
+2018-06-15 02:28:12 +0000]
Info: Retrieving plugin
Error: /File[/opt/puppetlabs/puppet/cache/lib]: Failed to generate
```

```
additional resources using 'eval_generate': SSL_connect returned=1 errno=0
state=error: certificate verify failed: [CRL is not yet valid for
/CN=Puppet Enterprise CA generated on pe-puppet-master at +2018-06-15
02:28:12 +0000]
Error: /File[/opt/puppetlabs/puppet/cache/lib]: Could not evaluate: Could
not retrieve file metadata for puppet:///plugins: SSL_connect returned=1
errno=0 state=error: certificate verify failed: [CRL is not yet valid for
/CN=Puppet Enterprise CA generated on pe-puppet-master at +2018-06-15
02:28:12 +0000]
Info: Loading facts
Error: Could not retrieve catalog from remote server: SSL_connect
returned=1 errno=0 state=error: certificate verify failed: [CRL is not yet
valid for /CN=Puppet Enterprise CA generated on pe-puppet-master at
+2018-06-15 02:28:12 +0000]
Warning: Not using cache on failed catalog
Error: Could not retrieve catalog; skipping run
Error: Could not send report: SSL_connect returned=1 errno=0 state=error:
certificate verify failed: [CRL is not yet valid for /CN=Puppet Enterprise
CA generated on pe-puppet-master at +2018-06-15 02:28:12 +0000]
```

PE console service is down

If the Puppet Enterprise console is overloaded, it can trigger an OutOfMemory error and crash. I see this most often when spinning up small Puppet Enterprise installations on a virtual machine or container on my local laptop. When the console is down, Puppet Enterprise users will receive an error, letting them know that the node manager service isn't running. Users should check the status of the PE console and the relevant logs if this message starts to come up in agent runs:

```
[root@wordpress ~]# puppet agent -t
Warning: Unable to fetch my node definition, but the agent run will
continue:
Warning: Error 500 on SERVER: Server Error: Classification of wordpress
failed due to a Node Manager service error. Please check
/var/log/puppetlabs/console-services/console-services.log on the node(s)
running the Node Manager service for more details.
Info: Retrieving pluginfacts
Info: Retrieving plugin
Info: Retrieving locales
Info: Loading facts
Error: Could not retrieve catalog from remote server: Error 500 on SERVER:
Server Error: Failed when searching for node wordpress: Classification of
wordpress failed due to a Node Manager service error. Please check
/var/log/puppetlabs/console-services/console-services.log on the node(s)
running the Node Manager service for more details.
```

```
Warning: Not using cache on failed catalog
Error: Could not retrieve catalog; skipping run
```

 This section only applies to Puppet Enterprise users.

Catalog errors

When a catalog compilation error is triggered, the Puppet Parser is alerting us that it cannot build a catalog from the provided code. A puppet run will fail and the agent will not configure anything on a node that fails catalog compilation. These errors trigger when Puppet cannot read the code, or cannot determine how to apply the resources supplied in the catalog. In the next sections, we'll cover the following common failures:

- Syntax errors
- Duplicate resource declarations
- Missing resources
- Autoload format
- Circular dependencies

 Enterprise Users: The configuration tab in the classification group will not be able to read classes that contain syntax errors, missing classes, or classes not found in autoload format.

Syntax errors

Syntax errors are the most common errors that we see when we develop code. It's easy to miss simple syntax when typing code, and to push failing code to a test environment. In the following example, the closing bracket to the class at the end of the file is missing:

```
[root@wordpress puppet]# puppet agent -t
Info: Using configured environment 'production'
Info: Retrieving pluginfacts
Info: Retrieving plugin
Info: Retrieving locales
Info: Loading facts
Error: Could not retrieve catalog from remote server: Error 500 on SERVER:
```

```
Server Error: Syntax error at end of input (file:
/etc/puppetlabs/code/environments/production/modules/profile/manifests/base
line.pp) on node wordpress
```

We can test for this failure long before it is deployed to our Puppet Master. The command `puppet parser validate` will give us the exact same message as the agent if we run it against the manifest. Users of the PDK will find that `pdk validate` runs this as one of the checks in the suite. The error from the agent run is replicated by Puppet parser validate in the following code:

```
[root@pe-puppet-master manifests]# puppet parser validate baseline.pp
Error: Could not parse for environment production: Syntax error at end of
input (file:
/etc/puppetlabs/code/environments/production/modules/profile/manifests/base
line.pp)
```

This is one of the simplest examples of a good practice to put into your CI/CD pipelines. You can find more good examples of adding this simple check in Chapter 8, *Extending Puppet with Tasks and Discovery*.

Syntax error checkers like Puppet parser validate scan through the code until they find a line that they cannot resolve. Often, these errors are on the line above the reported failure! Always check the line above the reported line. The following error was actually a missing comma on line 4 of the `example.pp`: `Error: Could not parse for environment production: Syntax error at 'source' (file: /Users/rary/workspace/packt/manifests/example.pp, line: 5, column: 5)`.

Duplicate resource declaration

Puppet builds our catalogs based on every resource declared in our manifests. In good Puppet code design, we have classes that include or contain other classes. During development, it's not uncommon to sometimes attempt to declare a resource that has been declared in a class that's already applied on the system. By design, Puppet will fail on a duplicate resource declaration, and for a good reason: How can the catalog decide which resource is the right resource to apply? In the following example, a resource is declared in two separate classes being applied to my node:

```
[root@pe-puppet-master production]# puppet agent -t
Info: Using configured environment 'production'
Info: Retrieving pluginfacts
Info: Retrieving plugin
```

```
Info: Retrieving locales
Info: Loading facts
Error: Could not retrieve catalog from remote server: Error 500 on SERVER:
Server Error: Evaluation Error: Error while evaluating a Resource
Statement, Duplicate declaration: File[/var/log/custom] is already declared
at (file:
/etc/puppetlabs/code/environments/production/modules/profile/manifests/base
line.pp, line: 6); cannot redeclare (file:
/etc/puppetlabs/code/environments/production/modules/profile/manifests/logg
ing.pp, line: 3) (file:
/etc/puppetlabs/code/environments/production/modules/profile/manifests/logg
ing.pp, line: 3, column: 3) on node pe-puppet-master
Warning: Not using cache on failed catalog
Error: Could not retrieve catalog; skipping run
```

In the preceding case, I had my logging directory set in my baseline profile. I iterated and designed a whole profile around logging, and included my directory in the logging profile. To fix this error, I'll simply remove the custom logging directory resource from my baseline profile.

 If you need to declare a resource, and potentially use it in multiple manifests, you may want to use a virtual resource.. Chapter 9, *Exported Resources* covers virtual resources, as well.

Missing resources

When we attempt to use a resource that is not available to our Puppet Master or Puppet environment, we can trigger a missing resource error, causing the catalog compilation to fail. While these are commonly caused by misspelling a resource type, they can also be caused by missing modules in an environment. In the following example, I'm attempting to use the NTP module with include ntp. Remember, classes are resources, too:

```
[root@wordpress puppet]# puppet agent -t
Info: Using configured environment 'production'
Info: Retrieving pluginfacts
Info: Retrieving plugin
Info: Retrieving locales
Info: Loading facts
Error: Could not retrieve catalog from remote server: Error 500 on SERVER:
Server Error: Evaluation Error: Error while evaluating a Function Call,
Could not find class ::ntp for wordpress (file:
/etc/puppetlabs/code/environments/production/modules/profile/manifests/base
line.pp, line: 3, column: 3) on node wordpress
```

```
Warning: Not using cache on failed catalog
Error: Could not retrieve catalog; skipping run
```

I'm simply missing the NTP class in my environment. I could resolve this by hand with `puppet module install`, but, if you're using r10k or Code Manager, enter the module entry and all of the dependencies into your environment Puppetfile:

```
mod 'puppetlabs/ntp'
mod 'puppetlabs/stdlib'
```

Using the Puppet module `install` method does make a module available to all environments, but I can only recommend using it on temporary Puppet Masters that are used to test code:

```
[root@pe-puppet-master manifests]# puppet module install puppetlabs/ntp
Notice: Preparing to install into
/etc/puppetlabs/code/environments/production/modules ...
Notice: Downloading from https://forgeapi.puppet.com ...
Notice: Installing -- do not interrupt ...
/etc/puppetlabs/code/environments/production/modules
└─┬ puppetlabs-ntp (v7.2.0)
  └── puppetlabs-stdlib (v4.25.1)
```

The Puppet module `install` grabs all of the dependencies for us, by default. R10k and Code Manager do not, so make sure that you include all of the dependencies in your Puppetfile.

Autoload format

If our manifests containing classes and defined types aren't in the right directories, our master won't be able to find them. In the following example, I'm attempting to use a new class:

```
[root@wordpress puppet]# puppet agent -t
Info: Using configured environment 'production'
Info: Retrieving pluginfacts
Info: Retrieving plugin
Info: Retrieving locales
Notice: /File[/opt/puppetlabs/puppet/cache/locales/ja/puppetlabs-
ntp.po]/ensure: defined content as '{md5}7265ff57e178feb7a65835f7cf271e2c'
Info: Loading facts
Error: Could not retrieve catalog from remote server: Error 500 on SERVER:
Server Error: Evaluation Error: Error while evaluating a Function Call,
Could not find class ::profile::baseline::linux for wordpress
```

```
(file:/etc/puppetlabs/code/environments/production/modules/profile/manifest
s/baseline.pp, line: 4, column: 3) on node wordpress
```

I know that I wrote my `linux.pp` manifest, but the master can't find it. If I run `tree` in the directory, I'll see that `profile::baseline::linux` is actually in the autoload directory for `profile::linux`. Remember, directories are what provide us with extra layers in our namespace:

```
profile/
└── manifests
        ├── baseline.pp # profile::baseline
        └── linux.pp # profile::baseline::linux <-- Can't find this
```

By simply moving my Linux baseline into the `baseline` folder, the master will be able to find this manifest:

```
profile/
└── manifests
        ├── baseline
        │       └── linux.pp # profile::baseline::linux <-- Found!
        └── baseline.pp # profile::baseline
```

Circular dependencies

Circular dependencies don't happen often in Puppet development, but when they do, they can be a major pain to troubleshoot. Circular dependencies happen when we create dependency chains with arrow indicators (->) or ordering metaparameters. In the following example, my three notify statements require each other in a circular chain - a -> b -> c -> a:

```
class profile::baseline::linux {

# notify {'baseline': message => 'Applying the Linux Baseline!' }

  notify {'a':
    message => 'Resource A',
    require => Notify['b']
  }

  notify {'b':
    message => 'Resource B',
    require => Notify['c']
  }

  notify {'c':
```

```
        message => 'Resource C',
        require => Notify['a']
    }

}
```

When this catalog is applied on the node, we'll get a statement letting us know which resources are in a dependency chain:

```
[root@wordpress puppet]# puppet agent -t
Info: Using configured environment 'production'
Info: Retrieving pluginfacts
Info: Retrieving plugin
Info: Retrieving locales
Info: Loading facts
Info: Caching catalog for wordpress
Info: Applying configuration version '1535603400'
Error: Found 1 dependency cycle:
(Notify[a] => Notify[c] => Notify[b] => Notify[a])\nTry the '--graph'
option and opening the resulting '.dot' file in OmniGraffle or GraphViz
Error: Failed to apply catalog: One or more resource dependency cycles
detected in graph
```

Notice the `--graph` flag that is indicated in the agent. If we run our agent again, with `puppet agent -t --graph`, we'll get a dot file back that details our ordering, and we will be able to highlight our dependency cycles. This file is written out to `/opt/puppetlabs/puppet/cache/stage/graphs/cycles.dot`. I can open this file in GraphViz (open source) or OmniGraffle and view my chain in a graph. The following diagram shows this notification cycle represented in OmniGraffle:

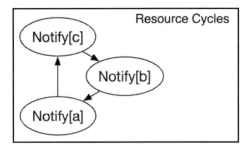

Debug mode – catalog

Sometimes, Puppet throws an error that isn't immediately obvious. In the next example, I'm attempting to install apache httpd, but I have misspelled the name of the package. If you haven't spent a lot of time working on a system that uses Yum, the error Nothing to do isn't exactly a very clear error:

```
[root@pe-puppet-master manifests]# puppet agent -t
Info: Using configured environment 'production'
Info: Retrieving pluginfacts
Info: Retrieving plugin
Info: Retrieving locales
Info: Loading facts
Info: Caching catalog for pe-puppet-master
Info: Applying configuration version '1535778801'
Notice: Applying the Linux Baseline!
Notice: /Stage[main]/Profile::Baseline::Linux/Notify[baseline]/message:
defined 'message' as 'Applying the Linux Baseline!'
Error: Execution of '/usr/bin/yum -d 0 -e 0 -y install http' returned 1:
Error: Nothing to do
Error: /Stage[main]/Profile::Baseline/Package[http]/ensure: change from
'purged' to 'present' failed: Execution of '/usr/bin/yum -d 0 -e 0 -y
install http' returned 1: Error: Nothing to do
https://yum.puppet.com/puppet5/puppet5-release-el-7.noarch.rpm' returned 1:
Error: Nothing to do
Info: Stage[main]: Unscheduling all events on Stage[main]
```

I may want to inspect exactly what Puppet is trying to get my system to do. I can use the --debug flag on the agent to inspect all of the actions that Puppet is taking underneath the system. I can see that Puppet uses rpm -q to check whether the package is already installed on the system. When it's not found, it executes a specific Yum command: run Yum without an error log (-e 0) or debugging (-d 0), and assume yes (-y) to install http. Finally, because this resource has failed, any resources requiring it will fail to install:

```
Debug: Executing: '/usr/bin/rpm -q http --nosignature --nodigest --qf
'%{NAME} %|EPOCH?{%{EPOCH}}:{0}| %{VERSION} %{RELEASE} %{ARCH}\n''
Debug: Executing: '/usr/bin/rpm -q http --nosignature --nodigest --qf
'%{NAME} %|EPOCH?{%{EPOCH}}:{0}| %{VERSION} %{RELEASE} %{ARCH}\n' --
whatprovides'
Debug: Package[http](provider=yum): Ensuring => present
Debug: Executing: '/usr/bin/yum -d 0 -e 0 -y install http'
Error: Execution of '/usr/bin/yum -d 0 -e 0 -y install http' returned 1:
Error: Nothing to do
Error: /Stage[main]/Profile::Baseline/Package[http]/ensure: change
from'purged' to 'present' failed: Execution of '/usr/bin/yum -d 0 -e 0 -y
```

```
install http' returned 1: Error: Nothing to do
Debug: Class[Profile::Baseline]: Resource is being skipped, unscheduling
all events
```

> The error `Nothing to do` wasn't actually solved. A quick search of your favorite forums will indicate some likely culprits, and in this case, `http` isn't a package in Yum. `httpd`, which is the Apache web server, is what I was looking to install.

Logging

Logging is one of the most useful forms of troubleshooting, if actively monitored. We can often identify problems in our infrastructure before they become problems that users report. By understanding the logging available to Puppet, you will know where to look for indicators of system degradation. In this section, we'll explore the log files available to Puppet and its sub components, and we will configure the log level in the Puppetserver.

The logback.xml file

Each component that we'll be logging on, other than the Puppet agent, will use Logback. Although this isn't a book on `logback`, we'll look at a few existing sections of `logback.xml` and some common settings that we can alter.

Main configuration

The main configuration includes the first and last line of the following XML file:

```
<configuration scan="true" scanPeriod="60 seconds">
```

The `scan` setting tells `logback` to rescan the configuration for changes and reload the service if changes are detected. The `scanPeriod` setting lets the configuration know how often to scan. We use these settings so that our log configuration is updated dynamically with the file; no service restart is needed.

Appender

The appender configuration section is what manages the log file. I've added comments to the appender for `puppetserver.log`, concerning what the individual lines are doing:

```
<!-- Setting the name for future reference and making a Rolling Log File -
->
    <appender name="F1"
class="ch.qos.logback.core.rolling.RollingFileAppender">

<!-- Logging to /var/log/puppetlabs/puppetserver/puppetserver.log -->
        <file>/var/log/puppetlabs/puppetserver/puppetserver.log</file>

<!-- Appending to, not replacing the log -->
        <append>true</append>

<!-- Roll the file over based on Size and Time -->
        <rollingPolicy
class="ch.qos.logback.core.rolling.SizeAndTimeBasedRollingPolicy">

<!-- What to name the file as it's rolled over, with date variables -->
            <fileNamePattern>/var/log/puppetlabs/puppetserver/puppetserver-
%d{yyyy-MM-dd}.%i.log.gz</fileNamePattern>

<!-- Maximum size of log file before rolling over -->
            <maxFileSize>200MB</maxFileSize>

<!-- Maximum Number of Files to keep - 90 logs -->
            <maxHistory>90</maxHistory>

<!-- Maximum Filesize of all files that will be kept. Up to 5 files with
200 MB -->
            <totalSizeCap>1GB</totalSizeCap>
        </rollingPolicy>
<!-- What to print for date and time with the message -->
        <encoder>
            <pattern>%d{yyyy-MM-dd'T'HH:mm:ss.SSSXXX} %-5p [%t] [%c{2}]
%m%n</pattern>
        </encoder>
    </appender>
```

In the preceding example, we're creating `puppetserver.log` with a rollover strategy. We'll keep up to 90 logs, but we'll rotate whenever a log reaches 200 MB in size, and we will delete logs if we have more than 1 GB of logs. We'll append the date to logs that we roll over, and we will print the timestamp from the log.

> You may see an appender to STDOUT. This actually prints to System.out and System.error, essentially appending to the Terminal.

Loggers

A logger in the logback.xml acts as a pointer for the logs produced by the application:

```
<logger name="puppetlabs.pcp" level="info" additivity="false">
  <appender-ref ref="PCP"/>
</logger>
```

This example connects to the puppetlabs.pcp log in the Puppetserver application, and collects the info-level logs. The additivity=false flag tells the log to replace the file, rather than append to it. Finally, the appender-ref tag tells the logger which appender to use for the logging configuration.

Root logger

There is also a special type of logger, called the root logger:

```
<root level="info">
    <appender-ref ref="${logappender:-DUMMY}" />
    <appender-ref ref="F1" />
</root>
```

The root logger acts as a default, allowing you to select the logging level and provide a list of appender-refs to apply the default settings to. Think of it as a default group policy logger, rather than a single configuration being applied to a log. All other loggers override the root logger for each value.

Puppet agent

The Puppet agent is on every node, and the log for the Puppet agent is stored locally on that node. This is the only log file that we work with that does not use logback, but uses system messaging, instead. The Puppet agent logs to the syslog of the operating system it runs on. Each operating system uses a different location, as follows:

- Linux: /var/log/messages
- macOS X: /var/log/system.log

- Solaris: `/var/adm/messages`
- Windows: Event Viewer

The information logged here is the same information that is output during a Puppet run. You can check on successful and failed resources being applied to the node in this log file.

 Enterprise Users: You also have agent logging available to view in the Puppet Enterprise console, which can be provided with filters, to help narrow down problems or statuses. You can find this log in the reports section of each node page.

PuppetDB

PuppetDB logging is managed by the config file located at `/etc/puppetlabs/puppetdb/logback.xml` on the PuppetDB server. This `logback` file contains entries for the following logs, which are in `/var/log/puppetlabs/puppetdb/`, by default:

- `puppetdb.log`: Information on the PuppetDB application
- `puppetdb-access.log`: Information on user and machine access to PuppetDB
- `puppetdb-status.log`: Current status of PuppetDB

 If you're looking for postgresql logs, they're contained in `/var/log/puppetlabs/postgresql`. This is standard postgresql logging.

Puppetserver

Puppetserver logging is managed by the config file located at `/etc/puppetlabs/puppetserver/logback.xml` on the PuppetDB server. This `logback` file contains entries for the following logs, which are in `/var/log/puppetlabs/puppetserver`, by default:

- `puppetserver.log`: Application activity with compilation errors
- `pcp-broker.log`: The log file for PCP broker activity on Puppet
- `pcp-broker-access.log`: The log file for users accessing PCP brokers on Puppet
- `puppetserver-status.log`: Status indicator for Puppetserver

Puppet Enterprise console

Console logging is managed by the config file located at `/etc/puppetlabs/console-services/logback.xml` on the PuppetDB server. This `logback` file contains entries for the following logs, which are in `/var/log/puppetlabs/console-services`, by default:

- `console-services.log`: Logging for Puppet Enterprise console
- `console-services-status.log`: Status indicator for the console

 This section is only useful to Puppet Enterprise users.

Summary

In this chapter, we discussed troubleshooting Puppet. We went over common errors seen in connections between the Puppetserver and Puppet agents. We looked at common catalog compilation failures, and how to debug them. We also covered `logback` and the log files on the master.

Other Books You May Enjoy

If you enjoyed this book, you may be interested in these other books by Packt:

Puppet 5 Beginner's Guide - Third Edition
John Arundel

ISBN: 978-1-78847-290-6

- Understand the latest Puppet 5 features
- Install and set up Puppet and discover the latest and most advanced features
- Configure, build, and run containers in production using Puppet's industry-leading Docker support
- Deploy configuration files and templates at super-fast speeds and manage user accounts and access control
- Automate your IT infrastructure
- Use the latest features in Puppet 5 onward and its official modules
- Manage clouds, containers, and orchestration
- Get to know the best practices to make Puppet more reliable and increase its performance

Puppet 5 Cookbook - Fourth Edition
Thomas Uphill

ISBN: 978-1-78862-244-8

- Discover the latest and most advanced features of Puppet
- Bootstrap your Puppet installation using powerful tools like Rake
- Master techniques to deal with centralized and decentralized Puppet deployments
- Use exported resources and forge modules to set up Puppet modules
- Create efficient manifests to streamline your deployments
- Automate Puppet master deployment using Git hooks and PuppetDB
- Make Puppet reliable, performant, and scalable

Leave a review - let other readers know what you think

Please share your thoughts on this book with others by leaving a review on the site that you bought it from. If you purchased the book from Amazon, please leave us an honest review on this book's Amazon page. This is vital so that other potential readers can see and use your unbiased opinion to make purchasing decisions, we can understand what our customers think about our products, and our authors can see your feedback on the title that they have worked with Packt to create. It will only take a few minutes of your time, but is valuable to other potential customers, our authors, and Packt. Thank you!

Index

Printed in Great
Britain
by Amazon